THE BRITISH
AIRCRAFT INDUSTRY

BRITISH INDUSTRIES
IN THE TWENTIETH CENTURY

General editor: Derek H. Aldcroft

THE BRITISH AIRCRAFT INDUSTRY

Keith Hayward

Manchester
University Press
Manchester and New York

distributed exclusively in the USA
and Canada by St. Martin's Press

Published by Manchester University Press
Oxford Road, Manchester M13 9PL, UK
and Room 400, 175 Fifth Avenue,
New York, NY 10010, USA

Distributed exclusively in the USA and Canada
by St. Martin's Press, Inc.,
175 Fifth Avenue, New York, NY 10010, USA

British Library cataloguing in publication data
Hayward, Keith
 The British aircraft industry. – (British industries
 in the twentieth century).
 1. Great Britain. Aircraft industries, history
 I. Title II. Series
 338.4'762913'00941

Library of Congress cataloging in publication data
Hayward, Keith.
  The British aircraft industry/Keith Hayward.
    p.   cm.—(British industries in the twentieth century)
  ISBN 0–7190–2816–7
  1. Aircraft industry—Great Britain. 2. Aerospace industries—
Great Britain. I. Title. II. Series.
HD9711.G72H38   1989
338.4'76291'0941—dc20   89–36265

ISBN 0 7190 2816 7 *hardback*

Photoset in Linotron Times
by Northern Phototypesetting Co, Bolton
Printed in Great Britain
by Courier International Limited, Tiptree, Essex

CONTENTS

LIST OF FIGURES

LIST OF TABLES

PREFACE
AND ACKNOWLEDGEMENTS

Attempting to encapsulate the history of an industry, especially one as complex as aircraft manufacturing, in one short volume is a trying task. The sins of omission alone begin to tax the conscience. The aircraft industry also lacks the range of authoritative secondary sources which would make a summary easier to assemble. There are plenty of detailed, often first-rate histories of aircraft and of aviation, but little which provides solid industrial, economic and political analysis. There is a temptation to follow scores of individual histories of both people and machines and I have tried to reduce to the bare outlines histories of key aircraft and engines. But in an industry where single programmes can dominate companies for decades, there has to be some reference to important examples such as the TSR2, Concorde, Airbus, the RB211 and so on.

Although this book is largely based on secondary sources, I would like to thank the many people working in, or associated with the industry who, over the years, have helped me to understand their business. I would also like to acknowledge the help and encouragement provided by Derek Aldcroft, the series editor; his observations and comments proved an invaluable aid to coherence. My thanks also to Laurence Corbett who, for the third time of asking, has disciplined one of my manuscripts. I am also very grateful to the Governing Body of the Staffordshire Polytechnic who granted me a period of Sabbatical Leave during which I completed this book. Any errors of fact or interpretation are, of course, entirely mine.

K.H.
Staffordshire Polytechnic

LIST OF ABBREVIATIONS

AFVG	Anglo-French Variable Geometry (aircraft)
BA	British Airways
BAe	British Aerospace
BAC	British Aircraft Corporation
BEA	British European Airways
BOAC	British Overseas Airways Corporation
BSE	Bristol Siddeley Engines
BTH	British Thompson Houston
CAD/CAM	Computer Aided Design/Manufacturing
DIB	Defence Industrial Base
DoI	Department of Industry
DTI	Department of Trade and Industry
ECU	European Currency Unit
E(E)C	European (Economic) Community
EFA	European Fighter Aircraft
ELDO	European Launcher Development Organisation
ESA	European Space Agency
GE	General Electric [US]
GEC	General Electric Company [UK]
HSA	Hawker Siddeley Aviation
IAE	International Aero-Engines
IRC	Industrial Re-organisation Corporation
JET	Joint European Transport
MAP	Ministry of Aircraft Production
MBB	Messerschmitt Boelkow Blohm
MDD	McDonnell Douglas
Mintech	Ministry of Technology
MoA	Ministry of Aviation
MoD	Ministry of Defence
MoS	Ministry of Supply
MRCA	Multi Role Combat Aircraft
MTU	Motor Turbine Union
NEB	National Enterprise Board
NGTRE	National Gas Turbine Research Establishment
PERT	Programme Review and Evaluation Technique
P&W	Pratt and Whitney
RAE	Royal Aircraft Establishment
RAF	Royal Air Force
R&D	Research and Development
RO	Royal Ordnance
SAM	Surface to Air Missile
SBAC	Society of British Aircraft (Aerospace) Companies

LIST OF ABBREVIATIONS

SST	Supersonic Transport
STAC	Supersonic Transport Aircraft Committee
UDF	Unducted Fan (propfan)
UTC	United Technologies Corporation
VG	Variable Geometry

GENERAL INTRODUCTION

Once the envy of the world, Britain's manufacturing industry now ranks among the weakest in the western hemisphere. Its relative decline has been in train for many years, with a noticeable acceleration in recent decades. At the turn of the century Britain was still the world's foremost manufacturing country, even if already facing a severe challenge from the United States and Germany. She accounted for around a third of the world's trade in manufactured products, and only slightly less in 1913. This share dropped sharply in the difficult and competitive climate of the 1920s, following the loss of markets during the war and the handicap of an overvalued currency with the return to the gold standard in 1925. It stabilised at around 21–2 per cent in the protectionist decade of the 1930s, rising again to a peak of 29 per cent in the post-war seller's market when Europe and Japan were still prostrate and there was a shortage of non-dollar goods. Thereafter it declined almost without interruption to a low of 7·4 per cent in 1984, a period during which some of Britain's main competitors, such as Germany, Japan, France and Italy, were increasing their share of world trade in manufactures.

A similar adverse trend is evident in the home market with respect to imports of manufactures. During the post-war years these have consistently risen faster than output or exports, with the result that import penetration has increased steadily and the surplus of exports over imports has diminished correspondingly. Imports of manufactures as a percentage of home demand doubled between 1955 and 1969, from 8 to 16 per cent, and then almost doubled again, to reach 30 per cent in the early 1980s. Manufactured imports now account for over two-thirds of total imports, as against 20 per cent before the war.

Even more disturbing has been the marked deterioration in the balance of trade in manufactures, especially in the 1970s and 1980s.

Britain had always earned a large surplus on this account which helped to offset deficits elsewhere in the balance of payments. Even as late as the mid-1960s the value of imported manufactures was still only 58 per cent of her manufactured exports. Yet by the early 1980s imports of manufactures exceeded exports for the first time in history. In 1980 a surplus of £5·5 billion was recorded, but four years later it had been transformed into a deficit of some £4 billion, equivalent to 8·25 per cent of manufactured exports and 1·2 per cent of gross domestic product. Since then the position has deteriorated further, with a deficit of no less than £10 billion recorded in 1987. Only a few major sectors of manufacturing, notably chemicals and pharmaceuticals, now show a positive balance on international trade. Yet Germany and Japan continued to record large surpluses on their manufacturing account. In 1984 Germany's surplus on manufacturing trade alone (£50 billion) was slightly greater than Britain's total exports of manufactures.

The attrition of the manufacturing sector is borne out by its declining share of total output and employment. The most dramatic shift has occurred in employment. In the 1950s and early 1960s, 40 per cent of all workers were employed in manufacturing; today the proportion is less than one in four. The peak in manufacturing employment was 1966, since when the numbers employed have fallen by no less than 40 per cent, with a loss of around 4 million jobs in this sector. Every major industry has suffered a steep decline in employment since the mid-1960s, with the most substantial losses taking place after 1979. The period from 1974 to the early 1980s also saw a collapse of manufacturing output, which until quite recently remained below the level recorded in the boom year of 1973. This was a far worse record than that of any other major industrial country.

Thus Britain's manufacturing performance during the twentieth century has been dismal, contrasting sharply with its record for much of the nineteenth century. It should of course be borne in mind that, given Britain's dominance in the past, some loss of share was to be expected as industrialisation spread, first to Western Europe and North America, later to Japan and the Pacific basin. Even so, the losses are too large and sustained to be explained away in these terms alone, especially since the Second World War, when other countries have managed to maintain or increase their share of trade. A second point to remember is that Britain has not been the only country to experience 'deindustrialisation', a contraction in the size of the manufacturing sector relative to the rest of the economy. Most of the advanced economies have witnessed a similar trend away from manufacturing, though none has seen such a pronounced shift as in Britain nor lost such a large slice of its trade share.

But the factor which has given rise to most concern is the dramatic shift in the trading position in manufactures.[1] The trend may have been aggravated by increased sourcing of exports from abroad by multinational companies with plants overseas. However, that could account for only a small part of the deterioration. In any case, it should be partly compensated by an increased stream of invisibles as profits accruing abroad are remitted back home. On the other hand, the decline in the manufacturing balance may be seen as an automatic response to movements elsewhere in the balance of payments account. Taking the period to the early 1980s as a whole, the UK balance has been close to zero, and the adverse trend in manufacturing reflects the autonomous improvements in non-manufacturing trade, that is, raw materials, food, fuel and private services. In 1950 the UK required a large surplus on the manufacturing trade account to offset large deficits elsewhere on the external account. As these declined or disappeared the former surplus on manufactures was no longer required; hence the deterioration in the latter represented a counterpart adjustment to improvements on the non-manufacturing side of the account rather than a reflection of industrial decline or failure. Rowthorn and Wells present a persuasive case for this scenario and argue that most of the deterioration in the manufacturing balance can be accounted for in these terms. They also maintain that even had the UK economy been more dynamic, and manufacturing more efficient, the balance of trade in non-manufactures would still have improved during this period and that it would have been offset by a corresponding decline in the manufacturing balance.[2]

This argument holds firm for the period up to the early 1980s. Thereafter it collapses, for obvious reasons. Improvements in non-manufacturing are not likely to be repeated in the future, especially on the fuel side. Nor is it likely that invisible items will be sufficient to plug the gap, even allowing for some under-recording on this account. As a result, the re-emergence of a surplus on manufacturing trade will be required in future to offset deterioration elsewhere and also to accommodate the import requirements of a growing economy. The crucial role of the manufacturing sector to the health of the economy has been stressed forcibly by Moore and Rhodes:

> it not only accounts for a large proportion of our exports but must also supply the bulk of the home market with manufactured goods which would otherwise have to be imported. Moreover it is the manufacturing sector to which we look as the main source of technical progress, economies of scale, increasing output per man and economic growth. The performance of this sector therefore impinges more than any other on the achievement of the general economic objectives of full employment, a satisfactory balance of payments and rising living standards. Any strategy for achieving these objectives in the future must prove itself capable of reversing the relative decline of UK manufacturing industries. An alternative strategy concentrating on the promotion of net exports of the service sector is unlikely to be an adequate substitute, although more exports from all sectors are needed.[3]

Unfortunately the prospects of the manufacturing sector re-emerging as a positive force in the balance of payments are far from promising. This is not so much because of its reduced size but more on account of the trend deterioration in relative efficiency since the Second World War. In the early 1950s Britain's manufacturing industry was generally more efficient than that of most other countries, with the notable exception of the United States. This is no longer the case. Productivity growth has averaged less than 60 per cent of that of the major industrial countries during the post-war period; by the mid-1980s the level of productivity was some 40 per cent below the average for Western Europe.[4] The decline in comparative efficiency has been fairly general, and only a few sectors of the economy, chemicals and pharmaceuticals in particular, can now boast performance levels comparable with best international standards.

In other words, because of its low level of efficiency British manufacturing is not well placed to compete in international trade, either in price or in non-price terms. Without a marked improvement in relative efficiency there is little prospect of the manufacturing sector resuming its positive contribution to the balance of payments. No amount of tinkering with the exchange rate or the wage level (that is, depreciation and wage cuts) can overcome what is fundamentally a supply problem arising out of an inefficient production system. Stoneman, for example, warns of the dangers of relying on wage cuts and devaluation to compensate for a continued failure to innovate and improve efficiency: the end result may be a low wage non-trading economy.[5]

The reasons for the poor supply capability of British manufacturing are numerous and have been debated endlessly. The proximate causes have been identified as underinvestment, a slow rate of innovation, low levels of skill formation, underspending on research and development, and the poor management of resources, especially labour. All these have contributed their share to the low rate of productivity growth. In turn, a whole range of economic and non-economic factors have been put forward to explain the underperformance in these key areas.

Any regeneration of the manufacturing system is going to be a lengthy process, since improving the supply capability of the economy is not something that can be effected overnight. In some cases it will no doubt require a radical overhaul and restructing of production systems rather than patchwork improvements to existing facilities. This could well result in a further destruction of jobs rather than the creation of new employment, since one of the major shortcomings of British industry in the past has been its wasteful use of labour. Even fast-growing sectors of activity have tended to show a static or declining employment profile over the last decade or so. In older sectors of manufacturing, where survival often depends on the complete renovation of production systems, the impact in terms of job loss can be dramatic.

Basically, therefore, the current plight of Britain's manufacturing industries is to a large extent the product of an accumulated backlog of inefficiency extending way back in time. It is an issue which will feature prominently in many of the studies of individual industries in this series, in the course of which we should be able to obtain a clearer idea of what went wrong and why. We may also be able to produce some success stories. On this optimistic note, therefore, it is appropriate to open the series with just one such.

D.H.A., 1989

Notes

1 See House of Lords, *Report from the Select Committee on Overseas Trade*, HL 238–I, July 1985.

2 R. E. Rowthorn and J. R. Wells, *Deindustrialistion and Foreign Trade* (1987), pp. 97–8, 101, 142, 151, 205.

3 B. Moore and J. Rhodes, 'The relative decline of the UK manufacturing sector', *Cambridge Economic Policy Review*, 2 (March 1976), p. 36.
4 A. Maddison, 'Long-run dynamics of productivity growth', *Banca Nazionale del Lavoro Quarterly Review*, 128 (March 1979); Rowthorn and Wells, *op. cit.*, p. 1.
5 P. Stoneman, 'Technological change and economic performance', in Department of Economics (University of Warwick), *Out of Work: Perspectives of Mass Unemployment* (1984), p. 56.
6 See the reports in the *Financial Times*, 13 March 1986 and 5 December 1988, by Michael Prowse and Jimmy Burns.

INTRODUCTION

The British aircraft industry, created by enthusiasts in the early years of the century and transformed into a strategic industry by two world wars, has survived and prospered through several cycles of 'boom and bust' to become one of the country's most successful and competitive manufacturing sectors. At its heart is the design, development and production of aircraft and engines, now dominated by two firms, British Aerospace (BAe) and Rolls-Royce. But below these two companies there is a huge number of electronics and equipment sub-contractors, about 2,000 aircraft-related suppliers and some 15,000 companies who supply the 'prime contractors'. In an age of 'integrated systems', and computerised, 'fly-by-wire' airliners and combat aircraft, the traditional distinction between airframes, engines and equipment has become steadily less relevant. With electronic and other equipment often accounting for about 40 per cent by value of the modern aircraft, airframe companies such as BAe have developed their own electronics and systems capability. In some cases, electronics firms such as GEC could credibly claim to lead the development of an airborne weapons system. Both aircraft and electronics firms have become involved in the development of missiles, 'smart' weapons and space vehicles. Indeed, the advent of missiles and space vehicles and the increasing use of ever more complex electronics during the late 1950s and 1960s transformed the aircraft industry into an *aerospace* industry which can encompass this whole complex of firms and technologies.

This book, however, focuses on the British airframe and aero-engine industries which will be collectively referred to as the aircraft industry or, after the Second World War, the aerospace industry. It could, in effect, be seen as a history of just two companies, Rolls-Royce and BAe, though we do not ignore Westland and Shorts. In reaching this concentrated industrial structure, we will encounter some of the most romantic names in British business history – de Havilland, Hawker, Vickers, Avro, Bristol and so on – links with an age of technical and commercial exploration and with events of national significance such as the Battle of Britain. Aerospace is still a 'glamorous' industry, with an aura of excitement and power which can capture the imagination of the thousands who visit the Farnborough and other airshows every year. Loyalty to firms, individuals and specific projects is high; men wept on hearing the news of the TSR2 cancellation in 1965, and not just for fear of redundancy. There is, of course, a danger that such feelings can lead to an over-enthusiastic commitment to technology for its own sake – and a dangerous disregard for commercial and economic realities. But those who work in it attest to the challenge and the drama of aircraft and engine development and a belief that they belong to an industrial elite.

Even allowing for the more sober calculations of contemporary aerospace development, the aircraft industry is not just another manufacturing sector. Its products are amongst the most technologically demanding and expensive in the world. It deals in weapons capable of potentially awesome violence as well as in products which have helped to open up the world to the package tourist. Moreover, aerospace is a rare capability, possessed by very few industrial nations. The UK is one of only three countries with a complete aerospace manufacturing capacity (defined as the ability independently to design and develop major civil and military airframes, engines and associated equipment). In total, some half a dozen states are important players in the global industry (see table 1). In Europe, only the French and perhaps the West Germans can match the UK in many sectors, but not one has the same range and depth of aerospace skills. Large commercial aircraft and engine development is even more concentrated, with just eight companies (excluding the Soviet Union) in the business. In recent years others, including Japan, have shown aspirations to develop a rounded aerospace industry. Aerospace is seen as a powerful 'technology driver', extending the state-of-the-art in materials, electronics and manufacturing standards. A domestic aircraft industry could provide both a market for high technology goods (a prime reason for Japan's interest in the sector) and technological 'fallout' into the economy at large.

Table 1: The world aircraft industry; 1985

	Turnover, millions ECU
USA	102,762
France	12,555
Britain	12,034
West Germany	6,524
Japan	4,652
Italy	3,070
Canada	2,869
Sweden [a]	745
Holland	533

Note: [a] Volvo & Saab only.
Source: European Community.

At the same time, aerospace is a highly competitive industry operating in a ruthless and highly politicised international environment. Development costs of some projects can run into billions of pounds, with commercial and technical risks of staggering proportions. A modern civil airframe and engine combination will have cost $3·5 billion to develop. The Airbus programme, in which BAe has a major share, has cost over $14 billion to date. The latest European fighter, the EFA/Eurofighter, will cost Britain, one of four national contributors, over £8 billion in development and production. Even a derivative of the Rolls-Royce RB211 civil aero-engine will need some £300 million. The industry operates in an unusual market where 'market forces' are constantly superseded by pervasive state intervention. The market consists of relatively few actors; a few hundred airforces and other military operators and some 500 airlines, many also owned by the state. It is a world of 'offset' trading, export credits, arms packages, 'controlled technology' and so on. Civil markets can be particularly volatile and affected by economic cycles, changes in regulatory practices and travel patterns. It can be years before investment costs are repaid, if at all, by sales. Defence markets, though in some respects more stable, are also vulnerable to shifts in government policy and the vicissitudes of the international climate.

The British aircraft industry has had to learn some difficult lessons from a number of spectacular commercial failures because alone it lacked the resources and the domestic market base to remain competitive. The British aircraft industry is now locked into a complex of international programmes where the costs and risks of development are shared between several states. Indeed, the British aerospace industry is perhaps better viewed as a central element in a European industrial system; for although British companies work with American firms, the US is the dominant force in world aerospace, and Britain, along with the rest of Europe, has had to combine in order to compete more effectively against the power of American industry.

It is sometimes asserted that the current high standing of the UK aircraft industry has been in part at the expense of other manufacturing sectors less able to demonstrate their 'strategic' value and thereby attract continuing support from the state. Aerospace, it is argued, has 'squeezed' out resources, both human and material, which might have been more fruitfully deployed in other manufacturing sectors. The ancillary benefits of a publicly supported aerospace industry such as the contribution to the balance of payments and technological 'fallout', are either overstated or unquantifiable and dubious. The aircraft industry has undoubtedly received very special attention from the state and perhaps the most important theme of this book is the industry's ambivalent but crucial relationship with successive governments since the early years of the century. In this respect, the British experience is not unique; indeed, it only reflects, though perhaps in greater depth, the prevailing pattern for the aircraft industry world-wide. As customer, sponsor and technological partner, the state has shaped the affairs of the aircraft industry like no other, save, for similar reasons, nuclear power. Neither has always been entirely happy with the relationship, but like two partners in a long and turbulent marriage, neither could face the expense and uncertainty of a divorce nor see an easy way to determine custody of the offspring.

The impact of government on the output, structure and context of industrial activity will, therefore, be a central, continuing thread in the narrative. The British aircraft industry was created by the state and was kept alive during the interwar years through a 'family' of ministry sponsored firms. The Second World War, of course, expanded and extended the relationship between state and industry almost to full symbiosis. After the Second World War, the state continued to assume a major responsibility for shaping and supporting the peacetime aircraft industry as a strategic and economic asset. As an extract from a memorandum submitted to the Plowden Committee in 1964 by Lord Portal, chairman of the British Aircraft Corporation (BAC), put it:

> . . . many new factors have accumulated in recent years, the combined effect of which has been to dilute the classical advantages of private enterprise. The industry is dependent to an increasing extent upon Government policy, Government decision making, and Government money; as a consequence one must accept participation of Government agencies in many domestic issues normally a concern to a Company's management only. It stands as an island of commercial activity surrounded by public authorities and is dominated by issues of public policy outside its control.[1]

For better or for worse, this relationship has dominated and largely determined the pattern of post-war industrial development. Even governments with a 'liberal' disinclination to intervene in other industries have found themselves locked into a close relationship with the aerospace sector. Ownership patterns have fluctuated, but in many respects 'nationalisation' and 'privatisation' have had little effect on substantive issues affecting the relationship between state and industry.

Another constant theme is the technological and cost dynamic and its effect on industrial structure. The Great War provided the stimulus which proved and refined the basic technical characteristics of the aeroplane and its high power/light weight piston engine. During the 1920s and 1930s, the growth of commercial aviation drove technological innovation in structures and aerodynamics, leading to the development of the stressed metal, multi-engined monoplane. The Second World War saw this technology reach a formidable maturity. But the primitive jet engine and the rocket-propelled missile developed during the war gave a foretaste of the step-change in aviation technology which followed the war (see table 2). In particular, the power and economy of the jet engine quickly revolutionised both civil and military aircraft. The introduction of jet engines vastly increased the size, speed and range of airliners, opening up new markets for air travel, a trend culminating in the turbo-fan powered wide-bodied aircraft which are now standard for most international operations. The supersonic, highly 'mission capable' military aircraft is the norm for any modern airforce. Helicopters and VTOL jets have provided an extra dimension to commercial and military operations. During the 1950s, the missile and space age added another complex facet to the industry. Finally, looking into the next century, the hybrid 'air-space' vehicle promises another level of technological complexity.

Table 2: Wing loading of aircraft, 1916–64

		Lbs. per sq.ft.
Biplane		
Sopwith Pup	1916	4·86
DH9	1917	7·55
Bulldog	1928	11·5
Monoplane		
Spitfire	1934	24·0
Jet		
Hunter	1954	70·6
Lightning	1959	83·0

Source: Aeronautical Journal, January 1966.

Table 3: Intergenerational costs
        (unit cost: 1973 $)

Spitfire	1934	300,000
Vampire	1946	500,000
Hunter	1954	600,000
Lightning	1959	2 million
Harrier	1969	5 million
Tornado	1979	8.7 million

Source: Science Policy Research Unit.

The increasing size and complexity of the aircraft, engine and missile has in turn generated the inexorable rise in intergenerational costs which have so increased the commercial and financial risks associated with aerospace programmes (see table 3). This, in its turn, has continually underscored the importance of scale as the basis for industrial success and survival and helps to explain why the UK industry first had to face rationalisation, and then, latterly, to look for overseas partners. In this respect, the effects of the 'learning curve' are particularly important; as the length of a production run increases the lower the cost of each unit becomes as the work force 'learns' how to assemble a new aircraft. Large fixed overheads are thus amortised over a larger number of aircraft or engines and if a company can expect a longer rather than a shorter run, it can afford to invest in more optimum manufacturing processes. This, in turn, allows it to fix lower prices than initial costs might otherwise justify. Nevertheless, all companies have to accept commitments to a process of long term R&D and contemplate development lead times which can exceed a decade. These factors have exacerbated the risks and uncertainty facing business and governmental decision-makers, whilst difficulties with the management and control of such complex projects, if publicly funded, have added to the tensions in the relationship between state and industry.

This book will pick out these central themes; the role of the state; the impact of technological change; the structural changes culminating in the internationalisation of development and production; and the problems of project management. Chapter One traces the development of the industry from its formation before the First World War, through its first wartime expansion and its interwar 'limbo' as a state pensioner, to its transformation in terms of scale and industrial importance during World War Two. This was the truly 'romantic' phase, of pioneer flyers and aircraft designers, often combined in one heroic individual, when the great 'names' of British aircraft manufacturing, Avro, Handley Page, Rolls-Royce and so on, were founded. The romance tended to hide a less than satisfactory technical and manufacturing position which was exposed, and only partly overcome, during re-armament and World War Two. This chapter also examines the wartime development of the jet engine and state sponsored preparations for a post-war industry with a much enhanced position in the economy.

The end of the Second World War represents the last clear watershed in the history of the British aircraft industry. Although there are subsequently many important milestones, from this point the story becomes too complicated, with several overlapping themes, easily to fit into sharply defined historical periods. Although the remainder of the book still reflects the historical chronology, each chapter will focus on a dominant theme. Chapter Two concentrates on post war developments, the progress of civil and military programmes designed to provide the basis for a competitive industry, and the industrial rationalisation of the 1950s and 1960s. It examines also the attempt to create British companies on a scale capable of sustaining the technical, industrial and financial demands of post-war aviation – a process which would not be fully completed in the airframe sector until the formation of British

Aerospace in 1978. Long before then, the goal posts had been moved and the *British* aircraft industry had aready become reconciled to international collaboration as a means of spreading the huge costs and risks of aircraft and engine development. The major collaborative programmes such as Concorde, the Airbus and the Tornado, the rationale for collaboration and its effects on the British aircraft industry, are examined at some length in Chapter Three. Chapter Four centres on the collapse and nationalisation of Rolls-Royce and the formation and subsequent evolution of BAe into a diversified high technology and engineering conglomerate; but again these domestic events are set against the international context of British aerospace activities. Finally, in Chapter Five, we will evaluate the current standing of the British aircraft industry and its place in the UK economy.

CHAPTER ONE

THE GROWTH
OF AN
INDUSTRY
1914–45

1.1 The foundation of an industry

The first powered flight in Britain was made at Farnborough, the site of the Army Balloon Factory, on 16 October 1908 some five years after the Wright Brothers. in December, J. T. C. Brabazon, later Lord Brabazon, became the first native born British pilot. In the summer of 1909, Blériot crossed the Channel, and the 'aeroplane came of age'.[1] In Britain, official interest in the new machines blew hot and cold, but enthusiasts such as A. V. Roe and Geoffrey de Havilland began to build their own aircraft. Some, like Frederick Handley Page, had an academic training, but most were 'intuitive' engineers – mechanics, tinkerers and novitiate pilots who simply wanted an aeroplane to fly. Friendships (and some rivalries) established during this formative period would link the industry's key personalities throughout the next four decades. In 1911 the Farnborough establishment became the Army Aircraft factory and in the following year, the Royal Aircraft Factory. The Royal Aircraft Factory played a major role in early British aircraft design and production. Geoffrey de Havilland, for example, was employed by the Factory, and his BS1 type became the 'ancestor of every scout and fighter thereafter'.[2]

Through its control over aircraft assembly for the Royal Flying Corps (or RFC, formed in April 1912), the Factory could impose a degree of standardisation on private constructors. The Admiralty, on the other hand, tended to look both to private industry and to the Royal Aircraft Factory for aircraft for the Royal Naval Air Service. Royal Aircraft Factory designs were also built by established engineering and armaments companies, such as Vickers and Armstrong Whitworth. From the outset, therefore, the state and the aircraft industry were linked in a close, interdependent relationship. Britain initially lagged behind both Germany and France, by then the leading world aeronautical powers. Although British airframes rapidly caught up, the development of a domestic aero-engine design was particularly backward. In 1914, none of the engines used by the RFC exceeded eighty h.p. and none were of British design. A government prize (the Naval and Military Aeroplane Engine Competition) of £5,000 for a suitable British-designed aero-engine was still unawarded by the spring of 1914. The Air Ministry turned to the motor industry and several French designs were 'passed on' to Napiers and Rolls-Royce. However, it was 1915 before these were in production and even these were dependent upon stocks of *German* magnetos.[3]

The First World War confirmed the aeroplane as a major weapon of war and accelerated the rate of technological change. Aircraft started the war as unarmed observation types; by November 1918, a four-engined Handley Page bomber was ready to carry a 1,650lb. bomb-load to Berlin. The industry expanded rapidly to serve the needs of the RFC and its maritime equivalent, the Royal Naval Air Service. By 1915, pressure from the Western Front, particularly following problems with the BE2c, forced the Royal Aircraft Factory to 'open up design to the trade' and the system of military requirements, specifications and invitations to tender was instituted. Companies were now free 'to create design departments of real strength' and a 'partnership between government and industry was formed which was to survive the war'.[4] The Royal Aircraft Factory became the Royal Aircraft Establishment, dedicated to aeronautical research for both the Services and industry – a role which left it considerable influence over British aircraft design. In 1916, a trade association, the Society of British Aircraft (now Aerospace) Companies (SBAC) was founded with forty-eight members; by 1918 its membership had risen to eighty.

Firms were able to open extensive new facilities, such as Handley Page's eleven-acre site at Cricklewood. The war had also stimulated the creation of a first-class engine industry, with Napiers and

Rolls-Royce dominating. The Rolls management, in particular, recognised that aero-engines could be an important area for future business – a decision helped by the existence of a factory full of specialised machinery at Derby.[5] Equally important, the war made aviation an integral part of national security and provided the technical basis for the development of passenger-carrying aircraft – a development graphically demonstrated by Alcock and Brown's 1919 transatlantic flight in a converted Vickers Vimy bomber. By 1918 the British industry was the largest and technically one of the most capable in the world, comprising 122 firms employing 112,000 people, producing on average over 1,250 aircraft per month.

However, the industry quickly learnt that a close relationship with the state could have its disadvantages – what government gave it could also remove. The abrupt cancellation of military orders at the end of hostilities and moves to tax wartime profits precipitated a crisis in the infant industry. Worse still, the Air Ministry held three years' supply of aircraft and engines for the RAF and there was little prospect of new orders of appreciable scale. The application of the 'ten-year rule' – the notion that Britain would not be involved in major hostilities for that period and renewed successively until March 1932 – cast a pall over prospects for future military business. The optimistic belief that opportunities for exports and an expanding civil market would carry the industry through also quickly evaporated. The new markets failed to materialise and in the UK at least, government was not willing to subsidise commercial air transport. In 1917, a committee looking at the possibilities of post-war aviation 'emphasised the need for an expanding civil aviation with, if necessary, state assistance'. It was largely ignored. Despite the creation of official machinery to oversee aviation, few politicians were really convinced that it was so important as to justify state aid for survival. The government failed to appreciate that a 'thriving civil aviation sector would lead to sound modern aeroplanes, and the effect of this would be felt beneficially by the RAF'.[6]

Firms that had mushroomed during the war depended upon government orders for finance and were grossly undercapitalised. Many wartime entrants left the industry, and those which remained faced harsh times. By the early 1920s, SBAC membership had fallen to 18. Even size was no defence; in 1920, the Airco manufacturing company of the Holt Thomas organisation – then the world's largest aircraft manufacturer – was forced out of business. Other pioneer firms, including Handley Page and A. V. Roe, tried to develop civil aviation interests, both producing aircraft and running airlines. Other attempts at diversification led companies into motor vehicles and general metal working – one firm producing milk churns. Glosters turned hangars over to pig-rearing and mushroom-growing. The de Havilland company survived through the timely input of capital from a rich enthusiast. Even Rolls-Royce at one point contemplated abandoning aero-engine production entirely and for the first three post-war years paid little attention to new technology. Until the 1930s, sales of Rolls' engines averaged only £200,000 per annum, although this was doubled by income from spares. For companies which had 'sprung into big business by reason of war and became used to dealing in millions it was difficult after the flush of victory to come down to smaller things – aviation had proved its power if not its economics'.[7]

By 1924, the government had begun to realise that the aircraft industry had to be maintained and civil aviation deliberately fostered for strategic and political reasons. The government introduced a series of loosely-related measures designed to encourage all aspects of aviation in Britain. However, the net result was half-hearted and in many respects counter-productive. The government subsidised the new Imperial Airways which was required to use British made aircraft; but its main task was the development of services to the Empire, not to compete with other airlines in Europe – a situation which would have a profoundly conservative effect on British civil aircraft design.

More directly, the Air Ministry provided just enough work to keep major design teams, built up during the war, from disintegrating. It allocated contracts to a selected number of companies – known as 'the ring' or 'family'. The 'family' was chosen arbitrarily, and its existence was justified by the view that competition amongst a wide group of design centres was more important than industrial rationalisation aimed at maximising production and financial capability. However, in order to help their chances of survival, companies tended to specialise in certain product areas. For example, Gloster, Hawker and Bristol concentrated on fighters; Blackburn, Shorts and Supermarine on flying boats; and Fairey on light bombers. Bristol Engines tended to work on radial engines whereas Rolls built liquid cooled designs. Outsiders found it very difficult, if not impossible, to obtain orders from the Ministry. Despite being technically superior to many in 'the ring', it took Nevil Shute Norway's firm, Airspeed, many years from its launch in 1931 to gain acceptance by the Ministry.

De Havilland was one of the few firms which chose in the 1930s deliberately to stay outside the 'family'. However, despite (perhaps because of) its independence, de Havilland had considerable commercial success based on a range of light aircraft (starting with the immortal Moth of 1924), the development of a matching light engine, the Gypsy, and its position as one of the world's largest producers of variable pitch propellers. Between 1924 and 1929, de Havilland grew from a firm of 300 employees worth £48,843 to an international company employing 1,500 and worth £400,000. Although it was hit by the depression, from 1932 its business revived with over half of its output going overseas.[8] But, overall the result of the 'family' system was an 'artificially large aircraft industry' supported by the state and it was this support 'rather than market forces which determined the size of the industry as well as its profitability and productive efficiency'.[9]

The interwar industry comprised fifty-two firms, but the sixteen largest, most in the 'family', accounted for 90 per cent of the work force which up to 1934, never exceeded 24,000 (see table 4) Between 1924 and 1938, some rationalisation did occur. In 1928 Vickers bought Supermarine for £300,000, with its brilliant designer, R. J. Mitchell, contractually bound to the company for five years. By the late 1930s, de Havilland was closely associated with Airspeed and finally bought the company in 1940. The most important of the pre-war mergers occurred in 1935, when Hawker acquired Armstrong Siddeley, A. V. Roe and Gloster to form the Hawker Siddeley Group. Even here, the link was mainly financial, with each centre retaining considerable autonomy and the ability independently to bid for Ministry contracts. In the early 1930s, an official committee attacked the system for its 'feather bedding' of the industry and promoted the virtues of rationalisation. However, the Air Ministry objected to any reduction in the size of the 'family' on the grounds that this would lead to price fixing and increased vulnerability to hostile action in time of war. The net effect was to emphasise design at the expense of production and obstructed the development of firms of equivalent size and scale to those emerging in the US.[10]

Table 4: Employment in the British aircraft industry, 1924–40

1924	11,735
1930	21,322
1934	23,775
1935	35,032
1936	75,000
1938	128,000
1940	750,000

The engine industry, although 'protected' by Ministry purchasing, was subject to less government intervention and direction. Lacking expertise in aero-engines, the RAE left the manufacturers largely to their own devices. Nevertheless, in 1926 the Air Ministry opposed Fairey's attempt to join the engine 'family' by acquiring a licence for the technically advanced Curtis Wright engine. The Ministry was already having the greatest difficulty in keeping the existing four design teams alive and further competition could have been fatal.[11] Napiers' failure to keep pace with technical developments, such as the use of new alloys, supercharging and improved fuels, led to a steady decline in their fortunes. The firm also made little effort to improve production efficiency and to cut costs. During this period, however, Rolls began to emerge as the most technically advanced of the engine 'family'. Rolls' commitment to new technology, driven by an imaginative and energetic management team headed by Sir Ernest, later Lord Hives, produced the Kestrel and the 'R' series which triumphed in the 1931 Schneider Trophy races and laid the foundation for the magnificent Merlin.

Bristol, which entered the field in 1920 through its purchase of the Cosmos Engineering Company, and steered by the dynamic Roy (later Sir Roy) Fedden, maintained an equally vigorous commitment to R&D and provided the only real domestic competition for Rolls-Royce. Fedden was also instrumental in setting up an apprentice school at Bristol and selling licences for the Jupiter engine to seventeen countries. He and his team were also responsible for the development of the 'sleeve valve' which considerably increased the power, efficiency and ease of construction of the piston engine. Unusually for his time, Fedden made several visits to the US and later to Germany to investigate new ideas. By 1939, 50 per cent of the RAF's engines were supplied by Bristol. However, for all of his undoubted talent, the abrasive Fedden was often in conflict with the Bristol Board and he left the firm during World War Two.[12]

Most of the aircraft industry was cut off from the full effect of market forces. In this sense, they were relatively insulated from the depression which hit many other manufacturing companies. For Vickers, aircraft construction provided one of the 'bright spots' of the late 1920s, with RAF budgets rising relative to the firm's more traditional naval and army customers.[13] The negative side of government dependency and 'penny packet' contracting was that by the mid 1930s, very few companies had any experience of mass production. Nor had they the incentive to build up their own research facilities (in 1935, only six companies had wind tunnels). Again the state filled the gap, with basic research undertaken by the RAE and the National Physical Laboratory. However, these establishments, for fear of competing with private industry, were not encouraged to work on production techniques. But dependence on Ministry and, worse still on Imperial Airways' specifications, had a serious effect on Britain's technological standing in the world aircraft industry. The RAF's main task during the 1920s was 'Empire policing' with little need for high performance aircraft, which would have required streamlining and advanced features such as retractable under-carriages. The Ministry was particularly resistant to the introduction of the monoplane. The biplane was certainly more manoeuvrable and, until the late 1920s, the theoretical speed advantage of the monoplane was limited by the low power of engines. But the use of grass airfields with a need for slow approach speeds, combined with Ministry conservatism, continued to constrain British designers well into the 1930s. In fact, the most significant stimulus for innovation during this period came from the Schneider Trophy air races which encouraged both the development of the Spitfire fighter and the Merlin engine. British aircraft were also holders of several world records for speed, altitude and endurance during the 1920s, but production aircraft tended to slip behind the rest of the world.

The Ministry did appreciate the importance of moving from wood to metal construction, and in 1924 ruled that it would no longer buy front line aircraft made from wood. However, many British firms were reluctant to make the change because working in metal was more difficult and four to five times as expensive as wood, requiring large and well-equipped firms with a skilled work force. These in turn depended on a substantial and continuous flow of production orders which was not forthcoming. The introduction of machine tools was similarly retarded. By the early 1930s, with a few honourable exceptions (Handley Page's commitment to basic research was especially noteworthy), the British airframe industry was technically inferior to its international competitors, a condition due almost entirely to the system of national procurement. Although similar mistakes, such as an over-emphasis on flying boats and reluctance to phase out the biplane, were made by other companies and countries, the position tended to be more acute and widespread in Britain.[14]

In the changing environment of the 1930s, a number of firms had the strength and commitment, as well as a cadre of brilliant and imaginative designers willing to adopt foreign innovations, to launch several advanced types as private ventures, or with only limited help from the state. Mitchell at Vickers-Supermarine and Sidney Camm at Hawkers both found the Ministry's reluctance to sponsor monoplanes increasingly absurd. Important examples of industrial 'anticipation' of Ministry contracts included early work by Vickers and Hawker on the Spitfire and Hurricane, and Vickers' 'geodetic' bomber airframe derived from Barnes Wallis' R100 airship which led to the Wellington.[15] However, while British firms, once stimulated by re-armament, would rapidly catch up in the design of military aircraft, in the case of civil aircraft there was no equivalent catalyst for change.

1.2 Civil aviation in the interwar period

The technological changes of the late 1920s and early 1930s had a profound effect on civil aircraft. Indeed, the search for a truly economic airliner to feed the growing demands for air travel, particularly in the United States, was a more dynamic stimulus for aeronautical innovation during this period than national security. The geography of the US, with huge continental distances between population centres, was an ideal context for air transport. The US government also encouraged the growth of civil aviation through mail contracts. Moreover, competition between several carriers put a premium on sound and efficient equipment and formed a sufficiently broad base to support a number of producers. Once established, the level of demand provided the major manufacturers with returns which justified further investment in large scale modern production facilities and a commitment to research and development.

Although the Air Ministry issued civil specifications and often paid for some or all of prototype development costs, the design of British civil aircraft was largely shaped by the requirements and attitudes of Imperial Airways. Its protected Empire route structure meant that it did not have to compete with other European airlines. Despite the great pioneering flights by Britons such as Sir Alan Cobham, by 1930 The UK/Empire route mileage was only 23,005 compared to Germany's 17,000 and France's 19,400 although both had less extensive imperial territories. In the same year, 385,910 people were carried by US airlines and 93,126 by German companies – in the whole of the British Empire the number was 58,261.[16] Imperial emphasised comfort over speed and its philosophy on long haul routes to the East was better served by flying boats. The flying boat, most notably in the form of Pan Am's Boeing Clipper flights helped to prove very long range routes , including trans-oceanic services, but in Britain they represented a dead-end development. The flying boat was destined to be outpaced by the long range land based airliner which, by the early 1940s, was emerging in the US. Imperial contracts undoubtedly provided a protected source of work for the British aircraft industry, but never in sufficient quantity or with a specification to justify private investment in designs capable of winning substantial export orders. Indeed, where independent British airlines operated against strong competition they usually bought American aircraft.

The gap between the UK and the US was underlined by the 1934 MacRobertson England-Australia air race. This was won by a specially built two-seater, the de Havilland Comet. In second place was a standard Douglas DC2 operated by KLM, covering the distance in just over seventy-two hours, some thirteen days faster than the Imperial Airways scheduled service. Despite the Comet's success, the embarrassing comparison between the DC2 and the standard British airliner did not go unnoticed in the UK. One feature of the period was the growing 'air mindedness' of the British public, a feeling actively fostered by the aviation community and its lobbyists. Its focus was, naturally enough, the aviator/designers, supported by the learned societies such as the Royal Aeronautical Society, pressure groups such as the Air League and professional bodies like the British Airline Pilots' Association. Broader dissemination of aviation fact and opinion came through *Flight* and *The*

Aeroplane. Through the 1930s, several MPs, such as Colonel Moore Brabazon and Harold Balfour, were ready to promote British aviation in Parliament. Finally, although the SBAC lobbied generally for the industry, it tended to be dominated by the larger airframe and engine companies, generally members of the 'family'. 'Outsiders', but members of the SBAC, often complained about this emphasis and consequently, the SBAC's overall strength as an industrial lobbyist tended to suffer.[17] Nevertheless, the inadequacy of British civil aviation began to attract political and public criticism.

In 1935, Airspeed took out a licence with Fokker, which had the European rights from Douglas to build the DC2. However, any relationship with an 'alien' was likely to cause difficulties with the Air Ministry and eventually Airspeed had to abandon the idea. De Havilland also lobbied hard to obtain Ministry support for a modern airliner. In 1934, the company wrote to the Air Ministry recalling that it had successfully produced civil types with the 'minimum of artificial financial aid'. But, the letter continued,

> it is strikingly apparent to us that immediate steps must be taken in this country to produce aircraft of better performance and of greater commercial merit than the successful foreign machines in the MacRobertson Race – and their inevitable developments. We interpret the signs of the times as indicating that the demand will probably need to be stimulated by some form of government assistance if our national prestige is to be maintained.[18]

De Havilland's pressure had some effect; in January 1936, the Air Ministry ordered two of its four-engined Albatross airliners for Imperial Airways. The cost of the prototype was shared between between the company and the state. The Albatross had a wooden structure but it proved to be an economical and useful twenty-three seater. However, the onset of rearmament was already being felt on the civil sector, with the Bristol 'Britain First' airliner being turned into the Blenheim bomber. In fact the shortage of suitable British airliners led the Ministry to allow British Airways, a second publicly owned carrier, to purchase a number of American and German aircraft. By 1939, Lord Reith, chairman of Imperial Airways, was also discussing the possibility of buying US-built aircraft.

The 1938 Cadman report on British civil aviation was highly critical of both Imperial Airways and the Air Ministry. It called for more emphasis to be put on developing routes in Europe and South America and on the need for an adequate range of modern British-built airliners. The government's response was the provision of £500,000 for airliner development and orders for several new types. There was also movement towards the creation of a Civil Aircraft Development Committee involving all interested parties to improve British civil aircraft design. On the eve of war in 1939, several new aircraft were either available in limited numbers or being developed. By then, however, the demands of rearmament precluded any large diversion of resources to civil work. Even so, it was doubtful whether even these designs would have been competitive with airliners already in production on the other side of the Atlantic, still less with the long range four-engined types in preparation. In 1941, civil production virtually ceased, and in May 1942 it was decided to rely upon American transports. The only exception was the York, as work on it had already begun and it would provide some insurance in the event of the Americans failing to deliver.[19]

This was a truly miserable period for the British civil aircraft industry. Its competitors, most notably the Americans, were better placed to exploit technological innovation and were usually better and more coherently supported by their governments. British firms also built for one of the most conservative and narrow-minded of airline customers. But the industry, with very few exceptions, also failed to recognise its own shortcomings in terms of organisation and commitment to new ideas in both product and in process technology. Above all, 'the British government again characteristically failed to promote and back a national "package" coupling long distance air transport development with commercially successful production of modern aircraft'.[20] These pre-war problems would mean, five years later, that the government and industry had considerable leeway to make up if Britain was to have any chance of creating a viable commercial aircraft industry.

1.3 Rearmament and the aircraft industry, 1934–38

In March 1934, Prime Minister Baldwin announced that the RAF was to have parity with the German airforce, a statement which effectively marked the beginning of British rearmament. During the 1920s, exports accounted for 20 per cent of airframe and 40 per cent of engine output, but from 1934 the home market began to absorb the bulk of production. The aircraft industry expanded rapidly, financed through increased share capital and helped by a generous payment system adopted by the Ministry. For example, in June 1935, Bristol had 4,200 employees; by Christmas the workforce had doubled. Overall, employment in the industry expanded from 21,322 in 1930 to 75,000 in 1936 (see table 4).[21] Although rearmament brought stability and rising profitability to the aircraft industry, it was evident that individual firms could not fulfil growing production targets. Even inclusion of 'second tier' firms, such as Airspeed, Miles and Percival, in the 'family' was insufficient to cope with the programme. With the introduction of 'Scheme F' in 1936, designed to provide 8,000 aircraft by 1939, the Air Ministry fully implemented its 'shadow factory' scheme. This had been first considered in 1929, and it entailed farming out airframe and engine production to other suitable manufacturing companies, primarily in the motor industry. Additional factories and plant were financed by the state and firms participating in the scheme received an annual management fee of £50,000 and a royalty for each unit produced – £75 in the case of engines.

However, as Sir Roy Fedden of Bristol Engines noted, many were 'unimpressed with the scheme as a business venture and showed no enthusiasm for taking part'. Even Fedden's own board was 'averse to the idea'.[22] Lord Nuffield, for one, would at first have nothing to do with it, and uncertainty about the ultimate disposal and financial responsibility for the new factories was not fully resolved until the outbreak of war. In the long term, several firms would benefit considerably from the new plant which would be used to support post-war expansion. Ultimately, the shadow system was the key to fulfilling both pre-war and wartime production needs. The Nuffield (Morris) organisation eventually managed the largest aircraft factory in Europe, producing 70 per cent of all Spitfires built during the war.[23] Other shadow factories were run by the airframe and engine companies, and for English Electric, it provided a way to re-enter the aircraft business. Not all of the industry was keen on the shadow system. Rolls-Royce preferred to work with a chain of subcontractors, the approach it had used in World War One, but agreed to participate after receiving assurances about quality control. Two important new Rolls facilities were opened at Crewe (where vehicle chassis production was re-located from Derby) and at Hillington in Glasgow. In turn, the Ministry recognised the virtues of Rolls' sub-contractor system and adopted it as a model for the rest of the aircraft industry.[24]

The increase in industrial capacity was impressive. In 1938, there was 4·9 million square feet of floor space available for aircraft and engine production; by October 1941, it had risen to 22·15 million square feet. But the years of small quantity work had taken its toll: 'management was geared to the difficult enough problem of small scale sales of aircraft in a period of depression and not to the quick production of what soon amounted to an embarrassment of contracts'.[25] A 1936 Ministry survey found that only three firms could be regarded as 'first class' in terms of the ability to carry through large scale production programmes. Following a visit to Germany, Sir Roy Fedden had compared 'Britain's small and inefficient plants' with the investment made by German industry and government. In particular, he criticised the 'basically wrong production mentality' of British firms. The management of several, including Blackburn, Boulton & Paul and Westland, was considered to be incompetent and changes were required before they were allowed to receive contracts. Even a substantial firm like Vickers had difficulties in adjusting to the new conditions. It had considerable difficulty in getting the Spitfire into volume manufacture. Under Ministry pressure, Vickers curbed the 'vice-regal' powers of Sir Robert McClen, who had run the Vickers aircraft division since 1928, and put a 'production man from the shipyards', Sir Charles Cowan, in charge.[26].

Naturally enough, the industry felt that a large part of the blame for these problems lay in a procurement process which had clearly failed to encourage modern production techniques or to provide the orders which would have sustained a proper level of investment. On the other hand, the stubborn independence of firms throughout the industry also got in the way of co-operation which might have helped to overcome some of its limitations. Even after the start of rearmament, the individualistic 'captains of the aircraft industry' would often oppose pragmatic solutions to national problems. The Air Ministry found firms reluctant to farm out designs to subcontractors for fear that hard won expertise would become common property; others did not want to produce aircraft they had not designed.

Some of the problems faced by the aircraft companies were

outside of their control. The machine tool industry was swamped by the demands of rearmament, especially by the need to equip the shadow factories. The solution was to import from the United States, and Bristol, for example, used its US office to buy machines direct from American manufacturers. More seriously, the aircraft industry had to compete with other sectors for scarce skilled labour. In 1936, the government found that there was no effective reserve of fully trained men, despite the high level of general unemployment. The Ministry of Labour announced that there were only 1,800 skilled engineering workers who were unemployed; the Daimler shadow factory alone needed 750. The absence of comprehensive training schemes and the longer term neglect of technical education was now badly felt. The skilled unions, such as the AEU, also opposed 'dilution'. Although many firms, such as Rolls-Royce, undertook their own training, especially of women, and 'converted' other skilled personnel to aircraft production, the only answer was often to poach labour by offering higher wages. The problem was partly solved by labour conscription and by the overwhelming priority aircraft manufacturing came to have during the war. At the peak of wartime production, six out of ten British engineering firms took on some aircraft work. Even then, the limited supply of skilled people would constrain development and production activity.

There was no excuse, however, for the fundamental weaknesses exposed in both management and in the Ministry procedures which had failed to encourage the growth of a more effective production system. Both sides in fact had a lot to learn about large scale production. Not until 1938 was it fully accepted that it was essential to 'replace the archaic supplier/customer relationship more appropriate to a military tailor's than to a national armaments industry reliant on government contracts for its survival'.[27] However, while the war would help to hide some of these problems, it would not wholly overcome the intrinsic limitations of aircraft development and production in the UK which were revealed during this period.

1.4 Design, development and production, 1938–45

The rearmament period and the war itself confirmed and deepened the partnership between industry and state. The RAF, the Air Ministry, the Ministry of Aircraft Production (formed in 1940) and the research establishments were all deeply involved in the design and development process, generating requirements based on combat experience in an increasingly systematic and sophisticated fashion. A wide range of both formal and informal contacts linked industry with its customers. In practice it was often impossible to identify exactly who was responsible for initiating projects. Even the so called 'private venture' aircraft – most famously the Spitfire, Hurricane and Lancaster – were private only in part. The development of an inadequate twin-engined bomber (the Manchester) into arguably the best heavy bomber of the war (the Lancaster) may have depended on the persistence and initiative of Roy Chadwick and Roy Dobson of Avro. But even here, their activities were not against the grain of official policy or interest. As the official history noted, 'co-operation between the firms and the Ministry was as complete as co-operation between industry and State could possibly be'.[28]

The state was also closely involved in the internal affairs of companies. The Ministry of Aircraft Production (MAP), especially under its first minister, the dynamic and ruthless Lord Beaverbrook, determined production priorities, encouraged design specialisation, distributed experimental projects according to competence and workload, and in the event of serious problems and failure such as at Fairey in 1942, it would step in to force managerial and organisational changes. In 1943, the position at Shorts was so bad as to force the government to nationalise the company. As the war progressed, Ministry officials were also stationed in factories to 'oversee' all aspects of development and production.

The Ministry had less need (and less technical competence) to intervene in the engine sector. Throughout the war, engine development remained, from the point of view of the British government, the 'one largely uncontrolled factor in the progress of British aircraft'. The best firms had an unchallenged reputation for delivering the goods; the more so if left to their own mysterious devices. On one occasion, when Rolls felt it was being pressed into something against its better judgement, Hives wrote to Lord Beaverbrook in no uncertain terms pointing out that Rolls had seen 'the rise and fall of Air Ministers', and that 'most of the Rolls-Royce successes have been achieved when we have acted contrary to the official recommendations'. As the company's historian observes 'the firm's technical record was so outstanding and the dependence

23

of the RAF on Rolls-Royce so great that even though those in authority thought that the production record might be improved by more direct control no-one was prepared to carry the responsibility for any failure which such interference might have caused'.[29] Only later in the war, and only in the case of major problems did the MAP intervene substantially in the affairs of an engine company when it effected the transfer of Napier to English Electric. Similarly, the government took steps to ensure a more effective exploitation of jet technology (see below).

Primary responsibility for development and production of aircraft lay with the 'family' of companies. In many cases, the 'founder' still played a major role in determining company policy, and in all, the key figures could trace their seniority to the earliest days of the industry. In operational terms, the central figure remained the 'chief designer' who would be responsible for conceiving new aircraft and working up major modifications in conjunction with the Air Ministry and the MAP. The chief designer was usually a principal member of the company, and as such he usually had a substantial say in overall corporate strategy as well as a decisive role in technical questions. With the partial exception of Fairey, the British did not adopt the US 'project team' approach where independent groups of specialists were responsible for different projects. These men were responsible for many fine products. Sir Sidney Camm was appointed chief designer at Hawker in 1925 and was still design director at Hawker Siddeley in the 1960s. Under his direction and leadership, Hawker produced several generations of fighter aircraft. They could also be difficult to work with; Sir Roy Fedden, for all his undoubted talent, was also abrasive and single-minded and parted from Bristol Engines in 1942, never having reached the board.[30] The problem was that the growing complexity of design *and* production required team work and a broader distribution of skills than the industry often possessed.

Many of the senior personnel, certainly a large number of the 'support' staff, had risen through the ranks of the company. Amongst the design and development groups, only a small proportion had received a university or college training in aeronautical and other engineering sciences. This reflected in part the paucity of such courses in the UK during the 1920s and 1930s, but also a strong preference on the part of the established designers/founders to recruit in their own image. There were exceptions; Sir Handley

Page was a highly respected aeronautical 'academic' and employed similarly 'theoretically' inclined people; Frank Whittle was a gifted practical and theoretical engineer who obtained a first class degree from Cambridge while working on jet propulsion; and W. E. W Petter of Westland and later leader, at thirty-five, of English Electric's newly-created design team, also held a first class degree from Cambridge. However, nothing could cover in the short term the absence of a middle rank of college-trained engineers which the US had in great profusion. Totally absent in Britain were the production engineers/managers and cost accountants which the US education system had provided and who were employed in great numbers by US firms. This problem was not unique to the aircraft industry; as Barnett observes, it reflected the 'deep seated British weakness in technical education and training which had already crippled Britain's older industries'. Indeed, the motor industry was as bad; Lord Nuffield was so prejudiced against 'intellectuals' that members of his organisation learned to hide any taint of university training.[31] However, it was a particularly serious problem for an industry thrust into the forefront of Britain's war effort.

The problem was accentuated by the fact that aircraft design and manufacturing was changing from a reliance on intuitive design skills and a 'finger in the wind' to a more systematic and scientific approach. During the war, the size and power of combat aircraft grew markedly; the range and payload of the bomber grew from under 4,000 lbs. over 1,200 miles to 5500 lbs. and more over 2,350 miles. The speed of conventionally powered fighters such as the Spitfire rose by over 100 mph. Moreover, the advent of airborne radar, navigation aids and other electronics-based equipment considerably increased the complexity of aircraft. For example, the Stirling bomber, not the most sophisticated of the 'heavies', had over 600,000 parts. One effect was the growth of specialist companies to develop and to produce large 'sub-systems' which hitherto had been built by the main contractor. For example, in 1936, Dowty Engineering took on the design of the Hurricane undercarriage and have grown into world class manufacturers of landing gear and control systems. Similarly, Rolls and Bristol Engines co-operated to form Rotol, a jointly owned company created to develop and produce propellers.

The Ministry's own conflicting requirements did not help. On the one hand, it wanted the most advanced aircraft for the Services – the 'doctrine of quality'. On the other hand, the introduction of new designs, or the incremental improvement of existing aircraft types, inevitably disturbed production. The Ministry also tended to 'duplicate' aircraft to fulfil similar roles, the Air Staff believing that it got a better product from competition between design centres. But as a result of 'accidents, delays in development, and of uncertainties in policy, the MAP found themselves by the beginning of 1943 having to provide for the continued production of at least three four-engined bombers, and of at least four aircraft of bomber weight, with the prospect of a fifth in the offing'. The policy did lead to the 'accidental' emergence of the best bomber of the war, the Lancaster, but the MAP found itself unable to transfer production capacity from the Stirling, the worst of the three, because of pressure from the Cabinet to avoid disruption in the build-up of a numerically adequate heavy bomber force.[32]

The sheer scale of the task entailed by the war effort was the crux of the matter. Firms which had been geared up for 'penny packet' quantities, centred on a chief designer, were stretched to the limit. Production requirements drained the design office of draughtsmen, and by the middle of the war, the acute shortage of drawing staff and other skilled personnel was causing problems for defence work and for preparations for a post-war civil programme (see below). Transfers between companies proved difficult to accomplish and ultimately these problems could only be met by training and by changing work practices. British designers also tended to be less practised in 'designing for production' and companies less concerned to plan for large scale production. The Mark VC Spitfire, for example, took 13,000 man hours to build compared to the 4,000 required for its German counterpart, the Messerschmitt Bf 109G.[33]

Design, development and, above all, production increasingly required integrative skills and a sophisticated management system. The 'hero designer' was becoming obsolete, and, if the head of a major company, a positive drawback to modernisation. Significantly, at Vickers, the 'shipbuilder' Sir Charles Cowan felt that the individualism of the 'chief' designer was 'a nonsense' and had begun to adopt more modern practices. Again, Rolls-Royce, a high quality *engineering* company with experience of volume production, was an important exception. From the early 1920s, it had frequently updated its organisation and was sensitive to changing requirements. In the mid 1930s, looking to boost its 'academic' base, Rolls began to recruit graduates. On hiring Stanley Hooker, with a D.Phil in airflow theory, Hives told him that 'I am no mathematician or scientist, but I have a feeling that we are going to need such people in the future. We need a more technical and analytical approach to some of our engineering problems, and I am going to look to men like you to give us that lead.' Above all, Hives saw the need to 'design for production' in order to ensure that Rolls engines were as efficiently produced as they were superbly engineered. This care extended to Rolls' shadow factories and subcontractors.[34]

The gap between the US and Britain was underlined by the 'Fedden Mission' to the US undertaken in the early part of 1943. Sir Roy Fedden, now working as a special adviser to the Minister of Aircraft Production, found that US firms employed proportionately larger organisations for research, design and production, with higher investment in testing and experimental facilities, than any British company. Other differences existed in the way in which drawings were used, leading to a much more efficient deployment of design and drawing staff. There was also a much closer relationship between design and production people. Fedden was equally struck by the systematic approach in the US to production planning, scheduling, plant layout and the use of statistical production analysis aimed at the improvement of overall performance. By comparison, an MAP visit to Vickers at the height of the war revealed incompetent and unqualified managers, shocking labour relations, poor shift control 'and no system of line production throughout the whole organisation'. Even the newest British factories fell short of the ideal for efficient production. Dispersion – to some extent dictated by security considerations – and the location of 'shadow' factories next to the geographically scattered car plants reduced the economies of scale which might have been achieved by concentration. Optimum factory layout was also constrained by the need for protection against blast damage. Similarly, while on a scale rarely seen in the British industry, the 'shadow' factories were still half the average size of the huge facilities being built under Federal contract in the US.[35]

By the end of the war, American techniques, drawing heavily on auto industry methods, were resembling those of the major car plants, with moving production lines and specialised tools which reduced handwork to a minimum. A similar association with the

British car industry to an extent helped the British aircraft industry break out of its 'craft' status. Rolls-Royce, for example, distinguished between the different needs of development and production and adjusted the use of its factories, plant and manpower accordingly. As Hives put it, Derby became a 'huge development factory' where design and prototype work could continue using crafted parts fitted by highly skilled men. Here they could do the jobs which would *upset the whole scheme of things in a true manufacturing plant* [Hives' emphasis]. Crewe, on the other hand, was used as a purely manufacturing plant with unskilled and semi skilled labour operating more fixed machinery and jigs. At Hillington, the design of which was helped by a firm of production consultants, the entire emphasis was on line production with modern systems of cost and production control. Rolls also established training centres for its predominantly female labour force. But generally British practice was still far below that of the most efficient American firms. Even Rolls was surprised to find that Ford UK, when called upon to produce the Merlin, worked to finer tolerances in the mass production of car engines than Rolls itself. Many senior managers were also unwilling to accept the findings of the Fedden mission until they themselves came into contact with American aircraft manufacturers. Sir Stafford Cripps, as Minister for Aircraft Production, thought otherwise and pressed hard to see its recommendations implemented.[36]

Production efficiency was detrimentally affected by several other problems. The resistance of the work force to the introduction of multiple shifts made it difficult for either firms or the MAP to improve the utilisation of capacity and to increase the flexibility with which the production of older types could give way to that of their successors. It was also evident that some firms 'preferred producing the well-established types' to taking on the demands and costs of new projects. Output was affected by absenteeism, wild-cat strikes and poor industrial relations. Even Rolls-Royce had difficulties with disputes over 'dilution of labour', pay scales and differentials. The Fedden mission also noted the lower morale of British workers and their generally inferior working environment compared to those in the US. On the other hand, people who worked in the industry during the war have attested to the commitment and dedication shown by those facing long hours on the shopfloor – a 'patriotic spirit' leavened by high bonus rates.[37]

The limitations of individual firms were exacerbated by the virtual absence of co-operation between companies. There was, of course, a close relationship between engine and airframe companies and the engine firms were required by the MAP to collaborate on the development of jets. But companies not linked by common ownership, such as Avro, Hawker and Gloster, worked 'more or less in isolation'. There was a degree of informal borrowing and learning, but there was little systematic exchange of ideas and experience. To a large extent, this reflected the 'rugged individualism' of firms and their design departments, and the lingering effects of competition. Harold Balfour at the Air Ministry compared the firms and their leaders 'to a lot of suspicious dogs sniffing at each other and refusing to co-operate, preferring to walk round in a sort of circle, each following the tail of the other and no-one giving any lead'.[38] These attitudes extended to preparations for post-war programmes, with each firm looking for contracts, unwilling to pool expertise and facilities to enter what, for most, would be the unknown territory of jet technology and large commercial aircraft.

1.5 Developing the jet engine

The jet engine was the single most important innovation in aviation to come out of the Second World War. Advances made in aerodynamics by the Germans were of considerable importance to post-war aircraft development, particularly in the area of high speed flight. German rocket technology would also form the basis for post-war missile and space research, but the jet was the driving force of a new generation of civil and military designs, massively increasing the size, power and range of aircraft.[39] The British did not 'invent' the jet engine – ideas for jet propulsion were considered in France, Switzerland and of course, in Germany, where the first (secret) flight of a jet powered aircraft took place in 1939. However, the jet would take the UK aero-engine industry, pre-eminently Rolls-Royce, to the forefront of world aviation and provide the basis for a bold, but flawed challenge to American post-war domination of the aerospace industry.

In Britain, Frank Whittle outlined the first definite proposal for a jet engine in 1929 while an RAF Cadet at Cranwell, registering a patent the following year. Whittle, later Air Commodore Sir Frank Whittle, was the son of a mechanic and small businessman who rose through the ranks of the RAF. Although a 'born' engineer, he also took a first class degree in engineering from Cambridge while developing his engine. Whittle's struggle to prove his concept and to establish jet technology in the UK is part of the folklore of British aviation history; but there has been a tendency to understate the real difficulties of pursuing fundamental research in wartime Britain as well as the intrinsic limitations of the Whittle design.

Whittle's work was preceded by research at the RAE by Dr A. A. Griffith in the mid 1920s. Griffith outlined several key concepts, including a design for a multiple blade axial-flow compressor and the idea of linking a turbine to a propeller – the turbo-prop. Work on the axial flow engine at the RAE stopped in 1930. Whittle was unaware of Griffith's research when he put forward his idea for a simpler single stage axial-flow turbine based on the tried and tested centrifugal compressor. Whittle's own theoretical work and investigations into turbine blade form were also highly original, and the simplicity of the Whittle concept proved to be one of its greatest virtues. Even so, Whittle's engine presumed the development of materials and structures capable of withstanding pressures and temperatures well beyond contemporary standards. In the long run, the multi-blade, axial compressor would be the basis of jet development, for unlike the bulky centrifugal engine, it had the potential to generate more thrust without increasing cross-sectional size. The Germans moved faster along this line of development and produced a more powerful axial flow engine. In service, however, the Me262 and other German jet aircraft were plagued by reliability problems (German engines had an operational life of less than forty-eight hours flight time) which Whittle-engined aircraft largely escaped.

Research at the RAE on the axial flow engine began again in 1936 in conjunction with Metropolitan-Vickers and provided the foundation for later development of axial engines in the UK. In the short term, the work suffered from a lack of facilities and competition from the more pressing demands of rearmament. Private industry was also very reluctant to enter the field.[40] In this respect, the 'outsider' Whittle acted as a catalyst for action, pushing against the odds his obsession with the turbine engine. However, as a serving member of the RAF, Whittle had to follow the demands of a service career as well as the spark of invention. His loyalty to the Service and its conventions also limited the degree to which he could defend and promote his engine in the face of commercial pressures.

In 1935, several industrialists and financiers, believing that Whittle's ideas might form the basis of a successful speculative investment, provided £10,000 to form Power Jets to develop a commercial jet engine. British Thompson Houston (BTH) was contracted to develop components for the new company. Although not prepared to fund the work, the Air Ministry allowed Whittle to become chief consultant to Power Jets in his 'spare time'.[41] Officials at the Air Ministry remained highly sceptical; but Whittle had one very well placed supporter in Sir Henry Tizard, then Chairman of the Aeronautical Research Committee (ARC), who pressed the Air Ministry to back a series of tests held during 1937. The ARC's subsequent report confirmed that Whittle's design promised a considerable increase in thrust using lower grade fuel than the piston engine, and recommended that the Air Ministry should support development. The Air Ministry was initially unwilling to provide money in advance of proof of design (which, without finance, Power Jets could hardly provide). A long wrangle over terms ensued, but in March 1938 Power Jets received a Ministry contract. This was a major step forward, but as the work now became subject to the Official Secrets Act, it became even more difficult to attract private capital.

In the spring of 1939, the Air Ministry, again urged on by Tizard, decided to pay for a flight-rated engine. In June 1939, a re-designed engine sufficiently impressed the Air Ministry and several senior officials, including Air Marshall Tedder, to initiate the development of an airframe. The Gloster Aircraft Company was chosen to build the E.28/39 and the operational fighter, the F.9/40 (Meteor) because 'most of the other firms were already overcrowded, and of the available design teams, Gloster's was probably the best'.[42] But industrial support for Whittle was still limited and Power Jets' financial base remained inadequate; its only assets were Whittle's patents and most of the fabrication work was done by BTH. Moreover, the continual struggle for money even after the Ministry contract was a constraining factor. Yet despite these problems, the E.28/39 made its first flight on 15 May 1943 and quickly confirmed the simplicity, reliability and above all the potential power of the Whittle jet.[43]

The Air Ministry, happier dealing with the 'family', was deeply suspicious of Power Jets and its private backers. There was a tendency for the official mind to seize on the inevitable difficulties of developing a radically new concept as evidence that Power Jets was a back yard outfit incapable of carrying through a major project:

> the historical verdict may be that the financial outlay was very low compared with both the value of the research work done by Air Commodore Whittle and with the cost of the work in the immediately succeeding period when jet propulsion was fully backed by the Air Ministry. In this respect both private business and H.M. Government failed to rise to the occasion.

Whittle's difficulties stand in stark contrast to the near ideal conditions which prevailed in Germany. Development was conducted by Heinkel, an established and well financed aircraft company, with solid support from German research institutes.[44]

By mid 1940, however, the Gloster/Whittle project had won a higher status, being defined by the MAP as one of a number of potential 'war winners'. It was now a question of how best to prepare the engine for production and get the Meteor into service. However, although Whittle's team was now recognised as a highly dedicated and competent *design* team, the MAP still held grave doubts about Power Jets' capability to manufacture production engines. The link with BTH was unsatisfactory and the recognised aero-engine firms were felt to be sufficiently tied up with conventional work. In any case, Whittle had strong views about allowing the 'orthodox engine' companies to muscle in on his work: 'It would seem to me grossly unfair that the Air Ministry should allow Power Jets to ripen the fruit and others to pluck it ... I believe that Power Jets as such could handle this job in its future stages better than some existing aero-engine firm, who would probably rather kill it than get on with it.'[45] Power Jets had already approached Rover as a possible partner and the MAP therefore turned to Rover and its shadow engine production facilities as a base for jet engine production.

In practice, the relationship between Power Jets and Rover proved equally unsatisfactory. The assumption was that the parties would abide by a 'gentlemen's agreement' and fully co-operate on development and production. Power Jets feared that it was being left at the mercy of a large industrial concern with little legal protection. An alternative, and, in some respects, logical solution would have been at this juncture to have transferred Power Jets to the RAE or another engine firm. But the personal difficulties involved were too great and potentially disruptive. Accordingly, it was accepted that Power Jets would remain formally independent, but supported by the MAP. In effect, Power Jets became an R&D centre for the nascent British jet engine industry. This did not, however, lead to any improvement in the working relationship with Rover.[46]

The MAP was beginning to take a wider view of jet propulsion. Having identified the jet as a potentially vital technology, the ministry wanted to get other firms and the RAE involved in development work. A Gas Turbine Collaboration Committee was established to encourage inter-firm co-operation. Research work was to be co-ordinated and data pooled to ensure that commercial interests did not hamper development. The War Cabinet also decided to include the jet engine amongst the technologies 'transferred' to the US where General Electric (GE) began to produce Whittle designed engines. Soon after, GE and Westinghouse began independent work on axial-flow engines. By early 1942, eleven British firms were involved in jet engine development. These included Rolls-Royce, Metropolitan-Vickers, de Havilland, Bristol and Armstrong Siddeley. De Havilland proved to be particularly successful; determined to break out of the constraints of small piston engine manufacturing, by 1943 the company was working on its own engine/airframe combination, leading in time to the Goblin-powered Vampire. This work also gave the company an important early indication of the civil potential of jet power. Armstrong Siddeley, strongly 'encouraged' by the MAP, abandoned piston technology entirely. The MAP in fact made it 'clear to them that their place in the aero-engine "family" was dependent upon such a change'.[47]

The most significant of these new entrants was, of course, Rolls-Royce. The firm realised from a early stage that its position as a major aero-engine company might depend on a successful adjustment to jet technology. In 1939, Dr Griffith had left the RAE to head research at Rolls into axial-flow jet engines. The company was aware that this was the most difficult approach to the problem, especially given its existing commitments to piston development and production. Consequently, in 1940 Rolls responded positively to Henry Tizard's suggestion that it should take a look at Whittle's engine. Hooker and Hives were both impressed by Whittle's design and the company undertook, free of charge, some fabrication work. In January 1942, Hives discussed with Whittle the possibility of a closer relationship 'in the national interest', but with both sides unwilling to make the first formal step, a 'golden opportunity was lost' to consolidate jet engine research under Rolls-Royce.[48]

Meanwhile, the production organisation put together at Rover's Barnoldswick shadow factory was 'still in a condition bordering on chaotic'.[49] Facilities worth £1.5 million were lying idle, and none of the few pre-production engines built for the F.9/40 prototype were fit for use. Some of the problems stemmed from the attempt to produce both airframe and engine 'off the drawing board' – a procedure which was often used to expedite progress in conventional projects but which was ill suited to a totally new concept. Rover also found it difficult to organise a production line for the jet, which although simpler than the piston engine, required new manufacturing techniques. In the event, Rover's system proved very effective, but the rapid transition from development to production overstretched the company's capabilities.

The relationship between Rover and Power Jets continued to deteriorate. Rover had hopes of entering the aero-engine field after the war and this engendered considerable tension between the two firms. Matters reached a crisis when Power Jets discovered that Rover was developing independently its own version of the Whittle engine, apparently with the tacit support of some officials at the MAP. In December 1942, the MAP accepted that the 'simple and inevitable' solution was to give the responsibility for producing the Whittle engine to Rolls-Royce. Rover had by now lost interest in developing an aero-engine business or, for that matter, in ever getting on with Whittle. Hives and Rover chief Maurice Wilkes arranged the deal over Whittle's head. Whittle, ill with overwork and unequipped to cope with this kind of high level manoeuvring, could only look on as Power Jets' future was sorted out by others.[50]

From 1 April 1943, Rolls took over the Barnoldswick factory in exchange for its tank engine factory in Nottingham. Rolls also acquired the services of Adrian Lombard, who became one of the finest engine designers of the post-war period. According to Stanley Hooker,

> this decision – which surely ought to have been taken at a national level much earlier – changed the whole tempo of the development of

the jet engine. Instead of small teams working in holes in the corner, in one stroke nearly 2,000 men and women and massive manufacturing facilities, were focussed on the task of getting the [Whittle] engine mechanically reliable and ready for RAF service.[51]

Fortunately, there was considerable mutual respect between the two sides and a close working relationship was quickly established. Power Jets remained an autonomous unit responsible for research and development of centrifugal compressors, but its exact role in the industry was increasingly uncertain.

By the middle of 1943, with more details of German developments becoming known and plans for the post-war industry under consideration, the Cabinet and Air Ministry began to consider future designs for jet aircraft. Research started on high speed aerodynamics and structures which generated ideas for a high speed interceptor and a twin-engined bomber. This work provided the MAP with the basis for turning the jet engine into 'an all purpose power plant, so that it would outclass the reciprocating engine in all conditions of flight ... a landmark in the history of the gas turbine and in the evolution of informed opinion'. Engine prospects for the near and more distant future 'were now clearly linked up with definite airframe requirements', and specific aerodynamic problems 'requiring speedy solution if further progress of jet aircraft was to be sustained' were identified.[52]

In July 1944, the Meteor entered service and was used successfully to intercept V1 flying bombs. Rolls-Royce and the de Havilland Engine company were producing centrifugal engines in quantity. In conjunction with Power Jets, Rolls had turned the basic Whittle design into the Derwent series and more important, had committed itself to a complete switch from piston engines to jets. As far as Power Jets was concerned, the last two years of the war proved to be something of a disappointment and left a residue of bitterness. It was increasingly cut adrift from production and was increasingly seen as an R&D organisation. It was eventually decided to nationalise the company and to merge it with the RAE's jet research facilities which, after the war, formed the National Gas Turbine Research Establishment (NGTRE) with a remit to provide research and advice for the industry on a non-commercial basis.[53] In focusing on research, the NGTRE would not constitute a potential threat to the private sector, but this would prevent Whittle's team developing and building full-scale engines. Nor was this what

Whittle had envisaged when he himself had suggested nationalisation as perhaps the best course of action for British jet engine development: 'I deluded myself into believing that, in a nationalised gas turbine industry, the Power Jets' team would naturally be at the apex of the pyramid.' In January 1946, Whittle resigned from Power Jets citing the shift to pure research as the main reason for his decision.[54]

Whittle received an *ex gratia* payment of £100,000 for his work on the jet engine and was knighted in 1948. He retired from the RAF, his health undermined by the war, and later emigrated to the US where he continued work as a consultant engineer. His company was undoubtedly treated in a rather shabby way, but sentiment should not confuse judgement. Power Jets had always been an anomaly and its peculiar status had provided both its strengths (stimulating original ideas and a burning passion) and its limitations (financial weakness and separation from the mainstream of aircraft and engine development). However, once jet technology had been recognised as the basis for Britain's post-war hopes in aviation it became imperative that the aircraft industry at large took on the challenge. Moving on from the Whittle engine to axial-flow designs would prove difficult and would require extensive and experienced engineering capabilities. It is difficult to see how Power Jets could have formed the *industrial* base for further development, especially given the entry of very well-funded and supported US firms into the jet business. Rolls, and to a lessor extent, de Havilland, Bristol and Armstrong Siddeley formed a more logical home for Britain's post war exploitation of the new technology.

1.6 Questions of post war structure and policy

By 1943, with the war effectively won, the government began to turn its attention to post-war reconstruction. The aircraft industry had clearly emerged as a strategically important industry and a major manufacturing sector. Three criteria emerged as the basis for planning in the aircraft industry – national security, employment and the contribution aviation could make to the UK's export trade which, overall, had to increase by 50 per cent.[55] Given the extraordinary wartime growth of the industry and the temporary pre-eminence of air power in British defence, some shrinkage was inevitable – but by how far? The exact level of demand capable of sustaining a given industrial capacity could not be calculated with any certainty. Military aviation would still predominate, but requirements would depend on the 'international or inter-UN settlement'. The market for military products in the dominions was equally uncertain, with likely competition from the US and demands for indigenous production. Although Britain was stronger relative to the US in military aviation, in the civil sector US dominance was 'inevitable'. It would take between eight and ten years for Britain to reach a comparable standard with the US, but it was imperative that policy should be based upon the assumption that 'this objective can be obtained and strive as far as practical to accelerate its attainment'.

Initial estimates suggested that the UK would need an industry with between 150,000 and 200,000 employees dedicated to defence programmes with a further 25,000 working on civil projects. This was already over twice the size of the aircraft industry in 1936, but the Air Ministry and Admiralty felt that 400,000 might be needed. The MAP believed it was 'probably wise' to assume a base at most of of 250,000, based on an output of between 10 per cent and 20 per cent of wartime production. The engine sector would certainly be much larger than before the war for industrial and strategic reasons. However, the Treasury was already signalling caution, warning that the larger estimate would imply a defence budget of over £500 million, then hardly conceivable in peacetime. In the event, even the MAP's figures proved optimistic (see Chapter 2).

The question of ownership was briefly touched on. Some Labour ministers in the wartime coalition wanted to see a larger proportion of the post-war industry under direct government control. Industry's slow pre-war mobilisation had, in their opinion, been due to a reluctance on the part of private enterprise converting to war production, and that on defence grounds a greater degree of government control would be justified. But while there was little support for radical industrial change in the formal relationship between state and industry, the state would still retain considerable scope for intervention. Although the 'family' would go, the Ministry intended to divide the industry into 'division one' and 'division two' firms, allocating orders and development contracts according to capability and capacity. The 'first division' would be the central design and development core for major projects. It comprised the two Vickers companies, Avro, Hawker, Bristol, de Havilland, Handley Page and Shorts. The 'second division' consisted of ten firms – Fairey, Armstrong Whitworth, Airspeed, Westland, Miles, Boulton-Paul, Saunders Roe, English Electric, Blackburn and Gloster.

It was felt that employment in first division companies should not fall below 4,000 and in the second, 2,000, leading to an industry total of 180,000 employees. Other firms could expect some assistance in the 'early stages' of the post-war period but thereafter would 'sink or swim' on their own. These standings were not fixed, and companies, 'if they repeatedly fail to give satisfactory service, may be demoted from the first or second class; conversely, it must be open to firms ... to graduate up if they prove their merit'. Special reference was made to English Electric; although its wartime production record had been top class, it could not be placed in the first division because it had no design staff. It was, therefore, up to the company 'to prove its ability to build up a design capability and that it has genuine ambitions to become first class' – an ambition which was quickly realised (see Chapter 2).

In view of the weaknesses identified during the war, the MAP increasingly emphasised the need for more technical education, skill training, and basic research in the industry. Government facilities would be improved and some consideration was given to the retention of a 'Ministry shadow factory' to 'stimulate design and development and to act as a yardstick for industry's efforts'. Less contentiously, other shadow factories owned by the state would be made available to companies to 'maintain war potential and for the construction of products for home and foreign sale'. The MAP also realised that much would have to be done to prepare the industry technically for the post war world. The industry's existing products were based on the practical application and subsequent modification of technical principles established during the early 1930s, largely by American firms. During the war, it was decided, with the critical exception of the jet engine, to limit the scope of new research activities to the improvement of established technological concepts. Another important area of innovation was in the application of airborne electronics, especially in the form of aids to bomber navigation, target acquisition and electronic counter-measures. But as Barnett observes, technically, the triumphs of the Battle of Britain and the bomber offensive were built in large part on 'foreign innovations and equipment'.[56]

Following pre-war practice, the British aircraft industry largely depended on outside bodies for advanced research on aeronautical and especially aerodynamic subjects. The Universities provided additional support, but the bulk of research data and often ideas for new items of equipment came from the RAE and other government research organisations. In other industries, and of course in the US aircraft industry, these functions were performed by in-house research staff. By 1943 the MAP, looking forward to peacetime reconstruction, increasingly felt that this was indeed something which might be better done independently by the aircraft industry. Some firms such as Bristol and de Havilland began to press the MAP for assistance in building up their own research capability, and as an ambitious newcomer, English Electric quickly invested in research facilities. In general, however, the level of provision for an adequate R&D base capable of absorbing the technical lessons of the war and exploiting the emerging gas-turbine based technology was worrying. By 1944, although plans were being made for the development of more advanced combat jet aircraft they would clearly take some time to materialise. Re-creating a British civil capacity would be even more problematic.

1.7 The Brabazon programme

It was evident from the MAP's deliberations that commercial aircraft would form an important element in plans for an expanded peacetime aircraft industry. However, the decision to rely on the US for transport aircraft, combined with the inadequacy of British pre-war civil designs meant that British companies had much to learn if they were to compete against the Americans, whose commercial industry had benefited considerably from wartime development and production. The nationalised airlines, BOAC (formed in 1939 from a merger of Imperial and British Airways) and BEA (created in 1946 to cover domestic and European services), would be required to 'fly British', but this alone would be insufficient to sustain a post-war development programme of significant proportions. The state would have to fill the gap.

Towards the end of 1942, the government asked Lord Brabazon to consider possible post-war requirements for civil aircraft. His committee's first report, submitted to the Cabinet in February 1943, confirmed the seriousness of the situation facing the aircraft industry without an adequate civil programme on hand at war's end, and outlined five broad airliner types which might form the basis of such a programme. A second Brabazon Committee was remitted to draw up a more detailed set of specifications which, after additional ideas from industry, led to nine projects (see table 5). Later, the Committee recommended several bomber conversions which could be used by British airlines as soon as the war ended, and the MAP itself added a series of other 'interim' types – more sophisticated derivatives of bomber designs.

Table 5: The Brabazon Types

Type 1	Bristol Brabazon (long range piston engined trans-Atlantic airliner)
Type 2A	Airspeed Ambassador (short range piston engined airliner)
Type 2B	Vickers Viscount (short range turbo prop airliner)
Type 2B	Armstrong Whitworth Apollo (short range turbo prop airliner)
Type 3A	Avro 693 (medium range turbo prop airliner)
Type 3B	Avro Tudor II (developed from interim aircraft replaced Avro 693)
Type 4	de Havilland Comet (originally designed as trans-Atlantic 'mail carrier')
Type 5A	Miles Marathon (piston engined feederliner)
Type 5B	de Havilland Dove (piston engined feeder liner)

The aim of the supplementary programme was to get some form of civil production under way as soon as possible. It was never likely to have much of a commercial impact on the well-established American airliners and the commercial prospects of the aircraft introduced under its aegis were further compromised by the delays encountered during development. In the event, only the Vickers Viking had any commercial success (see Chapter 2).

On 25 February 1943 the War Cabinet endorsed the 'Brabazon' programme, accepting that the UK should 'maintain a substantial aircraft industry after the war' and that 'British air transport after the war shall be on a scale and quality in keeping with our world position'. However, work on new civil types and the interim designs had to take second place to the war effort. The Cabinet was also concerned lest the US should discover preparations for civil projects which might threaten Lend-Lease. However, the government did accept the 'financial responsibility for the initiation of a programme of civil aviation upon a basis adequate to provide a minimum number of essential types of aircraft in the immediate post-war period'. Estimates of its cost, as one official noted, 'can only be a shot in the dark' based on the pre-war cost of developing the Flamingo.[57]

Allocation of Brabazon contracts by the MAP took account of military commitments, technical competence and the overall strength of companies to undertake major projects. Bristol was an 'obvious' choice for Type 1 – the eponymous Brabazon. It had spare capacity and the Ministry wanted the company to develop a capability for the design and development of very large bombers. Type 2 contracts went to Airspeed, Vickers and later Armstrong Whitworth. In the case of Airspeed, it too had spare capacity and the MAP wanted to encourage it to switch to metal construction for strategic reasons. Both Vickers and Armstrong Whitworth put forward turbo-prop designs. Vickers was well resourced, keen to get into the civil market and had the Viking to provide a useful 'learning' exercise. Armstrong Whitworth, on the other hand, was the weakest of the Hawker 'family' and the project received little support from the parent group.

The Type 5 Dove was a continuation of de Havilland's excellent series of small airliners. Although required to build an all-metal aircraft for the first time, de Havilland put £220,000 of its own money towards the £3 million needed for development and carried the cost of production and marketing. De Havilland was also well placed to build the Type 4, a jet powered 'mail carrier'. De Havilland's own work on jet engines gave a privileged insight into the potential and characteristics of the new technology. Helped by the vagueness of the original specification and the ignorance of many officials about jet engine development, de Havilland had considerable independence in the design of Type 4. The company also chose to use the 'Whittle' centrifugal compressor instead of waiting for the more powerful, but more complicated axial flow engine under development at Rolls-Royce. As a result, instead of a very specialised aircraft, the company produced a genuine airliner, the Comet One. De Havilland was further encouraged by the positive support it received from BOAC, seeing in the Comet the one truly revolutionary Brabazon project and the one most likely to challenge American domination.

On balance, the choice of firms to undertake Brabazon projects was not very sound; 'the choice of inadequate or heavily over-worked firms to take on these projects clearly raises the question as to whether they should have been started at all'. Few of the projects were commercial successes and some were total failures, obsolete before they flew. The programme's limitations were exacerbated by the inability of firms to co-operate and by the MAP's lack of power, or will, to enforce co-operation. In fact, the MAP's priority lay in maintaining a diverse collection of design teams for strategic reasons, and it saw no reason to enforce a rationalisation of industrial assets. Progress was also very slow, affected by shortages, especially of draughtsmen and other skilled personnel. There were also disputes with BOAC over both specifications and the priority assigned to the Type 1 which the airline felt to be unjustified. The Brabazon Committee frequently complained about the lack of progress, but measures introduced by the MAP to increase the supply of trained people were, by their nature, long term. It was as late as January 1945 before the Cabinet felt able to authorise a general change in R&D priorities to anticipate demobilisation and reconversion. Although civil aviation was then singled out as a special case, routine allocation of resources still favoured military supply. It was not until late in 1945 that civil projects 'really began to receive top priority' and even then only following very high level political pressure.[58] Nevertheless, although deeply flawed in concept and implementation, the Brabazon programme was of inestimable value in founding a post-war British civil aircraft industry (see Chapter 2).

1.8 The Second World War: an assessment

The British aircraft industry had a 'good war'. This was a reflection of the glory won by the RAF and its own merits. By the end of the war, over 126,500 aircraft had been delivered. At its peak in 1943, annual production was at 26,263 compared with 2,827 in 1938. In addition, over 18,000 major repairs were carried out. In 1935, the industry employed some 35,000 people with an output worth £14 million. In 1944 output was worth £800 million and the aircraft companies alone employed 300,000 men and women. In total, 1·7 million people worked on aircraft, engines and associated equipment. Capital investment in the industry had exceeded £350 million, of which £63·5 million and £39·6 million was spent on factories and plant respectively. The demands of aircraft production had also effectively created a light metal industry in Britain. In 1935, the annual production of aluminium was 15,000 tons – in 1944 it was nearly 26,000 tons per month. Here then was an industrial development 'without parallel in British history in terms of scale, speed and cost – and of state participation. Here was the centre of gravity of the entire British war effort.'[59]

These figures perhaps helped to hide structural and attitudinal weaknesses which, certainly by comparison with the US, impaired efficiency and which would seriously hamper post- war competitiveness. The increase in output was due almost entirely to the expansion of the workforce and the greater use of machine tools (largely imported). On a more precise measurement of productivity – in terms of structural weight produced per man – the US was 1·5 times more productive and even Germany was 20 per cent better. In his *Audit of War*, Corelli Barnett rightly demolishes some of the myths surrounding Britain's wartime achievements. There were fundamental problems associated with aircraft production and the design achievements were largely (but not entirely) dependent on foreign innovation.[60] There were, on the other hand, genuine successes in terms of industrial organisation. Overy, for example, notes how the shadow system produced 45 per cent of Britain's heavy bombers, two-thirds of her light bombers and, by weight, 23 cent of all aircraft production. By contrast, Germany, albeit with larger aircraft firms, failed to mobilise its car industry until well into the war and never ran at more than 50 per cent of capacity. Britain was also able to use scarce materials with greater efficiency.[61] For all its faults, the British system rarely faced the kind of internecine battles about priorities that pervaded Nazi Germany. Equally, although German designers came up with technically very advanced concepts, technical over-sophistication often tended to undermine military effectiveness. It should also be added that the best fighter of the war, the American P51 Mustang, rose from the mediocre thanks to a British engine, the Merlin.

Technically the industry was in far better shape than it had been in 1935, and the lead in jet technology promised much. However, there were important gaps, especially in the use of pressurisation, and the results of German wartime research would shortly show how much else had to be learnt if British airframes were to match British engines. The war had also effectively destroyed Britain's European competitors, at least for a generation of aircraft development. However, the commercial 'enemy' in the post-war period was not Germany or France but the US – and its industry too had prospered and expanded through the war. The war had increased the technological complexity of even conventional aircraft; the new jet age and Cold War technological competition would further accelerate the rate of innovation. With increased complexity would come rising development costs and still greater need to seek economies of scale. In this respect, the British preoccupation with 'strategic' capability and the refusal of both government and industry to countenance rationalisation was evidence of a dangerous degree of complacency.

The relationship between state and industry, already well established as the foundation of industrial development in the UK aircraft industry, was reinforced by wartime practice. The commitment to a post-war civil programme would further strengthen these links. In the years that followed, the state would remain industry's most important customer and the source of most of its development capital, as well as intervening in the structure and operation of companies. This dependence by the industry would continue to be a cause of friction, frustration and recrimination; but the alternative would have been even more unpalatable – full exposure to US competition, a Spartan mountain side of formidable ferocity.

CHAPTER TWO

RECONSTRUCTION AND RATIONALISATION

1945–52

2.1. Post-war reconstruction

The industry entered the post-war world with considerable prestige and popular esteem. Its designers and leaders had become household names and any weaknesses in the industry's structure or approach to its business were not readily apparent to the outside world. The industry had become a powerful economic and strategic element in British manufacturing, with strong political and official support. It was accepted that some shrinkage would occur, but the savage retrenchment of 1918–20 would not be repeated. Moreover, although there would be a reduction in domestic military orders, the Brabazon programme was designed to support a British attack on the civil market. In the longer term, new technically advanced military projects would also be authorised. Although the industry faced powerful competition from the US, the war had effectively removed any significant threat from other European companies for at least a decade. In short, the UK industry had an important commercial breathing space to assimilate the technological lessons of World War Two, replace worn out plant and machinery, and to modernise its production techniques.

Although the aircraft industry was clearly an important asset, it would still have to compete for resources in the general reconstruction of British industry and spending on the nascent Welfare State. Although the 1946–47 defence budget, at £1,667 million, was generous by pre-war standards, defence expenditure would be stabilised below 7 per cent of GNP and re-equipment plans would again be constrained by a 'ten year rule'. There was also considerable uncertainty about the future of defence requirements in the light of the atom bomb. The decision to develop an independent British nuclear weapons programme would imply the need for a major bomber programme, and some conventional aircraft, fighters and tactical bombers, would still be needed. However, time was needed to evaluate the lessons of World War Two and the new technologies it had spawned, as well as to build up research and development facilities capable of sustaining advanced work which had been neglected during the war. In the short term, demand for military aircraft would fall but it was hoped that full implementation of the Brabazon programme and the export of both civil and military aircraft would help to maintain a broad-based aircraft industry. In line with policy guidelines formulated towards the end of the war, the industry was expected to contract to about 180,000 employees. In the event, the immediate post-war level touched 114,300; even so, this was three times larger than the industry's employment level at any time between 1919 and 1938, and by 1949 it had reached just over 180,000.

Some firms attempted, with varying degrees of success, to diversify into other areas of engineering and sheet metal work including the construction of prefabricated housing. Most companies, however, were prepared to invest in mainstream aircraft development, sustained by some domestic military orders, Ministry development projects, the 'interim' civil production programme, exports and the promise of better things in the future. Some were better placed than others; de Havilland, for example, had three major programmes, the Vampire, the Dove and the Comet. As one of the first production jet fighters, the Vampire also sold reasonably well overseas. To support these and other programmes, the company improved its facilities at Hatfield and took over Vickers' shadow factory at Broughton, near Chester. This was one of the most modern factories in Europe and effectively doubled de Havilland's manufacturing capacity. Vickers' post war plans were based on the assumption that it would continue to be a major aircraft producer. Its chairman told shareholders that there was no reason why the company should not 'hold their leading position in the aircraft industry'. Investment was concentrated on the Weybridge factory and Vickers' research facilities were improved, including the construction of a large wind tunnel. The firm realised, however, that future development would be concentrated on a small number of high cost programmes with a commensurate increase in the level of risk. Interim projects like the Viking helped to tide the firm over, and the Viscount airliner and the Valiant bomber, both pushed hard by an aggressive design team led by George, later Sir George Edwards, would eventually provide a highly profitable base. In time Vickers, along with Bristol, became something of a civil specialist, but through its Vickers-Supermarine division, it maintained an important fighter aircraft design capacity.

Handley Page, still run by its founder, maintained a mix of civil and military programmes. In 1948, it acquired Miles Aircraft, then in liquidation, which formed the basis for a separate design and production organisation and which later went on to develop the Herald airliner. The firm was amongst the first in Britain to make use of German research data in designing the revolutionary Victor bomber with its advanced 'crescent wing'. Sir Frederick Handley Page, along with Sir Roy Fedden, was also instrumental in founding the College of Aeronautics at Cranfield.[1] In 1947, with the end of flying boat production, Shorts closed its English factory becoming Short Brothers and Harland of Northern Ireland. The firm remained largely in public hands, though Bristol later acquired a small share-holding when Shorts became an important subcontractor. Indeed, Shorts' main business was as a subcontractor to larger design centres, assembling Comet 2s for de Havilland as well as Britannias for Bristol. Its Belfast location also helped to ensure favourable attention from the government. Blackburn closed two of its wartime factories and concentrated production at Brough. Like Shorts, it did a lot of subcontract work, but it also had two important post-war programmes, the Beverley heavy military transport and the NA39 Buccaneer, a low level attack aircraft for the Fleet Air Arm. The main casualty of the immediate post-war period was Miles Aircraft, but there were a number of 'second division' firms with ambitions to become senior players. Scottish Aviation, which had produced Lysanders and other 'shadow' contracts during the war and had only been admitted to the SBAC in 1942, had the support of local MPs and unions in its efforts to attract Ministry of Supply (MoS) work. It became a subcontractor to Avro, de Havilland and Rolls, as well as developing its own Pioneer 'feederliner'.[2]

The most important and successful 'entrant' was English Electric. Its wartime production record had been exemplary and the company was selected by the MAP to assemble the de Havilland designed Vampire jet fighter. The MAP placed it in the second division because it lacked a design team but in 1944, when the company decided to remain in the aircraft industry, it set out to remedy this deficiency, recruiting William Petter from Westland to lead a new design team. Lacking both the tradition and the inhibitions of more established firms, English Electric had the advantage of a clean start with fresh ideas at a time when aircraft technology was in a state of flux. Equally important, the aircraft division benefited from being part of a stronger, diversified engineering company whose electrical and electronic interests gave a vital insight into the increasingly important role of electronics in combat aircraft design. The war had also provided new factories built under the shadow scheme. However, to support its claims to be a first rank aircraft manufacturer, English Electric invested in new design and test facilities, opening a large experimental centre at Warton aerodrome, seven miles from its Preston factory.

By 1948, the Warton test facilities included a Mach 0·9 wind tunnel and the largest structural test frame in the country. In July 1950, English Electric opened the first privately owned supersonic wind tunnel in Britain and probably the first outside the US. The firm also pioneered the use of computers in the design and development process, initially using the National Physical Laboratory's ACE machine and later its own DEUCE machine at Stafford. English Electric came to be associated with some of the most important post-war British military designs: the highly successful Canberra jet bomber – the first British military aircraft to be used by the USAF – and Britain's first operational supersonic fighter, the P1 Lightning. These two projects confirmed English Electric as a major actor in the UK aircraft industry: as the company's historians note, 'that one design team should have responsibility for two such important projects was remarkable. Its success can be judged from the fact that in the first five years its members conceived two aircraft which were to provide nearly 20 years of production work for the company.'[3]

The aero-engine industry was affected in much the same way as the airframe sector by demobilisation and government policy. There were eight manufacturers, of which five were of major importance: Rolls-Royce, Bristol, de Havilland, Armstrong Siddeley and Napier. Nearly all the companies developed new turbine engines under government contract. Many were for the same specification – the Rolls-Royce Dart, Armstrong Siddeley Mamba and the Napier Naiad were all aimed at the Viscount, a competition eventually won by the Dart. But for strategic reasons the government was particularly keen to get as many firms as possible interested in jet technology, pressing both Napier and Armstrong Siddeley into developing jet engines. In the event, only a few of these early projects were produced in substantial numbers, including the Rolls-Royce Nene, Dart and Avon; the de Havilland Goblin and Ghost; the Bristol Proteus and Olympus and the Armstrong Sapphire. Of these, the Rolls engines proved commercially the most successful and helped to underline Rolls' growing dominance of the UK aero-engine industry.

In 1945, Rolls was already by far the most important and technically competent of the engine companies, and unlike the others, independent of an airframe manufacturer (Rolls believed that this gave it a vital commercial advantage in securing orders from 'non-aligned' airframe manufacturers). In common with the rest of the industry, Rolls suffered a sharp contraction at the end of the war. Within fifteen months, Rolls shed nearly half of its wartime employees, reducing numbers from 47,000 to 24,000. Where many others in the aircraft industry looked to diversify into other fields, the company decided that its best policy was to concentrate on its traditional strengths in aero-engine and quality car production. Rolls had no intention of repeating its mistake after the end of the Great War when it allowed a technical lead to slip away. Rolls' 'Whittle' engines, the Nene and the Tay, were highly successful military engines and, under licence, helped the US firm of P&W into the jet era. The Nene also provided the basis for a Russian engine which powered the Mig 15. Rolls took over its shadow factories, with Crewe becoming the focus for car manufacturing and *Derby* the main centre for engines. Indeed, the decision to transfer jet development from Barnoldswick led to Stanley Hooker's departure; as Hives put it, 'Derby is the centre of Rolls-Royce not Hooker's bloody garage at Barnoldswick'.[4]

Along with Armstrong Siddeley and later Bristol, Rolls had begun to develop axial-flow jets. Rolls' axial engine, the AJ.65 Avon began as a private venture, but like the others was ultimately developed under Ministry contract. The axial flow compressor would greatly reduce engine diameter and allow higher compression ratios, thus increasing thrust and improving fuel consumption – a vital improvement if the jet airliner was to become a fully economic proposition. Although the Germans had developed axial-flow engines during the war, post-war development proved more tricky than expected and it took Rolls seven years to sort out the Avon (though this was in fact not much worse than comparable American programmes). By the mid 1950s, Rolls designs were powering most of the RAF's front line aircraft and had formed the technical basis for a range of civil engines. Rolls started the post-war period with little experience of selling piston engines in the civil market; as Sir Denning Pearson, Rolls' chief executive in the 1960s, described it, 'with the end of the last war we set out to build up from zero a civil aviation business'.[5] Rolls' initial lead in jet technology provided the key to a sustained and highly successful attack on civil markets.

De Havilland Engines, despite a similarly early start with jet engines, gradually slipped behind Rolls. The company did develop a supersonic engine, initially as a private venture and subsequently under Ministry contract, as well as producing a number of rocket engines. De Havilland also remained an important producer of piston engines and turbo-shaft engines for helicopters. However, de Havilland's engine programmes would be badly hit by the Sandys cancellations of 1957, and by the mid 1950s de Havilland's more advanced aircraft, including later marks of the Comet, were using Rolls engines.[6] By the mid 1950s, the only serious domestic challenge to Rolls was coming from Bristol and Armstrong Siddeley. At Bristol, Stanley, later Sir Stanley Hooker, led a sustained campaign to get on terms with his old firm. In this respect, Bristol was helped by the Korean emergency and a government decision to sub-contract production of Rolls Avon engines to Bristol; 'thus, by *force majeure*, the Bristol shops were equipped with the machine tools and techniques for mass-producing modern axial-flow engines'. Earlier, the company had a rather less happy time developing the Proteus turbo-prop originally designed for the Brabazon and Princess and later adopted for the Bristol Britannia. Its development was impeded by both design and organisational problems in a company still largely dominated by piston engine experience. Hooker was able to attract more skilled turbine engineers from his ex-employer and was even able to call on Lord Hives for emergency help. But as a result, the Britannia was late into the market, and Bristol only just broke even on the programme. Bristol Engines' own axial-flow design, the Olympus, was more successful.[7]

2.2 A fragmented industry

Although the ministry had separated the industry into 'first' and 'second division' companies this still left too many individual design centres and companies whose average size was far below those of the more important American firms. At the end of the war there were twenty-seven airframe and eight aero-engine companies. The industry was still dominated by powerful and strong personalities – the founders and 'hero designers'. Although many were now more distant from the 'sharp end' of design and production, they were powerfully placed to defend their companies in Whitehall. These men, and their equally independent design teams, would neither easily nor voluntarily look for rationalisation. As Sir George Edwards of Vickers remembered, 'never had it been less likely that such personalities would willingly have become subservient to each other – certainly not while business remained to be done'.[8] The Labour government, although committed to the nationalisation of many basic industrial sectors, was disinclined to take on the aircraft industry and its leaders. In any event, the government felt it had sufficient control over the industry through its control over purchasing and a selective allocation of contracts. As one junior minister averred in 1948, 'private enterprise does not exist in the aircraft industry'.[9] In fact, it suited government to maintain a number of separate design centres and a degree of surplus capacity – a 'surge capacity' – to expand rapidly in the event of an emergency. This was also supposed to provide a degree of competition, at least in terms of design and technical ideas.

Some rationalisation did take place. Airspeed could not cope with the Ambassador programme and was fully absorbed by de Havilland in 1951. The MoS, which absorbed the functions of the MAP in October 1945, eventually decided that there was no place for Metrovick Engines, and details of its jet engine design, the Sapphire, were handed over to Armstrong Siddeley. As noted earlier, Miles went bankrupt and were bought by Handley Page.

The Hawker Siddeley group, with Avro, Armstrong Whitworth, Gloster and Hawker, had a greater financial mass and a more diversified engineering base, but its individual aircraft companies still had considerable design autonomy and were allowed to compete independently for MoS contracts. Vickers, Bristol, and Rolls were also clearly of a size better able to compete in the post-war period. In 1947, the Minister of Supply, George Strauss, did ask officials to study the possibility of further rationalisation, but this was discontinued with the outbreak of the Korean war.

By the mid 1950s, although firms were taking more responsibility for their own R&D, the problem remained one of limited scale, duplication and inadequate co-operation between competing firms. Too many firms of very modest proportions were allowed to survive; although the extensive use of subcontract production shared out work and allowed firms to reduce the risk of over capacity, it discouraged the construction of large-scale and more efficient production facilities. 'Natural wastage' in the industry was too slow and hardly touched the heart of the problem – the need to establish firms large enough to achieve the economies of scale which would enable them to take on American firms. As Air Commodore Banks of Bristol Engines recalled, 'the government was clearly wrong to keep weak companies going. It is true that at that time everybody was feeling their way, but the government should have taken a stronger line with people who were unsuccessful.'[10]

2.3 The civil programme, 1945–56

The Brabazon programme, inherited by the Attlee government, was implemented virtually unchanged, consistent as it was with Labour's commitment to a planned, centrally directed approach to industrial recovery. The government believed that support for civil projects would help to maintain employment in a strategically vital industry and that exports of civil aircraft would make a valuable contribution to the balance of payments. Moreover, civil research and production could be integrated into an overall strategy for the industry through MoS contracts and supervision, helping to sustain design teams and the industry's strategic 'surge capacity'. The Brabazon programme entailed a close relationship with the Ministry using procedures similar to those applied to defence work. The MoS issued and supervised contracts and supplied most of the ancillary equipment needed for a project as an 'embodiment loan' to the contractor. More contentiously, the MoS acted as a procurement agency for the nationalised airlines as well as dealing with orders from private customers. The system was increasingly attacked by industry and airlines alike as cumbersome and inefficient. However, officials defended it on the grounds of both efficiency and equity, claiming that the Ministry was able to incorporate civil R&D into a broader research programme for aviation, encourage economies of scale and ensure that the civil programme was not prejudiced by military demands on scarce resources and facilities.

The airlines felt that their interests were being sacrificed in order to build up a British civil aircraft industry. Virtually all of the 'interim types' which British airlines were forced to buy were inferior to US airliners. The nationalised airlines, BOAC and BEA had little alternative, constrained as they were by the 'buy British' 1945 Civil Aviation Act. Others had difficulty in obtaining the dollar clearances needed to buy American equipment. Although the government was prepared to authorise a few exceptional and limited purchases of US aircraft, the airlines simply had to wait for the Brabazon programme to produce more advanced and commercially viable products. Even so, the nationalised airlines felt that if they had to buy British, they should at least have a more direct say in the procurement process. Contracts between the MoS and the manufacturers had no penalty for delay and contained little incentive to deliver more than the minimum. For their part, companies felt that Ministry intervention, the use of embodiment loan, combined with the changing requirements of the nationalised airlines, especially those of BOAC, made it impossible to work with tighter guarantees. But the MoS's interest was clear, 'it was not in the national interest to allow a first rate aircraft manufacturer to go bust', and the development of British civil aircraft had priority over airline efficiency.[11]

With hindsight, it is evident that many other aspects of the Brabazon programme were equally questionable. Too many of the projects had limited commercial appeal, reached the market too late, or were just technically inadequate. The eponymous Brabazon was an embarrassing failure; built at a cost of £13 million, it never saw airline service. It flew in 1949, by then hopelessly obsolete by American standards. Its construction did cause one of the finest assembly halls in Europe to be built at Filton (paid for by the MoS) and generated some expensive lessons about how not to design and build a commercial aircraft. Airspeed found it could not cope with the all-metal construction demanded of the Ambassador. Development was badly delayed and it entered service four years after an American equivalent which started later. The Armstrong Whitworth Apollo, although it only took three years to develop, had major technical flaws. The Princess flying boat was added to the programme in 1946, but two years later, BOAC finally decided that the days of the flying boat were over. However, to save Saunders Roe from bankruptcy, the Princess was retained as an experimental project until 1954 at a cost of £9·1 million. Both the Apollo and the Princess were marginal projects allocated to weak design teams and were typical of a refusal by the MoS to cut its losses on failing projects.[12]

The Bristol Britannia, another post-war addition to the programme, was rather more successful. Originally conceived as a turbo-prop insurance against problems with the Comet, in 1949 it was decided to develop the Britannia as a long range airliner for operation in 1954. However, development problems, primarily with the Proteus engine, led to serious delays and consequently the aircraft did not enter airline service until 1957. Although the Britannia won some export orders, by then the advent of the long range jet had destroyed any chance of a substantial market breakthrough. Indeed, of the range of new types developed during this period, only three, the Viscount, Comet and Dove, were superior to US aircraft. 440 Viscounts were sold world wide, including a number in the US. Its Rolls-Royce Dart engine was in production until 1986. Significantly, the Viscount survived an initial decision by BEA to order the Ambassador thanks to continued support from the MoS and Vickers' own financial commitment. The Comet, of course, was the technological crown of the whole programme. A gamble by the MoS, BOAC and de Havilland to go for a genuine jet airliner instead of a specialised, largely experimental design, produced the one clear opportunity to overtake the Americans. Its first flight in July 1949 seemed to symbolise both the aircraft industry's and the nation's recovery from the rigours of war. Its entry into service in May 1952 was an immediate success with passengers. In building the Comet, de Havilland learned much about modern production techniques and introduced several 'firsts' into British industrial practice.

Orders for the larger and more economic Comet Three were beginning to mount, including ten from the US 'flag carrier' Pan Am,
when a design flaw caused two fatal crashes. The subsequent
investigation by the RAE set new standards in aircraft safety, but
hopes that the Comet would be a huge commercial success were
dashed. Indeed, the crisis brought de Havilland to the brink of
collapse (see below).

The Brabazon programme essayed a 'good guess' about the
future; as one member of the committee recalled, 'it was a visionary
gleam ... a tremendous act of optimism and vision',[13] but many of its
premises were based on outmoded concepts which were further
invalidated by the war. Military transport needs, especially in the
US, not only stimulated a new range of large aircraft, but also
established an international air transport infrastructure which
American companies were best placed to exploit at the end of the
war. More important, the MoS was insufficiently selective and
ruthless in its approach to either contract allocation or the cancellation of ailing projects. Too many projects were awarded to firms
with no background in civil development or in building large
airframes. Indeed, most project choices and contract awards
reflected the interest in maintaining industrial capacity rather than
commercial logic. The government was also too quick to dismiss the
possibility of licence production of US designs as a means of covering the gap between the end of the war and the arrival of the jet and
turbo-prop types. Bristol, for example, was not allowed to build the
Lockheed Constellation. Compared with the £1·8 billion spent on
military development during this period, £78·7 million, with over
£12 million repaid in royalties, was a relatively modest sum to create
a British civil aircraft industry virtually from scratch. The programme provided work for British companies and, for the better
firms such as Vickers and de Havilland, valuable experience of civil
design and production which they were able to use in a subsequent
generation of airliners. On the other hand, few other manufacturing
industries had quite such generous support for new product
development.

It was increasingly clear, however, that the government could not
indefinitely treat the nationalised airlines as if they were adjuncts of
the RAF. Matters came to a head following the public inquiry into
an Avro Tudor crash in 1948. The Tudor development had been
affected by delays and technical problems which led to BOAC and

Avro blaming each other for the fiasco. The report concluded that many of the problems that had dogged development had been caused by the MoS system of procurement. The government responded with its own internal inquiry led by Sir John Hanbury-Williams. Hanbury-Williams recommended that the MoS should abandon its direct involvement in civil development, and allow manufacturers and airlines to negotiate in a more commercial fashion. If the government still wished to aid development, it should come after, not in advance of, orders from a major airline. The report, with its implicit condemnation of government and official practices – in effect challenging the socialist view that the public interest and the efficient operation of an industry were compatible – was nevertheless accepted by the Attlee Cabinet.[14]

A new approach was confirmed by the Civil Aviation Acts of 1948 and 1949. It would still be open for the state to support the 'design, manufacture and maintenance' of civil aircraft and engines. The nationalised airlines, however, were allowed to buy aircraft according to their own commercial criteria – subject only to 'directives in the national interest'. In practice, this caveat and the need to obtain approval from the government for loan capital clearly provided ministers with powerful instruments to intervene in airline procurement. Nevertheless, the Acts at least established a more commercial climate for civil development and the framework for launch aid for civil projects. In the event, the return of a Conservative government in 1951, with a commitment to limit intervention in industry, meant that firms would in any case be encouraged to finance their own civil programmes.[15]

The Conservatives believed that the aircraft companies should carry most, if not all of the burden of developing civil airliners. Although it was never specifically declared as such, the 'private venture policy' was increasingly evident in practice, strongly supported by the Treasury which had consistently opposed government assistance for civil aircraft development. Equally, a successful firm such as Vickers felt that Ministry contracts contained too many restrictions and demanded a usurious level of royalties. Consequently, Vickers was both willing and able to launch a larger successor to the Viscount, the Vanguard, as a private venture. Others were less well placed and, in any event, the private venture policy still depended upon projects obtaining launch orders from the nationalised airlines.

Even though direct aid for civil development was no longer forthcoming, an implicit 'buy British' policy still held for the nationalised airlines. Several airline chairmen accepted it as a duty to 'assist development of British transport aircraft'. But buying British could be an expensive business, with the airline carrying the cost of 'proving' an aircraft. BOAC's problems with the Comet and Britannia cost it nearly £3 million. The advantage in buying British was to have a decisive say in the specification of a new airliner. In practice, both BEA and BOAC demanded products 'tailored' to their requirements which other airlines tended to find less attractive. Ultimately, the ambiguities of the 'buy British' policy and the effects of 'tailoring' proved to have a disastrous effect on both the airlines and the aircraft industry.

In the case of de Havilland, its problems were accepted as something of an exception. The Comet disaster was a blow to industrial morale generally, but it left de Havilland with £15 million worth of unsaleable aircraft, useless jigs and tools. As one de Havilland worker recalled, 'it nearly flattened this place'.[16] The loss threatened one of Britain's major civil and, more important, military airframe companies with bankruptcy. The Treasury was willing to see the firm go under, but the government decided to mount a rescue operation 'to safeguard the public interest in the Comet and other projects'. The MoS ordered eighteen suitably modified Comet Twos for the RAF and advanced money for further development. Later, the government provided £6·5 million in direct assistance to ease a cash-flow crisis. Government aid to de Havilland eventually totalled £10 million in loans and contracts. Not unreasonably, the MoS insisted on delivery of the Comet Two transports before de Havilland could develop the Comet further as a commercial airliner. Although the Comet Four did beat the Americans into trans-Atlantic jet services, by then it had lost the sales battle to the Boeing 707 and DC8. The Comet airframe soldiered on and is still in service with the RAF as the Nimrod ASW aircraft.

Government aid undoubtedly saved de Havilland, but the company was unable to make up the lost ground. The Comet had triggered first Boeing and then Douglas into building their own long range jet airliners. Within four months of Pan Am placing orders in October 1955, the 707 and DC8 had over 220 sales. By the end of 1956, the technical and commercial initiative in long range airliners had passed once again to the US. In 1955, in a decision which many feel was a watershed in British post war civil aviation, BOAC rejected a civil version of the proposed Vickers V1000 long range military transport. The MoS fought hard to win support for the aircraft, but was successfully opposed by the Treasury, Air Ministry and the Ministry of Civil Aviation. Government spokesmen played down the likely consequences of the decision, arguing that the lack of a long range jet would not 'seriously damage' the British civil aircraft industry.[17]

Within months of turning down the V1000, BOAC asked for permission to buy the new Boeing 707, albeit with Rolls-Royce Conway engines. It is impossible to judge whether the V1000 would have been a commercial success, but the loss of BOAC's confidence in British long range jet aircraft was a blow to the industry. The government agreed to BOAC's request for Boeings on condition that the airline would buy a British aircraft for its specialised 'Empire routes' requirement. From a number of alternative designs, Vickers this time emerged as the winner, not only because the airline preferred its VC10 design but equally important, because Vickers was the only company prepared do it as a private venture. Again, while the VC10 proved to be a very fine aircraft, the 'Empire routes' specification required Vickers to produce a design which was less than optimal for other applications. This contributed to the aircraft's poor sales record and helped to undermine Vickers' profitability.[18]

The effects of these decisions, of course, were not immediately apparent. Nor, for that matter, could the extent of the impending threat of jet aircraft to either the Britannia or the Vanguard turbo-props be anticipated. On the face of it there appeared solid economic grounds for supposing that the turbo prop had several advantages over jet operation, certainly on short to medium range routes. By the end of 1956, despite the Comet failure and the cancellation of the V1000, the civil industry seemed to be in reasonable shape. Vickers was earning money from the Viscount and had hopes of comparable success with both the Vanguard and the VC10. De Havilland was poised to win a major contract from BEA to build a new medium range jet airliner and Bristol still believed that the long range turbo-prop Britannia had a future. But the economics of civil aircraft development were undergoing radical change. In the early 1950s, the break-even point for an airliner was between fifty and sixty sales – numbers which could be supported by the domestic market. However, aircraft such as the VC10 were substantially more complex and costly than airliners of the early 1950s and even a record £68 million launch order from BOAC would not cover development costs. Under these circumstances, it was even more imperative that British civil designs should be competitive and directed at an international market. The close links with BEA and BOAC, though in many respects comforting to British aircraft companies, were not in the long run conducive to the adoption of such a broad view.

2.4 The military programme, 1945–56

Although an important element in the industry's post-war recovery, the civil programme was still only a relatively modest proportion of its output. The bulk, about 70 per cent, of the industry's work was in defence, and military projects would continue to provide the cutting edge of technological development. As we have seen, several factors shaped the UK's post-war military programme: the limitations on defence spending; within this, the overriding priority attached to acquiring a nuclear strike force, and the supposed need to maintain a wide range of design centres for strategic reasons. The immediate technical consideration was to assimilate the technological lessons of the war, especially the results of German research work, and to anticipate the arrival of more powerful axial jet engines. All of this would have to take place within an environment of austerity and growing economic crisis which precluded the construction of an 'interim' post-war generation of military aircraft. The Berlin crisis of 1948 led to some increase in domestic demand. De Havilland opened a second Vampire production line at its Chester shadow factory and the MoS authorised an advanced version, the Venom, and a night fighter version of the Meteor. But Britain's worsening financial situation ruled out any adjustment to the long-term programme to hasten development of a new generation of fighters.

With the substantial exception of the jet engine, basic R&D had been sacrificed to the war effort. According to a 1955 White Paper, at the end of the war Britain 'had very few' advanced projects under development and, consequently, 'we were falling behind in the science of aerodynamics, though not in the field of gas-turbine engines'. It was, therefore, necessary to fill the gaps in practical knowledge and remedy the deficiencies in research facilities caused by the war. New test equipment and wind tunnels were authorised, but between 1945 and 1950, 'only limited new facilities were created'. The period was therefore dominated by a procession of research and development projects aimed at producing fighters and bombers for the mid-1950s but which also obviated the need for an expensive outlay on production. Specifications duly emerged which led to the English Electric Canberra jet bomber, the swept wing fighters Hawker Hunter and Vickers-Supermarine Swift and, most important of all in defence terms, the three V-bombers, the Vickers Valiant, Avro Vulcan and Handley Page Victor, Britain's nuclear strike force. In the short term, however, industry was left without major new production orders, although a lot of the research projects were of 'great value to aircraft firms, supplying them not only with contracts at no risk, but also with knowledge and experience which may be useful to them in other fields, particularly in the production of civil aircraft'.[19]

The proliferation of development projects, although relatively cheap, was inefficient and wasteful. During this period, twenty-six projects were started at a cost of £23·7 million out of a total military aircraft spend of £1·8 billion. At the same time, MoS penny-pinching delayed development and a number of aircraft, such as the Gloster Javelin, were already obsolete when they entered service and were unable to find export markets. A later review of the programme found that the Ministry had no criteria for deciding when to terminate a research programme, and that 'vested interests' were often evident in keeping projects going. Rather oddly, other projects were duplicated with a view to long-term savings. The Ministry claimed that it was trying to introduce more competition with a greater sense of financial discipline within industry. Consequently, several firms were awarded development contracts for the same specification as a 'deliberate policy in the full knowledge that it involved spending considerable sums of money on developing aircraft that would never go into production'. Any 'savings' that resulted were hard to prove, but failed competitive projects cost more than £5·5 million. Another reason for duplication was the so called 'reinsurance' programme – projects developed as a back up to more advanced designs. One example was the Shorts Sperrin, an interim jet bomber designed to shadow the V bombers. In the event, Vickers showed that its Valiant design was a better 'cover' for the Vulcan and Victor. The Sperrin was eventually cancelled, but not before the prototype had been built at a cost of £3·5 million, primarily because of sensitivities over employment in Northern Ireland.[20] In total, 'reinsurance' projects cost over £18 million.

The V-bomber programme proved to be a particularly elaborate case of duplicated development. The 1947 specification called for a fast (Mach 0·8), high altitude (45,000 ft) aircraft well in advance of the state-of-the-art. In particular, the designers were asked to anticipate developments in guided weapons over the next decade. Both the Victor and the Vulcan were highly advanced aerodynamically and structurally, incorporating a lot of German wartime data. Development was again limited by the paucity of test facilities which necessitated an elaborate series of test vehicles. Some industrialists, however, felt that enough was known in 1951 to have chosen between the Victor and the Vulcan. Sir Frederick Handley Page disagreed, citing the wartime experience of the Lancaster, Stirling and Halifax where the best of the three was only known after full development. His view, shared by the Ministry, was that a choice between the Vulcan and the Victor could not have been made safely at any time up to squadron deployment. In the case of the V-bombers, special considerations applied; the 'building up of a nuclear deterrent force quickly was considered of paramount importance, and if one production line was shut down, even though it was turning out a less successful aeroplane, the rate of build up would be slowed quite considerably'. This advice was repeated at each subsequent stage until 'it became too late to save money by cancelling either the Victor or the Vulcan'. The competition was real enough, and Avro certainly felt the pressure from Handley Page, redesigning the Vulcan wing to ensure that its performance would not fall behind that of the Victor. Industrial competition was reinforced by personal animosity between Sir Frederick Handley Page and Sir Roy Dobson of Avro.[21] But this was an elaborate and expensive way of acquiring a front line airforce and would be impossible to tolerate as development costs for military aircraft began to rise substantially in the 1950s.

With hindsight, the most important technological failing of this period was caused by the restrictions placed on supersonic research, a decision which set British fighter design back by several years. In

February 1946, the MoS cancelled the Miles M.52 supersonic research vehicle which would have been powered by a Whittle engine with 're-heat'. Officially the reason for cancellation was 'humanitarian'. The MoS's Chief Scientist said that 'flying at speeds greater than sound introduces new problems. We do not know how serious they are. The impression that supersonic aircraft are just around the corner is quite erroneous. We do not have the heart to ask pilots to fly the high speed models, so we shall make them radio controlled.'[22] A more likely explanation was Miles' inadequacies as a company. Not from the first rank, Miles' experience in advanced aircraft was, to say the least, limited and its financial position was decidedly shaky. In fact, theoretical work at the RAE had confirmed that supersonic flight was within reach, but the UK lacked the resources and facilities to match the US which pressed ahead with its 'X' series of rocket propelled research vehicles. In 1947, the MoS invited several better resourced firms to put forward supersonic designs which also had the benefit of German research data. In November 1948, the English Electric P1A design was chosen by the RAE's 'Advanced Fighter Project Group' as the basis for a supersonic interceptor. However, the production of supersonic aircraft was again delayed until the mid 1950s, by which time the US had already established a new generation of combat aircraft. As the MoS later admitted, 'it is easy to be wise after the event, but it is clear now that this decision seriously delayed the progress of aeronautical research in the UK'.[23]

In 1950, the industry's position was transformed by the Korean war rearmament programme. For the war itself, the RAF and Fleet Air Arm had to use obsolete aircraft or US-designed aircraft. However, the sudden explosion of the Cold War into open hostilities focused attention on the danger of a wider conflict with the Soviet Union. Aircraft planned for a leisurely introduction in the mid 1950s had to be brought forward and the industry was again called upon to expand production rapidly. However, the rearmament programme considerably strained the industry's resources, a situation which was aggravated by shortages of materials and machine tools and by an absurdly vague mechanism in the MoS for ranking the importance of projects. As had been the custom during World War Two, a number of aircraft were also 'ordered off the drawing board'. However, this time the aircraft and engines concerned were considerably more complex and the practice led to serious problems. For example, in November 1950, two Vickers-Supermarine Swift prototypes and 100 production aircraft were ordered simultaneously. Technical problems delayed the programme and even as late as 1955 the RAF would not accept the aircraft as having reached an acceptable standard. Some Swifts were eventually used in specialised roles, but the programme was effectively a failure at a cost of £33 million.

The Korean emergency again showed that the British industry was weak when called upon to produce aircraft in large numbers. Distributing work around design centres in the hope that a 'surge capacity' would be available when necessary proved to be no substitute for well planned production facilities. It was, nevertheless, a massive boost for the industry. Employment rose from just under 180,000 in 1950 to over 300,000 by 1956. Aircraft procurement increased from £78 million a year in 1950 to £240 million in 1954 and exports, stimulated by the war and helped by US offshore procurement policies, boomed. However, the use of 'cost plus' contracting, combined with the sense of emergency, did nothing to instil a commitment to cost control. For example, wage rate fixing for production work was often a matter of guesswork and shopfloor negotiation. [24] The immediate future, however, was likely to prove rather more problematic as the government was about to make a major shift in the direction of defence policy which would precipitate fundamental changes in the industry.

2.5 The Sandys White Paper and rationalisation

In the mid 1950s, there were still thirty-one full members of the SBAC and only three firms had dropped out of the industry since 1945. Ten firms had assets of less than £1 million and some employed only a few hundred people. However, the six largest firms, Vickers, English Electric, Hawker Siddeley, Rolls, Bristol and de Havilland accounted for well over 80 per cent of the resources and production capacity in the industry. By comparison, there were only twenty-three prime contractors in the US aircraft industry, with individual *divisions* of some of the larger firms employing up to 30,000 people. Hawker Siddeley, with its quasi-autonomous divisions – Armstrong Whitworth, Avro, Gloster, Hawker and Armstrong Siddeley Engines – was the largest British company with assets in 1955 of £19 million and employing 75,000. Rolls-Royce had £7.7 million in assets and 35,000 workers. The Korean War and its aftermath had swelled industry's order books, but changes in aircraft technology and consequent effects on project costs, combined with shifts in government defence policy, would have a profound impact on the British aircraft industry, its profitability, competitiveness and structure.

The technical demands of higher speeds and increased capability combined with the rising sophistication of electronic and other systems was having a dramatic effect on the complexity of programmes throughout the development and production cycle. This in turn extended the lead time of development and led to substantial increases in costs. As complexity and lead time grew, the effects of technological uncertainty, opportunities for managerial miscalculation, and cost escalation increased commensurately. The cost/complexity equation naturally affected the unit cost of and overall demand for military aircraft. For instance, in 1954 the RAF's force of 155 aircraft cost a total of £6·1 million; in 1958, 178 aircraft were valued at £29 million. In the early 1950s, the industry produced 2,000 or so aircraft a year, but in 1957 it had dropped to 968. By 1960, the total was down to 510 and, more significantly, this represented only 41 per cent of the weight of aircraft produced in 1953. In short, the RAF would be wanting more complex, more expensive, but fewer aeroplanes. The domestic base market was, therefore, bound to shrink, especially as many began to believe that aircraft as such would be 'superseded largely or partly by guided weapons'.[25]

In an environment of rapidly rising development costs – a phenomenon which was also affecting civil aircraft, albeit more slowly – it was even more essential for companies to achieve production levels which would generate economies of scale and sales which would amortise the cost of development. The fact of the matter was that in this respect British industry was falling even further behind the US. Between 1955 and 1961, US military production runs were three times greater than Britain's and four and a half times greater in transport aircraft. The US market was nine times that of the UK, and during the late 1950s and 1960s US companies accounted for 80 per cent of world production by value, exporting three to four times the British level. This justified, and paid for higher investment in plant and process technology. It resulted in better staffed and supported research facilities. Some of the competitive advantage of US firms over British was offset by the latter's lower labour costs – by about a half. In the UK, the situation was not helped by the peacetime system of procurement. When a design was accepted by the RAF or Fleet Air Arm, too few aircraft were ordered or, when ordered, were required in small batches according to budgetary or operational considerations. The result was inefficient production leading to increased overheads and unit costs. Up to 1955, twenty-three different types of aircraft had been ordered, each with production runs of less than 100.

Longer production runs also meant that non-recurring R&D costs were a smaller proportion of unit costs – a ratio of 1 : 3·2 in the US compared with 1 : 8·7 in the UK. The result was, on average, cheaper overall unit costs and quicker development times. Moreover, with a higher ratio of development to production costs, 'the worst off is the producer with the smaller total market. By the same token, the greater will be his total and proportionate losses, if he falls short of the sales target on which he has based his price.' US firms were able to build up production faster and, consequently, were able to offer keener delivery dates. As George Edwards put it, British industry always had to sell off the 'thick end of the learning curve'. British firms also complained that the rate of return on government contracts was insufficient to generate an adequate level of capital accumulation to allow for investment in R&D and new plant. Rates were still determined by a formula established in 1941 and were often insufficient to cover costs. There were occasions 'when it cost contractors more to borrow money to finance work in progress than the basic profit they were allowed under the profit formula'.[26]

The US aircraft industry was also supported by the US aid programme – between 1952 and 1961, 77 per cent of US military sales, worth $22 billion were financed this way. Exports of British military aircraft were also hindered by the over specialised nature of RAF and Fleet Air Arm requirements. Indeed, of the sixteen aircraft introduced between 1955 and 1964, only two were exported, the NA39 Buccaneer (to South Africa) and the Folland Gnat designed by William Petter and only reluctantly adopted by the RAF. Petter, in fact, advanced a radical solution; design smaller, less complex aircraft which could be exported more readily and build the more advanced products under licence from the US.[27] The attractions of building under licence American products would also continue to excite some interest, and in some areas, such as helicopters, become a significant alternative to indigenous development. But then, as now, the consequences for the level of British aerospace technology would have been serious, with additional political and economic problems associated with long term dependence on a foreign supplier.

Similar problems affected British civil aircraft 'tailored' to nationalised airline specifications. The worst case was the de Havilland Trident built for BEA where the airline asked for changes in the original specification which cut the aircraft's size and 'stretch' potential. This reduced the Trident's attractiveness to other customers who preferred the larger Boeing 727. In the civil sector, British problems were compounded by a general lack of experience in dealing with a global market, by poor market research and by sloppy ideas about customer support and service. Certainly, by comparison American marketing and sales tactics were more elaborate and sophisticated and only a few British firms, in particular Rolls-Royce, approached American standards. More-over, British industry was beginning to face other competitors, particularly from the rapidly growing French aircraft industry. The introduction of the Sud Aviation Caravelle short-range jet airliner would be the main reason for the Vanguard's failure to sell widely in Europe. Dassault would soon begin its successful attack on the world military market. Others, including West Germany, would also be looking to develop an aerospace capability.

Under these circumstances, even in 1956, as Korean production wound down, it was evident that some form of industrial rationali-sation was inevitable. Some industrialists could still believe there was no real problem: 'if analysed according to different types, ... the numbers are about right'. It could also be argued that a smaller firm could concentrate its efforts on a particular task, and the 'single guiding personality' could 'drive it through to success himself'.[28] Although overseas examples, most notably Dassault, might seem to confirm the value of a dominant leader figure with a small design team, the broader industrial trend was towards complex systems integration requiring considerable management skill and capacity. Production efficiency demanded economies of scale with commensurately large capital demands. Air Commodore Banks, of Bristol Engines, for example, recognised that British industry had to adopt US style and methods if it was to be competitive. Duplicated projects had to go, and a stronger centralised approach to programme management had to be endorsed. But how were the proudly independent companies to be pushed into rationalisation? In his view it was 'impracticably arbitrary to consider a ... banding together, by government decree, of the various and individual firms into larger units'. He argued that a 'sink or swim' philosophy was necessary to produce a successful industry. But equally, he warned that aid for civil programmes would be necessary to help the transition.[29]

The MoS was aware of the need for rationalisation. In 1953, officials picked up the studies of rationalisation which had been abandoned in 1950. Denis Havilland, Under Secretary at the MoS, wanted an end to a 'Buggins Turn' of thinly spread development projects and to create companies of an optimum size to handle the more complex aircraft of the 1950s. The MoS also believed that the best way to encourage consolidation was through the contract mechanism. In 1955, the Minister of Supply, Reginald Maudling rejected this advice, arguing that it should be up to industry to rationalise naturally as demand fell. However, a year later, MoS officials were able to 'go public' by giving evidence to the Select Committee on Estimates. Officials said that they wanted to see the growth of 'larger technical teams', referring to their knowledge of firms with a record of poor performance – 'candidates for relegation' – which would not be kept going by 'force feeding'. The question was, how and when? Even industrialists who advocated rationalisation might object if it was their firm which would be penalised, absorbed, or forced out of the aircraft business. The Select Committee on Estimates itself recommended that the Ministry should use a 'selective allocation of contracts to bring about the measure of coalescence in the aircraft industry which they agreed was desirable'.[30]

The Sandys Defence White Paper of 1957 provided the catalyst for rationalisation of the aircraft industry. Its predecessor in 1956 had already implied that a greater significance would be attached to guided weapons and had announced reductions in orders for fighter aircraft. But the Sandys White Paper stated that 'the new defence plan involves the biggest change in military policy made in normal times. In carrying it out, a certain amount of disruption is unavoidable.' It established that there were very definite limits to what the United Kingdom could spend on defence. The government was concerned that the costs of defence had reached 10 per cent of GNP and that this was having a serious effect on the economy. Its fundamental rationale was that the hydrogen bomb and the long range missile had rendered conventional defence obsolete. Britain would reduce defence costs by relying on missile-delivered nuclear deterrence, and guided weapons for point defence of key UK bases. The White Paper left room for only one major conventional military aircraft programme – the Canberra replacement, OR339. The Sandys review was a controversial and deeply flawed strategic concept, and by the early 1960s Britain would have returned to a more balanced concept of defence. In the short term, however, the 1957 White Paper had a significant effect on the UK aircraft industry.

In his history of the British Aircraft Corporation, Charles Gardner records how the Sandys White Paper 'was the biggest shock ever, at that time, to be administered to the aircraft industry'.[31] With 70 per cent of the industry's work dependent on military contracts, the Sandys review clearly anticipated a severe shakeout in the industry. It was predicted that the workforce would shrink from its 1957 level (and post war peak) of 311,000 to 150,000 by 1963. Even before the White Paper, the new Minister of Supply, Aubrey Jones had warned that 'some consolidation of resources' in the industry was inevitable, a process which the government would encourage by the 'selective allocation' of any remaining contracts'. He suggested that the continued prosperity of the industry would be through an increase in civil and export-orientated work.[32] But in threatening to deprive the industry of military projects which could be exported, as well as any prospect of aid for civil development, the government was expecting a lot from the industry.

The immediate impact of the Sandys review on the industry was slight. Few of the cancelled projects were at an advanced stage, and production of aircraft such as the Lightning, the V-bombers, the Hunter and Javelin was still building up. The value of sales to the government rose steadily through the late 1950s, and by 1964 had almost reached the 1955 level, the second highest of the 1948–64 period. Similarly, while between 1957 and 1964 there was an overall contraction of employment in the industry of 18 per cent, at 267,540 it was still one-fifth higher than at the outbreak of the Korean War (see Tables 6 and 7). It did lead, however, to the closure of the Gloster works by the Hawker group. Profits fell rather more steeply from £29·7 million in 1957 to £17·9 million in 1964, a drop of 40 per

Table 6: UK military aircraft R9D and procurement, 1948–64 (£ million)

	R&D	Procurement
1948	21	75
1950	30	78
1952	37	153
1954	60	240
1956	85	180
1957	95	170
Sandys Defence White Paper		
1958	85	140
1960	83	187
1962	107	203
1964	110	210

Source: Plowden.

Table 7: Employment in the aircraft industry, 1948–64

1948	171,800
1950	179,465
1952	36,420
1954	78,993
1956	307,632
1957	311,936
Sandys Defence White Paper	
1958	301,419
1960	291,355
1962	291,838
1964	267,450

Source: Plowden.

cent. Profits on capital employed fluctuated, but the trend was also downward – from 15·7 per cent in 1957 to 6·3 per cent in 1964 (the 1963 figure was 8·7 per cent, compared with an all-UK industry average of 11 per cent). For some companies, income from civil aircraft developed in the late 1940s helped to overcome short term difficulties, but much of this was re-invested in new civil aircraft, sales of which were disappointing.

In the longer term, the cancellation of several advanced projects had a marked effect on the industry in technological terms and on export opportunities in the military sector. Some projects were rightly terminated. The Saunders Roe rocket fighter was a highly specialised concept from a weak firm. Cancelling the Avro 730 supersonic bomber, with development costs estimated at over £100 million, was also a sound decision. However, with hindsight, the loss of supersonic developments of the Hunter left a highly lucrative export market to the Americans and to the French and left one of Britain's most successful fighter design teams scrambling for work. The decision also cost Rolls and other engine manufacturers the opportunity of developing re-heated versions of their existing designs. The disruption of an orderly progression of designs later put the industry in a position similar to that of the late 1940s, where British firms had to make substantial technological 'leaps' in order to match US development. The MoS had been looking at the 'building block' or 'shorter steps' approach prevalent in the US, but the Sandys review blocked the possibility of adopting a more incremental strategy of aircraft development. Consequently, when firms were called upon to build the more complex OR339, further 'leaps' in knowledge would be called for. The cost of losing this intra-firm 'learning' is hard to calculate, but it clearly contributed to later difficulties with the OR339/TSR2 programme.[32] On the other hand, the building block approach was expensive and certainly could not have been realistically applied across a complete range of military aircraft projects.

The adoption of a missile-centred defence was also founded on a relatively fragile technological base. Work on guided weapons had begun in 1944, but knowledge of German developments again stimulated research. By 1947, the MoS had 20 projects underway. As in the case of airframe development, the programme was characterised by duplication and fragmented effort, with several false starts and cancelled programmes. It was also technologically over-ambitious and, interestingly under the circumstances, 1957 was seen as the earliest date for the introduction of surface-to-air missiles. Industry was also reluctant to divert resources into missile development, but by the early 1950s, several airframe and a number of electronics companies were involved in guided weapons programmes. British development was aided by the 1950 agreement with the US governing the transfer of missile technology. In 1955, helped by US technology, development of the Blue Streak IRBM began. Owing to differing service requirements, two surface-to-air missiles (SAMs) were developed, the Bristol/Ferranti Bloodhound for the RAF and the English Electric Thunderbird for the Army. Airborne missiles, of course, depended on aircraft to carry them, and the Sandys White Paper cut that avenue of development. In time,

Shorts and Vickers would also develop a range of naval and army tactical missiles. However, the demand for guided weapons was likely to be an inadequate substitute for new aircraft programmes. Nor was it necessarily a cheap solution to British defence needs. The guided weapons programme cost over £400 million and was subject to substantial cost escalation, in some cases as high as 500 per cent (the Blue Steel stand-off missile).[33] Worse still, by 1960 the cost of developing the Blue Streak proved too great for a missile that was already obsolete and vulnerable to Soviet attack. Blue Streak was cancelled at a cost of over £200 million in favour of the US air-launched Skybolt.

The government hoped that civil production would take up any slack in the industry. But as a number of observers noted, it appeared to have overlooked the fact that civil and military development was closely linked. It was asking a lot of industry, with neither launch aid nor the security of future defence orders, to provide its own finance for civil programmes. Even in the US, civil aircraft projects were funded in part from the profits earned from defence contracts and helped by the inter-relationship between military and civil R&D. *The Times* noted that even if the industry did rationalise and would 'stand more firmly on its own feet', it could do so only 'so long as there is a defence interest'. In any event, the transition could not 'come overnight'. As *The Economist* put it, 'the MoS bears a heavy responsibility for shaping the industry's future, but as yet there is no sign of a policy towards the industry'.[34]

On 22 May 1958, the Minister Aubrey Jones outlined what the government expected of the industry. He told the House of Commons that it was 'fruitless to continue research and development expenditure unless the industry reorganises and strengthens itself to the extent necessary to meet the changed conditions with which it is now faced'. The government would 'encourage' the formation of stronger units which would also be better able to carry the burden of developing civil aircraft independently of government. Ideally, it would be even better if aircraft development was associated with a broader range of diversified industrial interests. The government would play its part in the development of very advanced programmes such as a supersonic transport, but the intention was to 'nudge or edge the industry to a greater degree of self-reliance'. The exact form that rationalisation should take, he said, would be left to industry. The proper course for government was 'something intermediate between full government authority and complete *laissez-faire*. What we need is a combination of impulse from above compelling the assumption of responsibility on the part of industry itself'.[35]

Jones was totally committed to rationalisation and had fully endorsed the advice which his predecessor had rejected. In August 1957, he invited an inter-departmental committee chaired by Sir Thomas Padmore of the Treasury to consider the question. The committee's report formed the basis for Jones' May 1958 statement. Indeed, he anticipated the Padmore Report by trying to direct BEA's order for a medium range jet towards the most suitable industrial combination. The airline clearly wanted de Havilland's Trident; the MoS preferred a joint design from Hawker and Bristol. Although de Havilland formed a consortium (Airco) with Fairey and Hunting to build the Trident, it was hardly a major realignment of industrial forces. The MoS had considerable doubts about de Havilland's financial strength and Airco's capitalisation of less than £100 million was also felt to be inadequate. However, Jones faced considerable opposition from the Minister of Civil Aviation, Harold Watkinson, who strongly supported BEA's request, and from several influential Tory backbenchers with aviation interests. In the event, the Cabinet (Jones was not a member) allowed BEA to buy the Trident.[36]

Jones' main lever for rationalisation was the OR339 contract. On 16 September 1957, senior representatives of eleven aircraft companies were told by the Permanent Secretary at the MoS, Sir Cyril Musgrove, that OR339 would proceed on the basis of consortia submissions. The order would go to a group of firms with one acting as a designated leader. The government hoped that this would lead to mergers and rationalisation. This triggered a complex round of proposal and counter proposal, manoeuvre and counter manoeuvre in the industry. Even within the Hawker Siddeley Group there were several competing designs, a confusion which probably cost Hawker a realistic chance of the contract. According to Handel Davies, then a government scientific adviser, 'there were about nine design submissions for OR339 and each one had to be evaluated in detail by teams of government experts. It became ridiculous and everyone in Whitehall and most of the senior men in the industry fully realised it.'[37]

One of the strongest contenders was the English Electric team at

Warton, the only British firm with experience of a production supersonic fighter, the Lightning. It had also been responsible for the Canberra. Its P17A submission with Shorts offered VTOL capability which quite impressed the RAF. Vickers had gained a high reputation for programme management with the Valiant bomber, and its Supermarine division provided substantial experience of fighter aircraft development. The Vickers Type 571 offered an integrated systems approach to OR339's advanced navigation and attack requirements. In mid 1958, the RAF merged the P17A airframe (without the Shorts VTOL platform) with the Vickers Type 571 systems package to produce the TSR2 specification. The decision was announced in January 1959, with Vickers selected to lead the programme, and English Electric as the main subcontractor. The choice of Vickers as project leader was much resented by the Warton team, but it seems to have been made on the basis of Vickers' track record in programme management. In the event, it took high level intervention to marry the two units. But the teaming of Vickers and English Electric clearly established the basis for a rationalised grouping. The companies had several complementary activities; in addition to its military aircraft division, English Electric had interests in electronics and guided weapons, and had begun to look for a civil aircraft capability, Vickers' strongest feature.[38] The TSR2 engine contract was awarded to Bristol Engines for a supersonic version of the Olympus engine. Although the Vickers/ EE team preferred a new Rolls design, Bristol was ready to merge with Armstrong Siddeley and de Havilland Engines, a move which had the support of officials at the MoS. With OR339 settled, the scene was set for a major reorganisation of the British aircraft industry.

2.6 The re-grouping

By 1959, it was evident that several companies were experiencing severe financial problems, often associated with civil programmes. Bristol was seriously affected by limited sales of the Britannia, and although involved in development work on a supersonic transport (SST), it had no money for new projects. As the MoS had predicted, de Havilland was finding it difficult to finance the Trident. The Hawker Siddeley Group had been particularly hard hit by the 1957

White Paper and the loss of the OR339 competition had left its main military design centre, Hawker, with only an uncertain VTOL fighter programme for the future (see Chapter 3). Even Rolls-Royce, having had considerable success in overseas markets, was finding private venture civil development increasingly hard to sustain. Vickers, despite its past success with the Viscount and the award of the OR339 contract, was also in trouble. Sales prospects for the Vanguard beyond BEA's launch order were rapidly diminishing in the face of more competitive medium and short-range jets. The VC10 still looked promising, but its development costs, much higher than expected, would be a further drain on resources. In 1956, the company had reported a trading profit of £3·1 million, but by the end of 1959 it was facing a substantial loss on its aircraft business and Lord Knollys, Vickers' chairman, complained of the 'great and disproportionate financial burden' of unaided civil development.[39]

Up to the 1959 General Election, industry's pleas tended to fall on deaf ears. The Minister of Supply, Aubrey Jones was determined to maintain the private venture policy and rejected several requests for launch aid even when accompanied by merger proposals. In his view, rationalisation would provide the basis for future growth and it was up to industry to recognise the inevitable and get on with the process of consolidation. However, his uncompromising stance was undermined by the several decisions to support civil projects in advance of the October General Election. After the election, Jones was replaced by Duncan Sandys who headed a new Ministry of Aviation (MoA) with a seat in the Cabinet. The MoA merged the MoS's responsibilities for the aircraft industry and military procurement with the airline and air transport brief of the Ministry of Civil Aviation. The formation of the MoA was, according to a government spokesman, 'a recognition that it had a special duty towards an industry like aircraft'. It was also designed to avoid the damaging inter-departmental disputes that had embarrassed the government between 1957 and 1960.

Sandys, however, not only shared Jones' view that rationalisation was necessary, but he also took a more active role in directing the process. His position was strengthened by obtaining Treasury approval for the formal re-introduction of launch aid for civil projects and other financial provisions to encourage rationalisation. In November he met leaders of the industry and told them bluntly that there was room only for two airframe and two engine companies. Once this had occurred, the government would concentrate its orders on the consolidated groups. The only exception would be where 'specialised requirements or social policy make it necessary to do otherwise'. He would act as an intermediary (or marriage bureau as he called it) to help firms come together, and promised to re-introduce launch aid for civil programmes.[40] The government also undertook to maintain a programme of basic research and to provide financial support for exports. The policy, with some modifications, was made public in February 1960.

The launch aid system re-introduced by Sandys continued to derive its legislative authority from the Civil Aviation Act of 1949. However, the government's view that launch aid in its new form would be a 'risk sharing' partnership between the state and industry was underlined by the procedures adopted by the MoA to vet requests for assistance and the limit set to the state's liability. Firms would have to assume at least half of the cost of development and all of the risk of any escalation to ensure that proper commercial disciplines were maintained. The government would get its money back through a levy on sales, albeit in a form which tended to favour the company. The Ministry would evaluate launch aid requests – taking account of factors such as the balance of payments and more direct commercial factors – as well as monitoring the progress of launch-aided projects. The first grants of launch aid were mainly used to ease the rationalisation process, and in a number of cases, such as the VC10 and Trident, the Ministry accepted that there would be little hope of repayment. Sandys also 'leaned' on BOAC to help Vickers with changes to the VC10 contract, a decision which would lead to a very bitter crisis in relations between airline and industry (see Chapter 3). However, the re-introduction of launch aid underlined a renewed partnership between the state and the aircraft industry in commercial projects which would rapidly expand through the 1960s.

Between November 1959 and January 1960, there was a flurry of merger negotiations and acquisitions which led to the creation of three main airframe and two engine groups (see Figure 1). De Havilland was bought up by Hawker Siddeley, which was looking for a civil capability to balance its military interests. For its part, de Havilland felt that it would be better able to maintain its own design identity with Hawker, rather than Vickers with its powerful civil

Figure 1 The new shape of the British aircraft industry

Airframe groups

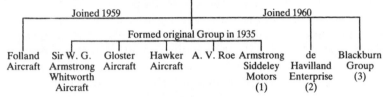

Helicopter group

Westland Aircraft

(Joined 1959) | (Joined 1960) | (Agreement to join reached in principle 1960)

(Saunders-Roe (Aviation interests) | Fairey Aviation (6a) | Bristol Aircraft (Helicopter interests)

Main engine companies
1 Bristol Siddeley – formed in 1959 by merger on 50:50 basis of Bristol Aero-Engines and Armstrong Siddeley Motors
2 Rolls-Royce

Companies unaffected by mergers (apart from Rolls-Royce)
1 Alvis
2 Handley Page
   Handley Page (Reading): formed in 1948 when Miles Aircraft was taken over.
3 Short Bros. and Harland: in which Bristol Aeroplane has a 15¼ per cent holding.
4 Scottish Aviation
5 Auster Aircraft
6 D. Napier and Son: part of English Electric Company (See 4 (b) below).
7 Boulton Paul Aircraft
8 Fairey Engineering (see 6 (b) below).
9 F. G. Miles
10 Lancashire Aircraft

(1) See Engine Companies. Armstrong Siddeley Motors ceased to exist in April 1959.
(2) Consists of aircraft, aero-engine and propeller companies and overseas interests.
(3) Formed in April 1959, as holding company for Group's aircraft, engine and electronic interests. Was previously Blackburn and General Aircraft, formed in 1949 after merger of Blackburn Aircraft and General Aircraft.
(4) (a) Formed in 1959 as subsidiary of English Electric Company.
     (b) Napier is not included in Aviation company, so is not part of new group.
(5) Originally Percival Aircraft which joined Hunting Group in 1944: became Hunting Pervical Aircraft in 1954 and Hunting Aircraft in 1957.
(6) (a) A wholly owned subsidiary of the Fairey Company in 1959 to look after its aviation interests.
     (b) Fairey Engineering (see 'Companies unaffected by mergers' above), remains a subsidiary of the Fairey Company looking after its missile and target aircraft interests.

design team. Blackburn, with its important NA39 Buccaneer contract and Folland also joined the new Hawker Siddeley Aviation (HSA) grouping. Sir Tom Sopwith, the company chairman and founder, stated that 'in making these offers we are trying to meet the declared policy of the government and although we are not particularly anxious to add to our aircraft interests in the UK, this merging of these companies will put HSA in an even stronger position to carry out any project which the government may have to offer'.[41] The TSR2 pairing of English Electric and Vickers formed the nucleus of the second airframe group, BAC. They were soon joined by Bristol, whose management had been told that the company would lose any chance of SST production work unless it merged. Vickers and English Electric held 40 per cent of the new group and Bristol 20 per cent. Hunting was directed by the MoA to explore the possibility of joining BAC. Hunting's links with the de Havilland-led Airco consortium had to be re-negotiated, but in May 1960, BAC acquired a controlling interest in the firm. Although a small company, Hunting had two very interesting designs, a jet trainer, the Provost, and a medium range airliner which turned into the successful BAC 1–11.

BAC, in fact, was a holding company for the aircraft interests of the three major shareholders but with an independent board responsible for all commercial judgements and project choices. A key problem to overcome was the treatment of existing projects, some of which were profitable, but others which were distinctly unhealthy. In the event, the company ran two accounts – 'Old and New' – which existed up to nationalisation in 1978. The exact distinction between 'old' and 'new' types was not easy to define and only goodwill enabled an easy transition. The VC10 and Vanguard, for example, were old account projects with Vickers carrying the financial risk while English Electric benefited from the lucrative Lightning programme. The TSR2, the Bloodhound 11, Thunderbird 11 and Blue Water guided weapons, a new medium range airliner, the BAC 1–11 and the SST, on the other hand, were treated as new account projects where costs and profits would be distributed between the shareholders. Its first chairman was the 'neutral' figure of Lord Portal of Hungerford. At plant level, however, there were local practices and loyalties to weld into a common enterprise. These were particularly difficult to resolve where teams had hitherto been in competition, especially between the English

Electric and Bristol guided weapons divisions. According to Charles Gardner, the company took four years to sort itself out, helped by a well funded public relations effort to educate both workforce and, more important, BAC's customers, that the company was more than a rag-bag of old interests. The new board quickly proved that it could take risks by cancelling the Vickers VC11 airliner and launching the BAC 1–11 supported by £9·5 million in launch aid and an order for ten aircraft from Freddie Laker's British United Airlines.[42]

Rolls-Royce was left largely untouched by the mergers, indeed it resisted pressure to buy up other companies which would bring unwanted extra capacity and little additional work. However, amalgamation of the Bristol, Hawker Siddeley, Blackburn and de Havilland engine interests into Bristol Siddeley Engines (BSE), created significant domestic competition for Rolls for the first time since the 1930s. This was underlined by the preference shown by the government to BSE in the award of several key contracts, including the TSR2, the SST and two VTOL projects. Given its dominant place in the British aero-engine industry, not a few airframe people were happy to see Rolls subject to some competitive pressure and having to lobby hard to obtain its 'fair share' of civil and military business (see Chapter 3).

Helicopter production was centred on a single firm, Westland, partly because neither of the larger groupings was prepared to take on a specialised helicopter business. The merger produced a group of 8,000 employees. A conservative R&D strategy, including licence work from the US, and substantial equipment and non-aircraft engineering interests, made Westland a very profitable company during the 1960s. However, later, its place as an independent producer of helicopters would make it increasingly vulnerable (see Chapter 4). Light aircraft construction was concentrated on the ill-fated Beagle company run by Pressed Steel until it was acquired by the government in 1966 (three years later Beagle collapsed at a cost of £8·5 million to the taxpayer). Only Shorts, Scottish Aviation and Handley Page remained outside the groups. Shorts, with 69 per cent of its shares owned by the state, was a special case. The Northern Ireland factor had often led the government to provide considerable direct and indirect support to the company. Other companies were encouraged by the government to place subcontracts with Shorts. It had been the beneficiary of a costly order for the Belfast, a military and civil transport which left it heavily in debt to the government. However, Shorts was also able to develop a useful missile capability and its own inexpensive and successful range of civil 'feederliners'.[43]

The main casualty of rationalisation was Handley Page. Where most of the 'grand old men' of British aviation had reluctantly conceded the logic of rationalisation, Sir Frederick Handley Page steadfastly held out for a valuation which no one else shared. As far as he was concerned rationalisation and nationalisation were roughly the same; the 'soul of a business lies in the creativeness of the individual and that progress is not achieved by elephantine size or by soulless bureaucracy'.[44] Like Rolls-Royce, Handley Page was affected by the government's manipulation of contracts in favour of the new groupings. But where Rolls had the technological and political muscle to fight back, Handley Page fought a losing battle with bankruptcy. Handley Page's stubborn independence caused the government some embarrassment, forcing it to intervene against a company competing in a 'free market'. Although Handley Page received launch aid to develop the Herald twin turbo-prop which was bought by BEA, the government awarded an RAF contract to the Avro/HSA 748, a decision based on the 'long term health of the industry' and consistent with the 1960 policy.[45] Sir Frederick died in 1962 but the firm continued to invest in new plant and designs. It was, however, an uphill struggle. The launch of the Jetstream feeder liner was estimated to cost £3 million, but an escalation to £13 million precipitated a cash flow crisis and the company finally ceased trading in 1970.

Sir Frederick Handley Page aside, the industry in general conceded that rationalisation was long overdue. It was, as Stanley Hooker put it,

> a time of great turmoil, rarely equalled in any industry. People in the great pioneering companies of this British industry were passionately proud and loyal to their great names, and powerful emotions had to be eroded if the mergers were to succeed. At top levels of management tough and astute tycoons fought for various interests – their employees, their company names, their aircraft projects, the financial deals and the fine print in the agreements. But at the technical and engineering levels it all took place with scarcely a ripple.[46]

Sir George Edwards of Vickers said that 'after twelve months' experience I would say we have done the right thing. I have always thought we had to get down to fewer units, and we can now see the advantages.' Sir George Dowty, president of SBAC also felt that 'the changes are for the better. Previously there was too much competition and overlapping of effort. Obviously this was wasteful', and it would put the industry in a better position to compete internationally. Sir Reginald Verdon-Smith of Bristol had been 'a protagonist of re-organisation for a long time', and felt that for 'a large number of medium-sized companies to be maintained in artificial competition by Government development contracts was an anachronism'.[47]

Rationalisation did not lead to significant improvement in the scale of production, even if it had produced somewhat stronger financial units linked to broader based industrial enterprises. HSA, with 50,580 workers, was the larger of the two airframe groups but more scattered, with nineteen centres to BAC's ten. Together they employed over 87,500 people out of an industry total of 259,000. No single factory employed more than 10,000, and only seven had more than 5,000 workers. Rolls-Royce employed 36,053 in nine factories, the largest at Derby with 18,606 workers. Before the mergers, the largest engine firm after Rolls had been Bristol Engines with less than a half of the workforce. BSE, however, now had 31,020 employees in four main plants (see Table 8). By comparison, Boeing employed 129,000, North American 92,000 and Lockheed 90,000. Of the fifty-five factories and facilities which comprised the industry, seventeen were still owned by the government, including those in BAC's Preston division and HSA's Chester factory. 38 per cent of the workforce was involved in airframe development and

Table 8: The aircraft companies, 1965

BAC (airframes)	30,169
BAC (guided weapons)	6,868
BAC (Total)	37,037
HSA (airframes)	36,793
HSA (guided weapons)	13,787
HSA (Total)	50,580
Short Bros	7,825
Handley Page	3,638
Beagle	1,702
Westland	8,702
BSE	31,020
Rolls-Royce	36,053

Source: Plowden.

construction, 28 per cent in engines and 9 per cent in guided weapons and space.

By August 1962, HSA had cut two design teams. But in the short term, the impact of rationalisation on the industry was relatively slight. There was a fall of 22,200 in the work force in 1963 as several production programmes tailed off and as a result of cancelled guided weapons projects. Consequently, BAC transferred guided weapons work from the ex-English Electric factory at Luton to the newer plant at Stevenage at a cost of 1,000 jobs. Indeed, a more severe round of job losses and plant closures followed the Labour Government's spate of cancellations in 1964–65 (see Chapter 4). Over the next decade, money would be put into new equipment, especially as the industry pioneered the use of computers in design and manufacturing processes. Already fifteen out fifty digital computers in Britain were devoted to aerospace work – five at MoA establishments. However, large new factories would have required a *national* investment which could, perhaps, have come only through government intervention in a commitment similar to French policy later in the decade.

With hindsight, the rationalisation process seems to have been over-protracted and a 'typically' British approach to industrial planning. It was well described by Keith Hartley as an 'excellent example of government induced concentration of an industry of a monopsonist using its powers to change the structure of an industry according to its own definite criteria'.[48] A Conservative Government, especially one with liberal economic inclinations, would have had difficulty in conceiving an alternative. Indeed, the return of launch aid, limited though it may have been compared to the Brabazon programme, was a clear reversal of the 1950s private venture policy. However, in the case of the TSR2, the strains of amalgamation and the simultaneous development of a highly complex project unquestionably contributed to the programme's difficulties (see Chapter 3). The weakest aspect of the government's policy was that it appeared to have little overall concept of an optimal shape of an industry capable of taking on the Americans or staying in front of its European competitors. Beyond a notion that larger must mean better, there was no attempt to identify the best use of industry's technical resources. The government also continued with the pretence that some form of domestic competition would be both possible and desirable after rationalisation. By contrast, the French approach would be to encourage technical specialisation and the creation of 'national champions'. But some form of rationalisation was long overdue; indeed it was already evident that the British aircraft industry would have to look for overseas partners if it was to cope with the rising costs and risks of development.

CHAPTER THREE

CANCELLATIONS AND COLLABORATION

1962–70

3.1 Drift and controversy, 1962–4

The new groups, although stronger than the fragmented industry of the 1940s and 1950s, still faced difficult times. The inexorable rise of development costs and the obvious limitations of the UK domestic market continued to undermine the industry's financial position. As Sir Roy Dobson of HSA argued, two groups made little competitive sense in the UK context, and he advocated some form of 'national projects' where the two firms could pool their resources.[1] Indeed, although much was made of the enhanced prospects for domestic competition, the Conservative government in practice tended to distribute contracts between the two main airframe and engine companies. As the Plowden Report later noted,

> in practice the technical merits of a submission rarely seem to have been the determining factor in the outcome of a design competition. More decisive has been the wish to share the available work as evenly as possible between the groups. Thus the two-group arrangement has served to cushion the effects of the competition which it is intended to stimulate.[2]

In the US, similar economic pressures were forcing consolidation, but the competitive position of American firms remained considerably stronger, buoyed by long production runs and lower unit costs. The French industry too would shortly be rationalised, but as part of a more co-ordinated, national technology strategy and with a deliberate attempt by the government to encourage specialisation. French firms, especially Dassault, with products which would tend to be geared to a wider market, would add to the competitive pressure on the British aircraft industry.

The strongest impression of the period is that, having engineered the regrouping and having reintroduced launch aid, the government had no coherent idea of what to do with the industry. In part, this reflected a wider uncertainty in Conservative policy about industrial and technological issues, but it also followed the oscillations of defence policy after the Sandys review of 1957. The missile-based strategy was discredited by the Blue Streak and Skybolt cancellations and undermined by shifts towards conventional force strategies in NATO. However, conventional forces were expensive and aircraft particularly costly. Although the cost of the British nuclear deterrent was much eased by the Nassau Accord of 1963 whereby the US would supply the UK with Polaris missiles, the strains of paying for conventional defence led the government to look for more cost effective ways of buying aircraft. It also sought to increase the capabilities of existing designs, most notably the TSR2, to cover a greater range of military tasks. Another option, and one which began to take on increased significance after the 1962 Anglo-French agreement to build the Concorde SST, was to collaborate in developing military aircraft. However, a heightened sense of *ad hoc* incrementalism in policy-making was reinforced by bitter inter-service rivalry over aircraft projects and by the growing controversy surrounding the escalating cost of aerospace programmes.

Both BAC and HSA, though welcoming changes in policy such as the reintroduction of launch aid, believed that the government lacked both an overall strategy for the industry and a clear idea of specific military requirements. Sir Reginald Verdon-Smith, who succeded Lord Portal as chairman of BAC, wrote later of a 'mood of growing frustration' with government policy during this period. Confidence was not helped by the bewildering succession of Ministers for Defence and Aviation[3] The response of one Minister of Aviation, Julian Amery was that it was 'very difficult to plan the future in this industry there are bound to be gaps and you can't eliminate them by planning'. However, in March 1963, heads of industry, airline chairmen, and Service chiefs met at Chequers to review with the Minister of Aviation the effects of rationalisation and future developments. They discussed, *inter alia*, the problems of controlling project costs, relations between the manufacturers and their government and airline customers, and the future of firms outside the main groupings. International co-operation was a main item on the agenda, and the government made it clear that it wanted to build on the Concorde Treaty and extend collaboration to military programmes. However, given the patchy experience with various NATO-sponsored programmes up to that point, the ground would have to be prepared more thoroughly with potential partners before substantive agreements would appear (see below). In the short term, the government had to confirm new domestic programmes and to see through development of the TSR2.

In the early 1960s, requirements were issued for an advanced jet fighter and a tactical transport, both based on revolutionary V/STOL concepts which had been financed largely by HSA with some support from the NATO Mutual Weapons Development Programme; but after two inconclusive NATO competitions held in 1962 for VTOL projects, the British government decided unilaterally to go ahead with two HSA designs, the P1154, a supersonic VTOL strike-fighter and the AW 681 a complementary VTOL military transport. However, matters were complicated by efforts to satisfy both RAF and Fleet Air Arm requirements for strike aircraft. Peter Thorneycroft, then Minister of Defence, was impressed by the US Defence Department's TFX (F111) programme aimed at achieving 'commonality' between the USAF and USN which aimed to reduce procurement costs. In both instances, this proved to be a case of mixing oil and water; even without the natural inclination of naval and air forces to prefer their own equipment, adapting ground based aircraft to carrier use incurred several design penalties. The Royal Navy was especially suspicious of the VTOL P1154 and its single 'vectored thrust' engine, and wanted instead the US McDonnell F4 Phantom. As HSA sought to reconcile the different requirements of RAF and Fleet Air Arm, progress was delayed and costs rose alarmingly. In September 1963, HSA was told to concentrate on the RAF version alone pending a later decision on a naval P1154. Labour's defence spokesman, Denis Healey claimed that Thorneycroft was being 'taken for a ride' by his 'quarrelling subordinates' in the Service departments. Thorneycroft's defence – that 'these men have made and are making a serious effort to develop a joint aircraft in order to save money' –

sounded increasingly threadbare.[4] In March 1964, he reluctantly abandoned 'commonality', the Navy got its Phantoms (with Rolls-Royce Spey engines and outer wings built by Shorts), and in August, HSA finally received full authorisation to develop the P1154 for the RAF.

The government also faced mounting problems with the TSR2, the centrepiece of its military aircraft programme. In particular, development costs were escalating and concern was growing that the programme was out of control. In a sense, TSR2 was not untypical of many technologically advanced programmes on both sides of the Atlantic. Cost escalation in aerospace programmes had emerged as a serious and endemic problem in the mid to late 1950s. In the UK, a 1958 MoS study of 100 defence projects showed an average cost escalation of 2·8, with some in excess of five times initial estimates. There could be several contributory factors: the inadequacy of estimating techniques; cumbersome procurement procedures; mid term changes in operational requirements; and contractors failing fully to appreciate costs and inflation. But the most significant reason was the greater technological complexity of major programmes and the difficulty faced by government and industry alike in adapting management and official monitoring procedures to cope with it.[5]

There were also specific contextual reasons why the TSR2 was proving even more intractable than other contemporary programmes.[6] For a start, development had to advance on several technological fronts simultaneously – particularly in the electronics and equipment areas. For reasons both of economy and of the radical changes in government policy seen in 1957, the idea of 'shorter steps' in development to reduce uncertainty and the technical difficulty of successive generations of aircraft accepted by the MoS in the mid 1950s, was never adopted. In the case of the TSR2, this problem was made worse by the addition of new missions to the specification, including a nuclear strike role. Secondly, and again despite official recognition of the need to define a single programme manager/prime contractor with clear lines of responsibility, the TSR2 was afflicted by an over-elaborate system of official oversight which effectively undermined managerial control. Although BAC was nominally the prime airframe contractor, many of the vital and most complex elements of the system were subject to separate MoA contracts. BAC found the development of the sophisticated electronics package, perhaps the most complex and uncertain element of the programme, especially difficult to control with the MoA acting as intermediary between it and the electronics companies. Similarly, problems with the supersonic Olympus engine were a major cause of delay and overall cost escalation (in 1964, Olympus cost estimates had risen from £7·3 million to £32·5 million). In both of these areas BAC lacked the authority either to control or to impose sanctions upon errant subcontractors. On balance, BAC had responsibility for only about 30 per cent of the aircraft's costs. Rather late in the day, in May 1964, the MoA conceded that BAC's position had to be strengthened and a senior BAC director was appointed project manager with the backing of new cost control and value engineering teams. The TSR2 was similarly affected by the tendency to use the project as an opportunity to defray the R&D costs of other programmes, such as the SST. Finally, senior management was inevitably distracted by rationalisation. Line managers and design teams also had difficulty in accommodating to new relationships and in coping with the disturbance which followed the mergers.

Matters were hardly helped by continual sniping against the project from the Treasury and some elements in the MoD and Admiralty. The latter persistently pressed for the adoption of the Buccaneer as a low cost alternative to the TSR2 which would also have helped to defray the costs of naval aviation. One trenchant critic of the TSR2 was Sir Solly Zuckerman who, as Chief Scientific Adviser to the MoD, had an important role in government R&D decisions in both Conservative and Labour governments. He contended that the TSR2 was a prime example of a military programme which 'slipped through' a more stringent net of project evaluation which he had helped to institute in the late 1950s. The Gibb-Zuckerman report of 1961 was one of the first systematic attempts in Britain to come to terms with the problem of military procurement in an age of complex and costly technology.[7] Its main conclusion was the need to invest heavily in both time and money during an extended technical-cost evaluation at the outset of a programme. The procurement process should also contain 'break clauses' which, although unsettling to the contractor, were essential if expensive mistakes were to be stopped:

we shall not achieve the best results unless the Government is also prepared to cut its losses and cancel projects even when a great deal of time, money and effort has been devoted to them. In these cases it is always tempting – because cancellations may be thought to argue incompetence – to go on in the hope that the effort already spent will in the end not always be wasted.

Wise words – but often honoured more in the breach than in the observance, and with the onset of collaborative programmes, even more difficult to sustain in the face of political pressure to go ahead with projects. Nevertheless, Zuckerman, supported by Lord Mountbatten, Chief of the Defence Staff, sustained a persistent campaign against the TSR2.

On the other hand, BAC shared with the rest of the aircraft industry a misplaced optimism about controlling large scale programmes. Even a sympathetic observer such as Charles Gardner recognised that it was beyond British capabilities at the time to 'evolve a project management system which ever looked like being able to control such a vast and complex undertaking and keep the costs within bounds'. Industry overall, including Vickers and later BAC, had 'only the slightest idea of the magnitude of the technical task ahead and of the costly snags they would hit'.[8] BAC did introduce several new techniques developed for managing complex programmes, including the PERT system, well in advance of many other British firms. But again without full executive authority, its position as 'prime contractor' was extremely awkward. In the final analysis, the fundamental problem was the level of complexity involved in the project. Most of the early estimates were rendered meaningless by the degree of technical uncertainty evident in the programme as late as 1963 and 1964. In this respect, TSR2 bears a remarkable resemblance to the problems encountered in estimating and controlling the costs of Concorde (see below).

The government's problems with the TSR2 and other defence contracts provided ammunition for Labour's campaign against Tory waste and mismanagement. The record of false starts in aircraft and missile projects was an obvious line of attack. The cancellation of the Blue Water tactical missile in 1962 brought the total cost of prematurely terminated aerospace projects since 1957 to £200 million. Harold Wilson, as leader of the Opposition and Chairman of the Public Accounts Committee ridiculed Tory defence policy. He likened one Minister of Defence to Helen of Troy; 'Helen's face,' he said, 'had launched a thousand ships, but at least they had been operational.' The claim that the government had lost control over defence contracts and that the aircraft industry was taking the taxpayer for a ride was underlined by the Ferranti affair. In February 1964, it was revealed that the company had made an 82 per cent profit on the Bloodhound missile programme. Ferranti duly repaid excess profits of £4·25 million, but a subsequent report by Sir John Lang found that the MoA's contract supervision and pricing procedures had been totally inadequate, especially in the new area of electronics and missiles.[9]

In the summer of 1963, the government's aviation related problems were further increased by news of BOAC's £50 million deficit. Although BOAC's financial crisis was caused by several internal and external problems, its choice of aircraft, and the role played by Ministers of Aviation in pressing for decisions which had helped the aircraft industry during rationalisation, had been major reasons for its difficulties. The BOAC affair rumbled on from 1963 to the summer of 1964 and deeply embarrassed the government. The affair led to a re-statement and clarification of the terms under which the government, in the national interest, could 'direct the nationalised airlines' to take uncommercial decisions, including the purchase of British airliners. Sir Giles Guthrie, BOAC's newly appointed chairman also forced the government to take financial responsibility for supporting the VC10 order, a move which, although it saved the VC10 programme, made selling the aircraft to other airlines even more difficult.[10]

It was all grist to the Labour mill. The Ferranti and BOAC affairs helped to fuel one of Labour's main themes for the General Election campaign of October 1964: 'the government,' Harold Wilson said, 'was swimming in shark invested waters' in its dealings with the aircraft and defence electronics industries. Aviation was now wholly identified with the expensive and grandiose ambitions of the 'wasted years' of Tory rule. As the General Election loomed, these attacks intensified as Labour sought to present itself as the Party which would regenerate the British economy through a more comprehensive, activist and technologically orientated industrial policy. Labour had long attacked the government for its a 'lack of balance' between R&D and production, the need for more public accountability of spending on aircraft projects and more emphasis on European cooperation. The lack of any forward planning was illustrative of the 'sloppy, slipshod way in which they (the Tories) have bungled so many of the economic problems which now face the country'. However, the Party had no positive view on what to do with the aircraft industry. Nationalisation was again rejected on the grounds that sufficient control could be obtained through government purchasing. Indeed, it was not until the spring of 1964 that the Party formed a small group to consider future options for the industry.[11]

The TSR2 was, however, increasingly the focus of Labour's attack on the Conservative government's military and aerospace policies. In 1963, Denis Healey described it as the 'biggest scandal since the South Sea Bubble', and accused the then Minister of Aviation, who held a Preston seat, of confusing national with sectional interests.[12] Labour's criticisms were reinforced by the government's refusal to publish details of the programme and its costs; as usual in these matters, ministers hid behind 'national security'. 'Other industries,' Fred Lee told the House of Commons in February 1964, 'were being deprived of money for modernisation which was being spent on aircraft and defence.' Labour intended to create a new ministry to spread the benefits of national R&D expenditure throughout the manufacturing sector. 'Prestige projects' such as TSR2 and Concorde would be scrutinised carefully, and an extensive review of national technological and industrial priorities should be expected. In short, Labour was putting the aircraft industry on notice that it would face another period of considerable uncertainty.

3.2 Labour and the aircraft industry

In October 1964, after thirteen years in opposition, the Labour Party returned to power bent on stimulating economic growth by encouraging industrial and technological regeneration. The government was overtly interventionist, encouraging the formation of larger industrial groupings – 'national champions' – in key manufacturing sectors to increase their competitive position. A Ministry of Technology (Mintech) was created to oversee the process and the Industrial Reorganisation Corporation formed to aid mergers and to provide an additional channel for state aid to industry. The aircraft industry, however, was generally regarded with some hostility by the new administration. Roy Jenkins, the Minister of Aviation, asserted that the industry had been 'feather bedded' for too long and that it was in for a 'few shocks'. He calculated that annually the industry received from the state a total of £1,350 for every employee – some 25 per cent of national R&D expenditure. In return, the industry's performance was steadily deteriorating; export earnings had fallen from 30 per cent of output in 1957 to less than 20 per cent, equivalent to 2·5 per cent of Britain's foreign exchange. The French aircraft industry, employing one third of the manpower had done almost as well.[13]

The government also felt that the industry had benefited too long from a built-in lobby in Whitehall, and in November 1966 the MoA was absorbed by Mintech. The MoA, it was asserted, had been insensitive to the commercial and economic consequences of overspending on aerospace: 'in pursuing its sponsorship function of the aviation industry, it [had] failed to give top priority to commercial objectives and to its wider responsibilities to the economy as a whole'.[14] Tony Benn, who took over the Ministry in February 1967, summarised the feelings of many in the Labour government about both the MoA and the aircraft industry. In a speech to the SBAC in 1967, he told them how Ministers of Aviation had been 'the most hated and feared Ministers in government. While their colleagues were grateful for anything they could wring from the Chancellor of the Exchequer, Ministers of Aviation ran off with sums of money that made the great train robbers look like schoolboys pinching money from a blind man's tin.'[15]

The government was therefore committed to a more fundamental review of the industry and of national commitments to aerospace projects. In December 1964, Jenkins announced that a Committee of Inquiry was to be set up under the Chairmanship of Lord Plowden to 'consider the future place and organisation of the aircraft industry'. In particular, he called upon the Committee to give special attention to the 'possibilities of international co-operation'. Ominously, he noted that decisions on future projects would not be postponed, but would act as 'fixed points' for the Committee's deliberations. In January 1965, at a dinner given by the Prime Minister Harold Wilson, the heads of the British aircraft industry described the damage that the loss of major projects could cause to design teams and to the level of technical skill in the industry. He was warned that serious cuts could cause BAC to fall apart. For his part, Wilson was able 'to encourage our guests on Anglo-French joint projects', but could not 'give them any reassurance' about domestic programmes such as the HS681, P1154 or TSR2.'[16]

In short order, the government axed the P1154, the HS681 and the TSR2. The Concorde would have gone too but for the provisions of the Anglo-French treaty (see below). On 2 February, Wilson told the House of Commons that the P1154 was not 'a practical proposition', it would be too late and it would cost too much: 'in these circumstances, and on defence grounds alone – quite apart from the cost argument – it will be necessary to extend the late government's purchasing programme for Phantoms and to use this aircraft as a partial replacement for the Hunter.' The AW681 was replaced by orders for the US Lockheed Hercules. Wilson said that the cancellations would save £300 million over ten years. In the event, much of the saving was eroded by the cost of re-engining the F4 with Rolls-Royce Speys and fitting other British equipment (see below).

As some compensation to Hawker Siddeley, the government announced that there was now a need for a sub-sonic VTOL aircraft, and that a 'limited development programme' would be authorised for the P1127 (Harrier). Fortunately, BSE had continued to develop its Pegasus engine and it had sufficient thrust to turn the P1127 into a viable combat aircraft. A substantial amount of equipment developed for the P1154 was also subsequently incorporated into the Harrier. In 1969, the Harrier was bought by the US Marine Corps under a fifteen-year co-production/licence agreement with McDonnell Douglas. Nevertheless, the cancellations led to 1,400 redundancies at HSA, the closure of the Armstrong Whitworth factory at Coventry and the loss of several well qualified design personnel. The AW681 may have been a questionable requirement, but the cancellation of the supersonic VTOL P1154 was a major setback to the UK military aircraft industry. Although the Harrier would prove to be a successful aircraft, demonstrating its value during the Falklands war, VTOL development has suffered from the lack of a high performance design. Although the British aircraft industry is still associated with VTOL development, technological leadership has now passed into American hands (see Chapter 4).

The cancellation of the TSR2 was even more controversial, leaving scars on the aircraft industry 'as deep and just as painful' as the

Comet disaster.[17] The aircraft was a major element of BAC's military work where overall 60 per cent of its business was in the high risk civil sector. In February 1965, Sir George Edwards wrote to Jenkins to emphasise the importance of TSR2 to BAC; cancellation would cut company profits by 50 per cent and seriously increase overheads on its other programmes. Effectively, the loss of TSR2 would 'put us out of business'. During the 1964 election campaign, Harold Wilson told Preston workers that 'our position on the TSR2 is exactly the same as the government's. If it works, and does what is expected of it at a reasonable cost we shall want it, though not for a nuclear role. We shall want it for its original tactical and reconnaissance roles.'[18] However, the qualification, 'at a reasonable cost' was the key phrase, and once in government, Labour spokesmen began to hint of difficulties. In January, Wilson told the House of Commons that the final figure for research, development and production would be at least £750 million with a unit price of £5 million. BAC was prepared to offer guarantees on delivery and cost, but these were not sufficient to sway the government.

The decision to cancel TSR2 was taken by the Cabinet on 31 March 1965. Wilson records that the meeting was divided three ways, with a group wanting outright cancellation and no American substitute. Supporters of the TSR2 were in a distinct minority. Richard Crossman (with a constituency interest in the aircraft industry) remembered it rather differently; in his diary he noted that a number of his colleagues were concerned that the government was 'cutting back on the British aircraft industry' in order to maintain an imperial defence policy which also left the UK 'in the hands of the Americans'. The announcement of cancellation was made during the April budget statement. Later, it was announced that the RAF's requirement for a long range strike aircraft would be filled by purchases of the US F111, costing some £300 million less than the TSR2. Roy Jenkins said that the TSR2, as well as the P1154 and HS681, had been designed too specifically for British use and would have had little chance of export success. Indeed, he described the TSR2 'as firmly geared to an exclusively British market as is a week's holiday at a Butlin's holiday camp but a good deal less value for money'. The government also argued, though without specifying where and how, that the physical and financial resources liberated by the cancellation of the TSR2 and the other military programmes would be better deployed in other manufacturing sectors. As George Brown, the Minister for Economic Affairs, put it, 'we are not out to run down an industry, but we are out to prevent this enormous waste of your money, and help the industry re-organise itself on a sound and viable basis'.[19] In the event, many skilled personnel went to work in the US or other aircraft industries.

Subsequent analysis of the figures suggests that the financial case for buying the F111 instead of the TSR2 was somewhat dubious. The total cost of £750 million may have been exaggerated by £250 million with the cost of general research attributed to the TSR2 programme. On the other hand, with three to four years of develop-ment work still to be done, there was a possibility of further cost escalation. In the event, Britain's deepening economic crisis and devaluation in 1967 led to a comprehensive defence review and the cancellation of the F111 a year later. Paradoxically, this too was a blow to some parts of the British aircraft industry which had hoped to win offset orders from the US. The most serious loser was Handley Page which had hoped to sell the Jetstream to the USAF. The loss of this potential business helped to drive the firm into bankruptcy.[20] One bright spot was that the US, as part of the offset arrangements covering the purchases of American aircraft, had helped BAC to enter the Saudi Arabian defence market with very substantial long-terms gains for the UK aircraft industry (see Chapter 4). With the benefit of hindsight, the potential costs of the TSR2 seem small compared to those of the Tornado, its eventual successor. But the long-term logic of national development and production of such a complex aircraft on the basis of such a small domestic market was increasingly questionable. As Bill Gunston grudgingly put it: 'TSR2 served as a watershed that separated the days when Britain could do anything – or thought it could, from a new and harsh world in which the nation's self-confidence in aerospace evaporated, so that it became afraid of embarking on a major programme without overseas partners who were supposed to reduce the risks and costs.'[21]

The truth of the matter was that, no matter how good the TSR2 might have been, enthusiasm for expensive all-British technology had to be tempered by increasingly straitened economic circum-stances. In the short term, the path of international collaboration was not always a smooth or even necessarily a cheaper option, but it was the most realistic alternative to a steady, but inevitable industrial decline. As Healey put it, international co-operation would form 'a sound basis for the re-organisation of the industry's resources and capacity, certainly on a reduced scale but also in a manner better calculated to serve the defence and economic interests of the country ...' Jenkins was equally blunt: 'there had been too many domestic projects based on the inadequate British market'. The cancellations, he said, would 'clear the ground' before 'rebuilding' the industry on the basis of joint projects. Even the Marshal of the Royal Air Force, Sir John Slessor admitted that 'the lesson of TSR2 is the need to break through our traditional British attitude of complacent self-sufficiency into the sphere of collaboration and integration with the very efficient aircraft industries of Europe'. To an industrialist like Sir Stanley Hooker, these decisions at least ended ten years of 'the worst mismanagement of the RAF's equipment and of the British aircraft industry that could possibly be imagined'.[21] Although not immediately apparent, collaboration would bring long term commitment to programmes and stability for the industry. It did, however, require both the government and British companies to learn some hard lessons in industrial and technological diplomacy.

3.3 The Plowden report

The Plowden report, published in December 1965, provided a diagnosis of past failings and suggested possible remedies.[22] It outlined the difficulty of maintaining an aircraft industry in an environment characterised by extensive technological change and beset by ever-increasing development costs, where economies of scale had increasingly favoured American producers. From 1957, profitability in the British aircraft industry had declined to a point well below the average for manufacturing industry generally. Much of the industry's capital had been obtained by borrowing, with 47 per cent of assets financed through loans compared to 4 per cent in British industry generally. Rationalisation had made little difference to the structural limitations of British companies. Only Rolls-Royce was in a sufficiently healthy position financially to compete effectively in world markets. In sum, aerospace was a risky business and its hazards had 'borne particularly hard upon countries such as the United Kingdom with relatively modest economic resources'. Overall, again with the exception of aero-engines, 'the picture is depressing'. It was, therefore, 'not surprising that some people should ask whether it is worthwhile having an aircraft industry at all'.

The report went on to consider why Britain should have an aircraft industry. First and foremost, it was a strategic asset providing some degree of autonomy in defence equipment, although there was no longer a case for providing all of Britain's military requirements from domestic sources. Secondly, it was a major employer, but mainly of skilled people who could readily find jobs elsewhere. Thirdly, there was a technological 'fallout' from the aircraft industry and the nation would suffer in the short term should the industry disappear altogether, or even in the event of a 'large and speedy contraction'. On the other hand, the more government invested systematically in the promotion of advanced technology in the economy, 'the less it need rely on the stimulus of the aircraft industry'. Fourthly, the industry made an impressive contribution to the balance of payments through exports and by 'import savings'. Finally, there was the 'infant industry' argument – that is to say, aerospace would eventually pay its way, but needed help against the powerful US industry. But, as the report commented, 'it is not easy to think of the British aircraft industry with its sixty-year history, its present employment of 260,000, and its past peak employment of over a million, as an infant'. According to Plowden, none of these arguments provided conclusive evidence for maintaining an aircraft industry: 'we do not believe that the benefits conferred on the nation by the aircraft industry will be so large or unique as to make it worth maintaining it in existence regardless of cost...' Yet, on the other hand, it was 'exactly the sort of business activity on which Britain should concentrate' with a high conversion ratio of imported to exported material, and defined as a high value added, skill-based capital intensive industry. The fundamental need, therefore, was to increase efficiency, to achieve competitive economies of scale and to reduce the cost of aircraft development.

The most important step toward these goals was international collaboration. Plowden welcomed the steps which had already been taken in this direction, but past examples of collaboration had been random and had led to inefficient forms of work sharing and management. Plowden now called for Britain to 'seek a comprehensive programme to include most of the aircraft projects on which the industry will be working'. This should include all advanced combat aircraft and especially long range, large or especially complex civil aircraft. A programme of this scale would provide the scope and flexibility for distributing work more efficiently. Despite a long association with the US, it was evident that American firms were not ideal partners for British industry. They had no 'overriding need' for co-operation in development and production, although there was still scope for selling British engines and equipment for use in American aircraft. Cooperation with Europe was therefore the most promising direction for British industry. The national aircraft industries of Europe 'all suffer from the same basic problem that their home markets are too small none of them is likely to survive alone for many years as a significant force in world aviation'. Even existing bilateral collaboration might be too limited and it was imperative to achieve a European-wide pattern of co-operation. Plowden went on to suggest that Britain should take the initiative and call for a conference of European aviation ministers to formulate a long term policy for aircraft manufacture and procurement in Europe which would lead 'in time to the creation of a European aircraft industry, with Europe as its basic market'.

In this context, it was absurd to maintain the pretence of competition in the UK market:

> Against the background of an austere future for the industry, mergers between the two airframe groups or between the main aero-engine groups would no doubt offer scope for economising in overheads and design facilities, and for rationalising production. Mergers would also remove the present temptation to Government and industry to create work in order to keep separate organisations alive and strong.

Government would inevitably retain a vital role in determining the structure and performance of the industry. The industry differed from most others in that it depended on government 'for its very existence', and the basic question was 'whether the Government should continue to act so as to keep an aircraft industry in existence'. Government had a right to monitor expenditure and the progress of sponsored projects but this was often to the detriment of industrial efficiency.

Plowden's answer to the dilemma (though not unanimously – Aubrey Jones, the ex-Conservative Minister of Supply, wrote a dissenting appendix) was some form of public ownership of the aircraft industry, either by nationalisation or by a public shareholding. Nationalisation, on the one hand, would acknowledge the dominant role of government in the industry's affairs, but on the other it would justify a relaxation of official intervention in commercial and managerial issues. However, nationalisation might deter private capital from investing in projects and the resultant political controversy would certainly not help the industry at such a critical juncture in its history. On balance, Plowden urged the government and industry to negotiate some form of public shareholding which would facilitate a reduction in government's detailed intervention in industrial decisions and programme management, but which would enable the state to play a formal role in the direction and planning of industrial activity. Lord Plowden later summed up his report's underlying thesis: there was 'no reason to regard the size and activities of the industry in recent years as immutable and sacrosanct'. The objective of future policy should be to ensure that it would be able to 'thrive with no more protection or support than given to comparable industries in Britain'. The aircraft industry was an example of 'the choices facing the British people. We cannot do everything. We cannot go on living in the past.'[23]

The government accepted in principle most of the report's recommendations. In February 1966, the Minister of Aviation, Fred Mulley, told the House of Commons that although the overall level of government support for the industry would fall, it endorsed the general case for retaining an aircraft industry with a comprehensive design and development capability. The government would certainly seek further to rationalise the industry and to negotiate some form of public participation in the airframe sector. But above all, the government recognised that the industry had to 'turn to collaboration as the principal means of improving the relationship between the size of the market and initial production costs and as the key to remaining a major force in aviation'. Above all, and in one of the best remembered phrases of the day, Mulley asserted that 'Britain is unlikely to be justified again in embarking alone on an expensive new project'.[24]

However, such a commitment to collaboration in advance of any firm agreement on specific programmes was seen as a dangerous limitation to Britain's negotiating position with its prospective European partners. For example, the SBAC wanted a precise definition of the nature, extent and means of collaboration on joint programmes, bearing in mind that we must retain our national capability to design and manufacture our own requirements in time of need ... collaboration can be advantageous only if Britain can negotiate from a position of strength; we must therefore continue to undertake the basic research and development work to enable us to influence the choice of joint projects and, in the last resort, in individual cases, to carry them through independently.

There were also fears that industrial effectiveness would be undermined by politically determined work sharing agreements which would have a particularly detrimental affect on the far stronger British equipment industry. As Sir George Dowty put it, 'the developing collaboration with countries such as France on new aircraft projects has brought about unfortunate decisions to parcel out this work on the basis of not what is best but what seems to be politically expedient'. BAC's Sir George Edwards did not 'recall a French minister say[ing] that it would not be possible for France to undertake projects on her own any longer and that they could only start if she had a colleague country on which to lean. It is no good going to the table with one's own government openly professing inability or unwillingness to go it alone.'[25]

This theme was picked up by the Opposition; the previous government had been pursuing an effective collaborative strategy, and the P1154 and TSR2 were to have been the last generation of purely national military aircraft. These would have provided a stronger base for collaboration, but Labour had withdrawn projects from the industry before it had 'caught the European tide. If we dismantle the industry before we go into Europe, we shall have nothing with which to get into Europe and no nucleus around which the European industry can be built our view is that we need to maintain a strong British industry until we can establish a lasting partnership with Europe.' Others, including *The Economist*, felt that Plowden had not gone far enough. It urged not only outright nationalisation, but felt that there was a strong case for complete specialisation within a European context, with Britain concentrating on aero-engine development.[26] In general, the Plowden report was stronger on grand ideas and objectives than on providing a detailed (and politically realistic) means of achieving them. To call for a more systematic approach to collaboration was one thing; to convince the French to submerge their industrial ambitions in a

European industry was quite another. Hopes of achieving a more integrated British industry also proved more problematic and moved in a direction not anticipated by Plowden.

3.4 Early steps towards collaboration and the Concorde

The basic aim of European collaboration is to recreate some of the conditions which are said to underpin American competitive strength – superior R&D resources, a large domestic market and the advantages of long production runs. By pooling national resources, sharing costs and broadening initial markets, European firms might be better placed to resist US domination of the aircraft industry. It was recognised from the outset that getting two or more nations to work together would involve delicate political questions relating to vital national industrial and technological issues such as work sharing and technology transfer. Equally, the prospect of higher costs consequent on developing and producing aircraft in two or more countries – with different languages, management styles, industrial standards and levels of competence and efficiency – was accepted as a necessary, but hopefully containable problem. In any event, collaboration was intended to cut the overall cost of aircraft development to each participating country. As Julian Amery said in 1962, co-operation would indeed bring 'marginal additions to some costs'; but these would be 'outweighed by the major economies which followed from the elimination of duplicated national effort'.[27]

The first examples of European collaboration occurred during the 1950s and centred on a series of co-production programmes of US-licenced designs involving German, Italian, Dutch and French companies, an experience which for some was a way to rebuild a national aerospace capability. Although some British equipment, notably engines, was incorporated in these and other European aircraft, British industry largely concentrated on domestic programmes. In 1957, an exchange of letters in *The Times* raised the question of international collaboration. Three Labour MPs suggested that co-operation with Europe was the only realistic way for the British industry to match that of the US. They were concerned that British firms seemed to be ignoring opportunities for working with their colleagues in Europe. The president of the SBAC, C. F.

Unwins, replied that British industry was not 'aloof' or hostile to the idea of co-operation and he pointed to a number of links between BSE and Snecma as well as de Havilland's contribution to the Caravelle. But the future 'lies more in the natural evolution of independent alliances between companies with common interests than in the dry and formal concepts of international regrouping'.[28] However, active British interest in co-operation remained limited. The French were particularly aggrieved that despite Britain's part in the Caravelle, it was not seriously considered as a contender for BEA's medium range jet airliner requirement filled by the Trident. On the other hand, Dassault rejected a proposal from Rolls to offer the Germans an Avon-powered Mirage to compete with the Lockheed F104. Co-operation on military projects was, of course, unlikely while the Sandys' doctrine was in the ascendant, although the Germans had been interested in building the Saunders Roe SR177, and internationalising OR339 was certainly not on the agenda.

By the early 1960s, attitudes were beginning to change, but the views of senior industrialists were still mixed. Naturally enough, rationalisation was absorbing most of their time and energy, but even so some were quite doubtful of the principle. Sir Aubrey Burke, deputy managing director of HSA said that he had 'had experience only with one, comparatively small, consortium and they were all Englishmen working together. On the basis of that experience I would expect designing aeroplanes by international collaboration to be exceedingly difficult. You cannot design aeroplanes by committee. There must be one man in charge.' His colleague, Sir Roy Dobson also appeared to be less than keen about collaboration; subcontracting with other countries was possible, 'but when it comes to putting the machine together and flying it, that must be done here'. For others, such as Sir George Edwards, the onset of internationalisation was a natural and logical extension of rationalisation. Air Commodore Banks was equally in favour of a 'whole-hearted link up'. In his view, it should have been 'underway from the end of World War Two, but it is still not too late to get the process underway'. As far as *Flight* was concerned, it was a 'fundamental part of the future'. Of course, saying that collaboration was necessary, even desirable, was one thing, but starting a joint project was quite another. Sir Reginald Verdon-Smith of BSE summed up the problem nicely: '... we have arrived at the stage ...

where international co-operation is necessary. But to say that it is necessary does not mean that it is easy. All concerned in these international projects find them very complicated and it is said that the engineering involved is simple compared with the political and administrative problems.'[29] By the early 1960s, the SBAC had joined the European trade association AECMA, but the Farnborough air show remained closed to foreign aircraft until 1966, and then invited only if they contained a substantial element of British equipment.

The various NATO-sponsored design competitions had shown just how frustrating co-operation could be. Too many were speculative proposals which stemmed from an approximate coincidence of national requirements. The NATO NBMR-3 competition for a VTOL strike-fighter held in 1963 was a classic example of the problems involved. The British P1154 was declared the 'technical winner', but the NATO committee also said that the Mirage 111-V had 'equal merit'. The French certainly did not want the P1154; the British refused to accept the Rolls engined Mirage; and the Americans then decided that VTOL was not needed when its industry had an aircraft like the Phantom to promote. NMBR-3 was 'a bizarre sort of contest because not one of the competing European countries had actually promised to buy the winning aircraft. It was just vaguely assumed that the prize for the winner would be vast orders for his aircraft.'[30] A similar outcome followed a NATO competition for an ASW aircraft; in this case, the British turned down the Franco-German winner in favour of developing the Nimrod. The truth of the matter was that collaboration was as much about politics as responding to an industrial or technological logic. To launch an international programme successfully, governments had to recognise a mutuality of interest. It did not have to be the same set of interests or a matching set of priorities, but there had to be a strong convergence of political forces. For the creation of the European Launcher Development Organisation (ELDO), it was the British looking for a suitable role for the redundant Blue Streak missile which helped to fulfil European aspirations of joining the space race. In the case of the SST – the Concorde – it was the coincidence of national industrial interests, technological ambitions and a major British foreign policy goal.

British work on an SST had begun in the early 1950s, largely as a result of initiatives taken by the RAE. In 1959, the government received an official report from the RAE's Supersonic Transport Aircraft Committee (STAC) which recommended the launch of a supersonic airliner. Although extremely optimistic about technical questions (such as the sonic boom), sales and costs, the thrust of the report and the political battle waged on behalf of the SST within Whitehall implied that without an SST, the UK civil industry would be unable to sustain a competitive challenge to the Americans. As Morian Morgan, the RAE's deputy director put it, failure to proceed with the SST 'could have a profound effect on the pattern of our aircraft industry and on our position as a leading aeronautical power'.[31] Aubrey Jones, then Minister of Supply, immediately saw that a project of this scale had to be internationalised. Its likely costs, although largely a matter of guesswork, would be at least twice as high as the VC10, perhaps £100 million, and would be bitterly opposed by the Treasury. As the French were also interested in an SST – a 'super Caravelle' – they welcomed Jones' initial approach made in the Spring of 1959. However, Jones' Cabinet colleagues were not so keen, and British companies were asked to submit designs for a national programme based on the STAC report.

Between the summer of 1959 and the autumn of 1961, the government underwent its 'conversion to Europe', and decided to apply for EEC membership. The new Minister of Aviation, Duncan Sandys, was strongly in favour of both building the SST and joining the EEC. MoA officials also realised that a collaborative context would help the political case for the SST. It would also outflank a hostile Treasury. The companies working on the SST were now requested to consider a collaborative programme but at this stage with either France or the United States. If there was to be an SST, the Treasury preferred the American option for financial and commercial reasons, but a majority within the MoA looked to Europe. In the event, the US chose a more ambitious (and costly) project than the British thought wise. The French, on the other hand, responded positively to British overtures, and from this point co-operation with the French became the basis for SST development. By the summer of 1962, with negotiations surrounding Britain's application to join the EEC at their height, the SST rapidly became a symbol of British good faith as a 'truly European' nation. As Julian Amery, Minister of Aviation during these final stages put it, building Concorde and entry to the EEC were 'really part and parcel of the same thing'.[32]

The Bristol/BAC 223, a Mach 2·2, 100-seat, London to New York airliner designed by Archibald (later Sir Archibald) Russell, had emerged as the basis for the British programme. The aircraft would be powered by a civil version of the Olympus being developed for the TSR2. In April 1960, BAC and the French firm Sud Aviation (later Aerospatiale) began to hammer out a joint design. The French and British teams had widely differing views about fundamental issues such as range, payload and timing. In particular, the French wanted to press ahead more rapidly and produce a short range SST which the British, already conscious of the importance of trans-Atlantic requirements, thought was a commercial absurdity. Negotiations dragged on throughout 1961 and most of 1962. The situation was not helped by a degree of corporate and personal rivalry between some of the principals. Neither side was willing to concede 'leadership' to the other – an early example of how the designation of a 'design leader', although offering potentially better management options, could cloud collaborative programmes. Later, as more sophisticated structures evolved, the need for 'design leadership' located in one company largely disappeared. In the event, it took heavy pressure from the two governments to force BAC and Sud into coming up with a joint programme. Even so, it was initially agreed to 'have a common basic aeroplane in two versions', BAC's long range aircraft and Sud's simpler medium range design. Later, the French came to accept that their medium range type made little commercial sense but only after incurring needless delay and unnecessary complication.[33]

On the engine side, matters proceeded rather more smoothly. Bristol Siddeley Engines and Snecma, the French engine company, quickly reached preliminary agreement based on the Olympus. According to Sir Arnold Hall, then managing director of BSE , 'we went to talk to my friends at Snecma to see what they felt about it all. The result of these conversations was that we concluded that, if at any time there were an aircraft project, the two companies ... would work together on the engine...' By November 1962, the two firms had already been working on a joint design and had sorted out their respective development responsibilities. Indeed, BSE's established links with the French were highly influential in the original decision to adopt the Olympus instead of a new engine based on Rolls design.[34]

The Anglo-French Treaty committing both countries to 'develop and produce' a SST, soon to be named Concorde (the 'e' was conceded by the British in 1967), was signed on 29 November 1962. For a programme of considerable technological complexity and organisational novelty, the document was, at two pages, singularly brief and superficial. Programme costs and profits would be divided equally between the two countries. The British would 'lead' the engine programme with 60 per cent of the work, balanced by a French 'lead' on the airframe, also with 60 per cent of the work. Each country would build different elements of the airframe, but there would be two production lines and two prototypes would be built. Costs were estimated at between £150 and £170 million for what were then two versions. Perhaps inevitably under the circumstances, the collaborative machinery set up to oversee Concorde was cumbersome, top heavy with senior officials and industrialists. Decision-making was 'collegial' and nothing could be agreed which was not acceptable to both sides. In the early days, decision-making at all levels was far from easy. Differences of management style and temperament meant that exchanges were ritualised and formal. But ultimately, the questioning of basic procedures and attitudes on both sides proved to be highly productive and mutually informative, and purely national positions on technical matters began to disappear.

It was evident from an early stage that personal affinity was crucial in building the trust needed to run a trans-national programme. For instance, Sir George Edwards got on well with General André Puget, head of Sud. As he noted, 'there was a fair amount of antagonism in different parts of the organisation and had there not been this goodwill between Puget and myself at the top I think the project might well have suffered a different fate'. Later, Geoffrey Knight and Henri Ziegler would together strengthen and simplify programme management acting as a bi-national team.[35] But neither side's position was ever wholly compatible. The British were usually more concerned to minimise the financial burden of development in achieving specific technological and hopefully commercial targets. The French gave greater priority to building up a European aerospace industry led by France, to using the programme to modernise their industry and to strengthening areas such as avionics where French industry was decidedly weak.

Despite these problems, BAC soon came to appreciate one

crucial aspect of joint ventures – once started, they were difficult to stop. In the case of Concorde, unilateral cancellation was constrained by the terms of the Treaty which lacked a specific 'break clause', but political commitments and interests could be equally compelling. When the Labour government wanted to cancel Concorde along with the P1154 and TSR2, the French threatened to sue in the International Court of Justice for compensation. The British government, seeking to apply a second time for EEC membership, backed down. Similar concerns intervened in 1970 when Edward Heath's government reviewed what was by then a horrendously expensive project. Only in 1974 did both governments agree finally to cap their expenditure by limiting production to sixteen aircraft. By then, the extent of the aircraft's commercial failure was known, its sales prospects destroyed by environmental problems (especially the prohibition against overland supersonic flight) and by the massive increases in fuel costs of the early 1970s.[36]

The Concorde was certainly a classic example of cost escalation – by 1974 its probable cost had risen to £1,070 million with a further commitment of £200 million to follow for production. There were a number of specific reasons for such a miscalculation – inflation, currency adjustments, large scale design changes and a major problem in 'civilianising' the Olympus engine. But to a great extent, and like the TSR2, it was a function of sheer technological complexity. The Concorde was, and still is, one of the most advanced aircraft the European industry has ever undertaken, perhaps one of the most innovative and demanding projects in aerospace history – combining military power and performance with a commercial airliner's reliability and safety. One British civil servant rated Concorde second only to the US manned space programme in technological complexity and many of 'the difficulties of cost estimation and cost control should be considered in this light'. Largely because of its political importance, it also broke all the 'rules' of the Gibb-Zuckerman procedures. The project was started, with two governments 'locked-in' to full scale development in advance of an adequate design study, with cost estimates which were described by one official as 'very provisional indeed'. Official mechanisms for cost control and monitoring simply could not cope; indeed the system tended to be too intrusive and ultimately counter-productive. As Sir George Edwards put it, 'I suppose it was a defensive mechanism ... so that they at least thought they'd got a reasonably direct control of the money-spending procedures and the programme monitoring'.[37]

It is impossible to judge whether a single national programme would have fared any better. It would certainly have been cancelled at a relatively earlier stage. Even within the UK, relations between the British government and the prime contractors were often difficult. The main bone of contention was the degree to which the government could reasonably and realistically expect private firms to assume a share of the risk in developing such a complex aircraft. From the start, it was evident that launch aid was not applicable to the Concorde or its engine. BAC made it clear that the SST was such a leap in the dark that it would be 'improper' for the company to risk its shareholder's money on the project. As Knight later told a Commons Select Committee, Concorde was not a 'fit project for shareholder's investment, [any] more than I think the US space activity is'. Initial development was funded by a 'cost-plus, fixed-fee' contract. On the other hand, the government wanted to avoid an 'agency' relationship, where the contractor had little or no incentive to keep costs under control. By 1968, a loose system of target costings and rewards for beating them had been established. However, as the Public Accounts Committee found, penalties for exceeding estimated costs were very modest. It was hoped to tighten up the production phase, but when the prospect of a long production run faded away, this again proved largely nugatory. Again, the fundamental problem was the sheer complexity and uncertainty associated with the programme so that it was, perhaps, 'outside any form of contractual control'.[38]

In the view of one analyst, for a 'true' expenditure of over £2000 million, the British government obtained very little in the way of measurable benefit.[39] Even the aircraft industry was divided over the desirability of developing the aeroplane; Sir Arnold Hall, chairman of HSA felt that Concorde had drained resources away from other projects. The programme undoubtedly raised serious questions about the accountability of large scale publicly funded civil programmes. It focused critical attention on the level of support which the aircraft industry had received since the Second World War. Together with the RB211 affair, the Concorde undoubtedly helped to confirm the Labour Party's commitment to nationalisation (see Chapter Four). In the longer term, the project has remained something of an albatross hanging over the aircraft industry. Whenever governments have been faced by requests for launch aid the cry of 'no more Concordes' has often been heard. On the other hand, though equally negatively, it did provide lessons in how not to run a collaborative programme.

In the early 1960s, however, Concorde symbolised a break-through in Anglo-French relations and offered the prospect of future collaborative programmes. As Julian Amery put it, the most significant development

> may be the lessons which France and Britain will learn from working together on every aspect of a joint project of this size. Our two countries were pioneers in the early days of aircraft production. Then, they were also rivals. But now the time has come to join forces, if we are to hold a leading position in the air routes of the world.[40]

In 1964, talks were held between British and French ministers aimed at developing a wide range of civil and military projects. In due course, these negotiations formed the basis for a package of collaborative programmes launched by the incoming Labour government. The ultimate paradox of the Concorde is, perhaps, that probably only a programme of such importance could have so readily broken down national barriers; but its very complexity per-haps made it a poor choice with which to practice the complicated arts of international aerospace co-operation.

3.5 The Anglo-French military package

The negotiations with the French started by the Conservatives and taken up by the incoming Labour government took on new signifi-cance after the cancellation of the P1154 and TSR2 and the Plow-den report. In due course, a package of joint projects with the French emerged encompassing two combat aircraft, several heli-copters, missiles and a wide-bodied medium range airliner. The helicopter package of 1967 was, in effect, an example of *contra achats*, where each state undertook to buy a piece of equipment largely designed and developed by the other. The British took the French Puma and Gazelle in return for the French accepting the WG13 (Lynx). There was in addition a missile package (the Martel), where a common airframe was equipped to different national requirements.

The most important of these Anglo-French programmes was the

Memorandum of Understanding signed between the two governments on 17 May 1965, linking an advanced attack/trainer (Jaguar)
with a much more advanced and complex multi-role combat aircraft
(AFVG). The French firm of Breguet was to 'lead' Jaguar airframe
development with Rolls 'leading' on the Adour engine. The roles
were reversed on the AFVG, with BAC 'leading' Dassault and
Snecma taking charge of the engine with BSE as its British partner.
As collaboration evolved, the notion of design leadership would
eventually have little practical significance, but at the time much
was made of such 'leadership' roles. In particular, neither Dassault
nor Rolls, which took over BSE in 1966, were really very happy
with the idea of 'following' anybody, especially on the AFVG,
regarded as technically and industrially the more important of the
two projects. *Flight* was also worried about the vagueness of the
MoU and the fact that it was full of break clauses, a clear indication
that at least one lesson had been learnt from the Concorde episode.
The British government, however, was very pleased with the
outcome. Denis Healey, the Minister of Defence said that 'Franco-
British co-operation was in the logic of things', while the Minister of
Aviation, Roy Jenkins described the package as the 'essential
foundation for the future of the British aircraft industry'.[41]

The Jaguar's complicated gestation showed that the meshing of
two sets of national requirements could be difficult and protracted.
It started life as a high speed trainer but following the P1154
cancellation the RAF pressed for a more formidable supersonic
ground attack/trainer. Both airforces subsequently abandoned the
idea of a supersonic trainer and each country developed an
alternative sub-sonic jet trainer – in Britain the HSA Hawk while
the French developed the Alpha Jet with the Germans. As the
Public Accounts Committee observed in 1971, 'but for fortuitous
circumstances the Ministry would have found themselves with an
unnecessary, over-sophisticated and expensive supersonic trainer'.
They hoped that in the future the government would be able to
obtain 'cost effective aircraft from good planning rather than good
fortune'. At an industrial level, the Jaguar worked out very well.
Both BAC and Breguet badly needed the business and had every
incentive to pool their efforts in a smooth and effective manner. In
the light of the the Concorde experience, it was decided to base
programme management on a clearly defined centralised structure.
In May 1966, SEPECAT, registered as a French-based holding

company, was formed to run the programme with BAC and Breguet acting as sub-contractors to the jointly owned company. Rolls and the French engine firm of Turbomeca adopted a similar organisational structure to develop the Adour. With a joint initial production run of 400 with exports to follow, the Jaguar was the 'first example of how Europe could combine to get American-type production runs and the competitive costs which flow from such an arrangement'.[42] BAC found Breguet easy to work with, and the French company certainly benefited technically from collaborating with BAC. However, in 1967, Dassault took a majority holding in Breguet with a complete merger following in 1971 and relations between the two companies became more problematic, especially as Dassault was producing a competitor. Nevertheless, the Jaguar programme showed that collaboration could produce an effective aircraft with only a modest increment in overall development costs and the collaborative framework would provide a model for future international programmes.

The AFVG, however, was the more important of the two projects. The Jaguar was a modest concept which could have equally been launched as a national programme. The AFVG, on the other hand, was very much more a 'TSR2' replacement designed to meet roughly complementary French and British requirements for a long range strike/interceptor fighter. It was based on work done by BAC's Warton design team on variable geometry wing technology. BAC's interest in variable geometry (where the wing would change its position to accommodate different flight conditions, thus allowing a more flexible range of missions) went back to studies begun in 1945 by Barnes Wallis. His more advanced concepts suffered from a lack of interest in the UK, finally falling to the Sandys' axe in 1957. In 1959 the Weybridge Military Project Office took over Wallis' VG work and used it as the basis for a design for a 'TSR2 successor'. In 1964, all Weybridge VG work was transferred to Warton, contributing to the formation of one Europe's foremost military aircraft design centres.

Changing military requirements in both Britain and France hardly helped to provide a stable base for co-operation. But the lukewarm attitude adopted by Dassault and the French government to the whole project was in the event fatal to the aircraft. To the French, the AFVG seems to have been little more than a politically useful balance to the Jaguar, and interest was sustained in the

AFVG for no longer than it was required to commit the British to the Jaguar and the 1967 helicopter package. But for the British government the AFVG was the operational and industrial heart of the UK's aircraft programme. As Healey told the House of Commons in February 1967, 'without this project there would be no design work for the British aircraft industry after work on Concorde finishes, and without that design work there would be no future for the aircraft industry not only in Britain, but in Europe. That is the sense in which this is the core of our long term aircraft programme.'

In June 1967, the French exercised their rights under the 1965 MoU to review and to withdraw from the project before a final commitment, due at the end of 1967, had to be made. They cited the rising costs of the programme – up from £200 million in 1966 to over £300 million by 1967. The reaction in Britain was that the French government, egged on by Dassault, had deliberately undermined the AFVG. Early in 1967, BAC had become aware of independent work by Dassault on a similar variable geometry design, the Mirage 3G. Unknown to BAC, Dassault was also working on a conventional advanced fighter, the F1, which would eventually fill the French requirement. The collapse of the AFVG was deeply embarrassing for the government, vigorously attacked by the Conservatives for putting all its aircraft eggs 'in the collaborative basket'. Cancellation of the AFVG left a gaping hole in both the RAF's future plans and in BAC's design and development organisation. The Plowden doctrine, they claimed, had been shown to be wanting: 'no French government would have put its defence and technological future in the hands of an unconditional veto from a foreign government'. Labour had now spent over £250 million on cancelled aircraft developments, more than during the 'wasted' years of Tory rule. Denis Healey put a brave face on things and recalled the 'indifference to costs' that had been the hallmark of the Conservative's handling of aircraft projects. He looked to the Jaguar and the Martel missile programme as a better indication of the future pattern of collaborative ventures. He tried to show that the French had had genuine doubts about the costs of going ahead with the project. However, there was no hiding the fact that the government, and Healey personally, had been thoroughly discomfited by the AFVG affair.[43]

The AFVG crisis cast a pall over collaboration, especially with the French. The British had certainly believed that a formal commitment to proceed had been made in January, and as such had been warmly welcomed by many in the industry. As Sir George Edwards put it, 'the consolidation of joint products like Concorde, Jaguar and the AFVG has restored a poise and purpose to the British aircraft industry which has been lacking since the round of major cancellations'. A *Flight* editorial probably reflected industry's bitter reaction to French actions: 'we support European collaboration, but not at the price now being paid. It amounts to a betrayal of the nation and of half a decade of British technology, devotion, leadership and investment.' These events confirmed for many in the industry that 'collaboration from strength' was essential. Sir George Edwards accepted that co-operation was undoubtedly the best course of action for the British industry, but this was not the same as saying 'that Britain should never be prepared to build a transport or military aircraft on her own again. We should always retain this ability, and demonstrate our willingness to use it. All successful collaboration must be based on mutual respect, which in turn relies on strength and the ability to be independent.' As the SBAC averred, in the light of the AFVG affair, it was now even more essential that mistakes should not be made in an over-hasty search for new partnerships: 'we cannot afford to jeopardise our technical leadership in the interests of winning new partners for joint programmes'.[44]

3.6 The MRCA/Tornado

With the end of the AFVG programme, the government continued to support work on VG at BAC while Denis Healey tried to assemble another international programme to fill the gap in both BAC's workload and the RAF's operational requirements. The main European need was for an F104 replacement, but most of the F104 users, including the Germans, wanted a relatively simple and cheap aircraft. The RAF, on the other hand, wanted a more expensive multi-role strike-fighter using VG and entailing a greater degree of complexity. However, the German industry was particularly keen to upgrade its design and development capabilities and working with Britain had obvious attractions. The British government steered a protracted series of international discussions towards the RAF's position, with the result that Italy, West Germany and the

UK joined together in launching a tripartite programme. In December 1968, the air staffs of the three countries agreed to a joint specification for a Multi-Role Combat Aircraft (MRCA), later named Tornado. BAC, Fiat (later Aeritalia) and MBB of Germany formed the industrial team, establishing a German-registered holding company, Panavia, based in Munich. Later, after the British government had successfully pressed for a British engine, Rolls, Fiat and MTU formed a similar organisation, Turbo Union, to design and develop the RB1999. Two NATO-based procurement agencies, NAMMO and NAMMA, were created to monitor the programme and to act as a forum for inter-governmental decision-making.

The development costs and work shares were to be based on the number of aircraft each country ordered. Initially, this meant that Germany, with 600 aircraft, claimed a dominant role in the programme, a demand which caused BAC some vexation given the inexperience of the German aircraft industry at this time. Although German companies had been involved in some advanced design and research work since the early 1960s, this was the first major combat aircraft they had taken on since the Second World War. BAC believed that the British government may have been prepared to concede this point to the Germans in order to demonstrate to their partners the 'strength of the British resolve to join the Common Market'.[45] German 'leadership' of the project caused some irritation in Britain, though largely amongst outside observers. This was later exacerbated by a cut in the German order to 400 aircraft, the same as the RAF's (the Italians wanted 200). Changes were effected in the composition of Panavia, with BAC and MBB each finally taking a 42·5 per cent share of the airframe with Fiat (Aeritalia) 15 per cent. In practice, the British share of the airframe has been about 47·6 per cent.

British equipment and avionics firms were even less happy with the Tornado work-sharing agreements. In order to complete Germany's entitlement, a number of important systems contracts were awarded to German companies. In some cases, lacking the necessary technology and expertise, they resorted to licences of American technology. For example, the attack radar was based on a Texas Instruments design derived from equipment used by the F-111. This was also cheaper than developing a wholly new programme centred on European, that is to say, British technology. On the other hand, several British companies, particularly Ferranti, were awarded major contracts for Tornado systems. The blunt truth, however, was that without the project the British military avionics industry would have been in a very bad way indeed; a share of a confirmed programme must be regarded as being considerably better than a hundred per cent of a cancelled project. As the MoD put it,

> participation in this project is certainly going to develop our own capability in very many areas. I think there are some areas in which our industry is not going to participate and in the case of the radar there will be a loss of experience in development. But on the whole the industry will gain in standing from this project.[46]

Panavia and Turbo Union have proved particularly effective in diluting questions of design leadership and forging lasting transnational links between the six firms involved. Lessons from both the Concorde and Jaguar programmes were applied. The holding companies had proper Boards and a staff system with a continuity of membership – for example, Panavia's managing director from 1969 to 1978 was the MBB designer Gero Madelung. In practice, nationality has rarely been a problem and BAC in particular found relations with MBB and the Italians much easier than with the French. The Panavia structure so satisfied the airframe industry's concerns about design leadership and technology transfer that some industrialists began to see it as the basis for a more comprehensive re-grouping of European aerospace. In the event, this was a little premature, but the co-operation generated in the Tornado programme has continued into the next generation of European fighters (see Chapter 4).

The Tornado has evidently satisfied all of its primary requirements and technically stands comparison with US aircraft. Although rising costs forced a reduction in the initial production order to 809 overall, this was still an unprecedented base market for a European military programme, offering economies of scale approaching those of the United States. Subsequent export orders have pushed the total production run towards a thousand units, including an Air Defence Version developed for the RAF. It has unquestionably been an expensive aeroplane; total programme costs will exceed £30 billion. Managing such a complex programme across three currencies at a time of growing economic instability has not been easy. This, and the need to duplicate some aspects of production, has entailed extra costs. The alternative, buying from the US, even if cheaper in the short term, would, however, have entailed heavy balance of payments costs and would have ended British and European hopes of staying in the business of building advanced combat aircraft. As one MoD official put it, 'if one had attempted any other solution it would probably have meant complete domination and absorption by the American aircraft industry'. The Tornado ensured the continuity of British military aircraft design and production, giving state-of-the-art experience in one of the most challenging areas of aerospace. However, as Charles Gardner observes, it was 'a long wait for the famous Canberra replacement, the OR339 of February 1958'.[47]

3.7 Airbus

Complementing the Anglo-French military package, the Labour government also encouraged the development of a new medium range, wide-bodied airliner – an 'airbus'.[48] In the early 1960s, BEA and the RAE began to consider specifications for such an aircraft, and both BAC and HSA were interested in developing an aircraft to meet this general requirement. BAC wanted a project to follow the 1–11, and HSA had its 'de Havilland' Comet and Trident expertise to protect. In France, Nord Aviation, Sud Aviation (later to merge as Aerospatiale) and Bréguet were following similar lines of development. As it was clear that the government wanted a collabo-rative programme, by 1965 both BAC and HSA had teamed up with French companies – HSA with Nord and Bréguet and BAC with Sud. The Germans, seeking an *entreé* to the civil aircraft business, joined the official negotiations in 1966. By March 1966, talks between the three governments had led to an outline specification with HSA, Sud and a German consortium Deutsche Airbus selected as the 'industrial partners'. BAC, with its existing links with Sud, felt that it had lost out to a 'Buggins' turn' on collaborative projects operated by the British government. Up to that point, BAC had indeed won the lion's share of collaborative projects and HSA lobbied very hard to secure the Airbus contract. Roy Jenkins, the Minister of Aviation, suggested that HSA was 'a strong candidate for any future project'.(49) HSA, however, could fairly point to its considerable experience in building medium-range airliners as justification for its selection as the British contractor.

The three companies rapidly established a cordial working relationship, and in October 1966 announced details of a 225–250 seat twin-engined aircraft – the A300 Airbus. The final decision to go ahead with the project was delayed until September 1967 while the three governments sorted out which engine to use. The French and the Germans preferred a licence-built version of the American P&W JT9D. This had commercial merit and would have linked Snecma and BSE in a joint programme. The main opposition came from Rolls-Royce and the British government. Rolls was concerned to head off competition from a Euro-American programme, and more important, having failed to win an order from the US for its new turbo fan engine, it needed the Airbus contract to maintain its position in the civil engine business. In support of Rolls, the British government argued that it made no sense for a major European project to rely on American engine technology. Rolls' take over of BSE in summer of 1966 also undermined the JT9D option (see below). Indeed, the British government made its participation in the programme conditional on the choice of a Rolls engine. In the event, the French accepted a trade-off between a Rolls-led engine programme based on the RB207 design and Sud leadership of the airframe. On 25 September 1967, the three governments signed a Memorandum of Understanding launching the Airbus. Programme costs were estimated at £190 million, with an in-service date of 1973. The governments also agreed that the project must have the support of their national airlines and that they would not finance a competitor. Both of these undertakings caused problems for the British government. BEA was not interested in an aircraft of this size in the timescale envisaged by the Memorandum of Understanding. In fact, BEA preferred BAC's 2–11 design, powered by the smaller Rolls RB211 turbo fan and made it clear that it would resist any attempt by the government to force it to buy the A300. However, the British government refused BAC's request for launch aid and BEA had to have Trident 3Bs as an interim aircraft until the A300 was ready.

Although one British minister described the Airbus as the foundation for a European challenge to American domination of civil aviation, within twelve months the British government was looking for an excuse to pull out. Crossman describes a Cabinet meeting in June 1968 which considered the Airbus to be a 'repetition of past mistakes'. There were problems with the Airbus design: by early 1968, it had grown in both size (to 350 seats) and in cost (up to £285 million). The German national airline Lufthansa had joined BEA in opposing the prospect of a 'forced' purchase, and no other airline had shown an interest in buying the aircraft. As a result, British officials were increasingly doubtful of the project's commercial viability. The need to protect Rolls' technological position had also diminished, following its contract with Lockheed for the RB211. Rolls' interests and energies were increasingly devoted to developing this engine on a very tight schedule and the RB207 was becoming something of an embarrassment (see Chapter 4). In July 1968, the Airbus design team was given six months to produce a more realistic proposition, and in December revealed the smaller 250-seat A300B. Although the A300B would use the RB211, it was hinted that a choice of engines (American) might be offered to airlines. This made commercial sense, but it provided a pretext for the British government to question the whole programme. According to Tony Benn, the Minister of Technology, this was a 'new situation' which would have to be studied at length, with the possibility of opting for a direct British competitor, the BAC 3–11.

The loss of the BAC 2–11 had been a blow to BAC's hopes of building a 'family' of aircraft to follow the success of the 1–11. The company continued development work, closely following BEA's requirements. The result was the BAC 3–11, a 245-seat wide-bodied airliner with two RB211 engines. The British government tried to get the 3–11 considered as an alternative to the A300B, but this was unacceptable to the Germans and French who demanded that Britain make up its mind about the A300B. In March 1969, British procrastination was overtaken by a bilateral agreement between France and Germany to re-launch the Airbus and officially, Britain was out of the Airbus programme. HSA was obviously very disappointed by the outcome, but decided that it had to stay with the Airbus or lose its civil design capability. HSA, therefore, with some assistance from the German government, negotiated a private contract with Airbus Industrie, the French registered holding company formed to co-ordinate development and to market the aircraft. HSA's contribution would prove vital to the programme, with its advanced wing design proving to be a major reason for the aircraft's eventual success. The BAC 3–11 did not in the end benefit from

Britain's departure from the Airbus. Labour lost the 1970 General Election before it could authorise BAC's request for launch aid. The incoming Conservative government, faced by a growing financial crisis at Rolls-Royce, combined with the escalating cost of Concorde, decided that public investment in civil aerospace had to be contained and that launch aid for projects like the 3–11 would not be granted.

By the late 1960s, it was evident that Labour's commitment to collaboration was diminishing. Negotiating agreements and then maintaining industrial coalitions in the face of divergent national technological and political interests had often proved more difficult in practice than the theory had suggested. The French had been particularly adept at shaping collaboration to suit their interests and bailing out of programmes that did not. The AFVG affair was especially galling for the British and did much to undermine the Plowden doctrine. Relations with the French were further strained in 1969 when they re-structured their part of the joint helicopter programme, again citing economic problems and cost escalation. As a result, the whole package was thrown out of balance. Westland felt they had been 'thoroughly conned' and the experience would condition later relations with the French (see Chapter 4). As *Flight* observed, 'nobody blames France for being ruthless in the interests of France. The real gremlins of collaboration are those who appease this ruthlessness at the expense of the British aircraft industry.'[50] On the other hand, Britain's effective withdrawal from the ELDO programme in 1969 and the government's handling of the Airbus/ BAC 3–11 affair did little to help encourage a positive image of Britain's commitment to Europe.

Part of the problem was that collaboration was not an easy option, especially in terms of reducing the overall costs of aerospace development. This was most dramatically demonstrated by the Concorde, but other joint projects had a similar, if less dramatic tendency to incur additional costs, although it should be noted that one analysis suggests that collaborative projects were no worse than European national programmes.[51] The difficulties of monitoring international programmes added to the uncertainty associated with large and complex aerospace projects. The Downey Report of 1968 underlined the continuing importance of good project evaluation and clear leadership in project development if expensive mistakes were to be avoided. However, Downey accepted that 'advanced development by its very nature can never be susceptible to precise estimating'. But the report was especially concerned that collaboration, with the difficulties of harmonising several national procurement philosophies, different cost and profit margin allowances, the pressure to 'lock in' parties to an agreement at an early stage, and the tendency to manage through committee, 'militated against incisive management'. As one minister admitted, 'it is very difficult to put arrangements for cost control into a Memorandum of Understanding between two countries. Cost control is a technique rather than a subject for inclusion in an agreement.'[52]

An even more sceptical view of collaboration was expressed in 1969 by St John Elstub in his report on the *Productivity of the National Aircraft Effort*.[53] Elstub cast considerable doubt on the effectiveness of collaboration as an answer to the basic economic dilemmas of aerospace development in the UK. Problems with *le juste retour* (work shares directly related to the national contribution to costs), prolonged negotiations leading to delay, and the need to compromise specifications were seen as sources of intrinsic inefficiency in collaborative programmes. Elstub was also worried that any trend towards a closed European market might insulate European manufacturers from the 'healthy effects of competition'. It could equally lead to transfers of technology, creating for British firms 'competitors of tomorrow when they have fortified themselves technically through contact with the most experienced aircraft industry in Europe'. The report concluded by suggesting that 'collaboration can only be really effectively achieved if the initiative in seeking opportunities and negotiating partnerships is taken by industry ...'

In this respect, Elstub identified the main weakness of collaboration during this period – the great majority of joint ventures were indeed creatures of government. As such, political interests would inevitably stand alongside industrial and economic criteria. Although the Labour government claimed that commercial principles should be applied to joint ventures, in practice, political considerations were never far away. Denis Healey conceded as much in evidence to a House of Commons Select Committee:

> the main case for collaboration is based on the economies which the collaborating countries can hope to derive from successful collaboration. I do strongly agree [that] there may also be great political advantages in collaboration. How far these are going to determine

the way in which our defence collaboration with Europe develops over, say, the next ten years I would not care to hazard a guess. But I would like to maximise the programme in this direction for political reasons as well as economic ones.[54]

Indeed, Labour's own commitment to technological collaboration tended to reflect the government's changing views about Europe. It too had seen aerospace as a way of building bridges with Europe, even if its use as a 'bargaining card' to gain entry to the EEC was not successful. The high point of Labour's interest in European technology was Harold Wilson's 1967 Guildhall speech, with its references to the dangers of 'industrial helotry' *vis à vis* the Americans with his call for a 'European Technological Community'. Crossman's references to the ELDO programme illustrate quite clearly how the government's wider diplomatic interests shaped decisions relating to Britain's participation in the programme. The government's disenchantment with collaboration and the retreat from Plowden matches a similar disillusionment with the EEC. This can be judged by Tony Benn's second speech to the SBAC when he said that while the 'facts drive us to collaboration', there was 'no automatic bar or rigid policy laid down by us that rules out all-British projects'. Harold Wilson was even blunter, asserting in 1969 that collaboration was 'a desert track littered with the whitening bones of abortive joint projects mostly undertaken at high cost'.[55]

Yet there was no going back to the narrow nationalism of the 1950s. The economics of aerospace left little room for such luxury, although a more pragmatic approach to collaboration was more fashionable. In his 1970 Lubbock Lecture, Sir George Edwards underlined the necessity of defending British interests in co-operative programmes. Industry had to have the design and development capability to define its own programmes which could form the basis of commercially sound joint ventures. The gradual weakening of the British industry would help neither British interests nor those of a European industry. As Edwards put it, 'European technology cannot do without a strong, broadly based British aircraft industry. To strengthen Europe we must give away some of our knowledge and our competitive position. This we have accepted in the interests of a worthwhile European aerospace industry. What I will never concede is that we must be permanently cast in a junior role.'[56] The initial contact with Europe had left scars, but over the decade there had been a marked and significant shift of orientation and the two core programmes of the 1970s and 1980s, the MRCA/Tornado and Airbus, had been launched.

3.8 Industrial restructuring under Labour

After collaboration, the main thrust of the Plowden recommendations was directed at questions of industrial restructuring, in particular the advantages of a merger between BAC and HSA. The aero-engine companies, though dependent in the long term on the strength of domestic airframe development, had performed reasonably well internationally and could be left alone to operate independently. However, the most important example of industrial restructuring was the 1966 merger between Rolls and BSE, while an attempt to complete the rationalisation of the airframe sector with some form of public ownership was a complete failure

Rolls, of course, was the dominant and more successful of the two British companies, in the early 1960s supplying engines for well over half of the non-Communist world's jet airliners. Since 1957 Rolls' civil business had overtaken its military work – from 40 per cent to 67 per cent of turnover. However, technological innovation in the form of the high by-pass ratio turbo-fan engine, would require an expensive commitment to R&D if Rolls was to remain a major force in civil engines. The formation of BSE in 1960 had provided a stronger domestic competitor for Rolls-Royce – or at least the basis for more potent opposition. With some justice, Rolls-Royce felt that the Conservative government had tended to favour BSE in awarding key contracts, in particular for the SST and TSR2. Although Rolls had been able to keep up its private venture investments, most notably in launching a civil version of the Spey, by the early 1960s the rising cost of development was beginning to strain the company financially. The re-introduction of launch aid in 1961 brought Rolls little relief and its management felt that the government was failing to recognise the 'grave financial risks the company was taking' in developing its civil and military programmes without adequate government support. Rolls contrasted this with the 'favourable conditions' its US competitors were receiving from their government to develop new families of engines. Equally, where the airframe companies had received 'emergency aid' for projects like the Super VC10, Rolls still had to carry all of its development burden. Denning Pearson, Rolls' chief executive, wanted support for Spey and Conway development and 'in the long term a major military project to redress the balance between our civil and military work, such as the twin Spey in the P1154 and tactical transport. If we can get neither of these contracts, then the future of Rolls-Royce as an independent firm is grim indeed.'[57] In the event, Rolls' lobbying was successful and it won the contract for the AW681. It also fought hard and equally successfully to supply a re-heated Spey for the Royal Navy's Phantoms.

The change of government in 1964, in contrast to much of Labour's views about aerospace, brought a more sympathetic view of the company's position. Although the government rejected an Anglo-French 'Spey-Mirage' alternative to the F-111, it confirmed that Phantoms for both the Navy and the RAF would have Rolls engines. These 'anglicised' F4s proved to be substantially more costly than buying the same aircraft 'off the shelf'. Although other British equipment was also involved, the greater part of the additional cost came from developing and integrating the Spey into the American airframe. The Minister of Aviation, Roy Jenkins admitted that the cost was substantially above those inherited from the Conservatives, but 'we have decided in the interests of the industry and the firm, to go ahead with this proposal'. The industrial arguments underpinning the decision were underlined by Sir Ronald Melville, the Permanent Secretary at the Ministry of Technology. 'Anglicisation' would reduce the dollar cost of the purchase over the aircraft's lifetime, but it would also protect Rolls' technological position; 'so far as the Ministry of Technology is concerned, we have a strong industrial reason for maintaining Rolls Royce as a British organisation which is powerful industrially and can export.'[58] In a similar vein, the government defended Rolls' position in negotiations associated with the collaborative projects started during this period.

The take-over of BSE was triggered by the threat posed by the possibility that BSE and Snecma would enter the large civil engine market by building the P&W JT9D for the Airbus. In the event, the merger was welcomed by both BSE and the government. BSE's chairman, Sir Reginald Verdon-Smith was in favour of a single British aero-engine company and the MoA wanted to 'avoid unsurmountable difficulties of sharing projects particularly when Europe is involved'. Rationalisation would bring several economic, technological and competitive advantages, not the least of which would be to remove the danger of an American 'Trojan Horse' implied by the BSE/Snecma arrangement. In September 1966, Rolls made a formal offer for BSE costing £63·6 million, £26·6 million of which was in cash to HSA. The valuation included about £20 million in 'goodwill' and shares in BAC and Westland, which Rolls later sought unsuccessfully to sell. The price also took into account estimates of future profits from BSE projects which proved to be considerably over optimistic. In fact, Rolls-Royce would have to provide additional capital to support the Bristol side of the business at a time when its own liquidity was under pressure from its fateful contract with Lockheed (see Chapter 4). Moreover, the advantages of rationalisation were slow to emerge and were still not apparent at the time of Rolls' eventual bankruptcy. Serious differences of style and philosophy between Derby and Bristol made amalgamation of design teams difficult.[59]

At the time, however, the merger was seen as a major step towards the creation of an internationally competitive aero-engine company which would benefit both the British and European aerospace industries. In terms of employees, Rolls was now the world's largest aero-engine company, though in turnover, it was still well behind GE and P&W. It was by far and away the most technically capable engine firm in Europe. But this was not necessarily an advantage in dealing with the Europeans, a point which was recognised by some ministry officials. For example, Rolls' dominance of European engine technology only served to increase French fear of dependence and their scepticism of Rolls' commitment to collaborative programmes such as the Airbus. With hindsight, it is evident that the determination to prevent P&W obtaining a European foothold led Rolls into a precipitate and ill-judged act. Although the merger was not the main cause of Rolls' later problems, it would be a significant contributory factor. According to the official investigation into Rolls' bankruptcy, 'despite the compelling considerations which led to the acquisition, from the Rolls-Royce standpoint the transaction cannot be considered a financial success'. On balance, the merger proved to be 'something of a "shot gun wedding" and the strains upon Rolls-Royce finances by the conjugal relationship did nothing to strengthen Rolls-Royce in its subsequent times of trial'.[60]

Many in the British airframe industry were equally disturbed by the emergence of such a powerful element in the industry – made the more so by the collapse of merger/nationalisation talks between BAC and HSA. The government wanted to encourage a merger between BAC and HSA and to have some form of holding in the new company. This would help to strengthen companies which had been hard hit by cancellations and the cost of new civil programmes. For example, despite launch aid of £9·75 million, the £30 million needed to develop the BAC 1–11 was putting considerable strain on BAC's finances. Residual competition between HSA and BAC, most notably over civil airliners, was also complicating government policy. Integration and rationalisation was not necessarily opposed by the industry; in a memorandum to the Plowden Committee, Lord Portal stated that conditions seemed 'to point to a new alignment in which the industry is recognised as being essentially a national enterprise, is brought under one unified direction and is established, preferably by voluntary negotiation, on a basis more suited than at present to the essentially international pattern which aviation is assuming for the future'.[61] However, Portal and other industrialists, while they wanted a greater commitment to planning and more stability in government procurement policy, did not want public ownership in any form.

Formal talks between HSA, BAC and the government began in October 1966, and in November, the Minister for Aviation announced that 'the national interest would be best served by a merger of BAC and HSA' with the government assuming a substantial minority interest by acquiring BAC. He added that the government's role in this process was essential, for unlike the Rolls/BSE merger 'this is not a matter that can be left to be settled as a result of commercial forces'. However, the merger depended on achieving an agreed valuation of BAC shares and assets and to a large extent on BAC co-operating with the process. BAC indicated that if the government wanted an interest in BAC, it would have to be a full scale bid, and BAC was not inclined to be 'friendly'. The BAC board and its operational divisions did not want to fall under HSA control and any takeover would lead to large numbers of resignations by key staff. English Electric also laid claim to BAC's guided weapons division. With BAC's financial prospects improving following orders for the 1–11 and with confirmation of the Saudi Arabian arms deal, BAC's three major shareholders became less eager to sell. Matters were further complicated by the Rolls Royce/BSE merger. Rolls did not want to hold BSE's shares in BAC, and offered them, as the terms of BAC's incorporation required, to English Electric and Vickers. If they did not want them, Rolls was prepared to sell its stake to HSA or to the government directly .[62]

It was increasingly evident, however, that the government lacked a clear plan for the merger/purchase. At one point, a Government Aircraft Investment Company was considered as a way of consolidating the government's existing interests in Beagle, Shorts and a share of BAC/HSA. But the new Minister of Technology, Tony Benn did not like this 'BP' solution, arguing that it left the government with insufficient control over the company. However, the valuation placed on BAC was never close enough to tempt the shareholders. BAC wanted £75 million, the government went as low as £25 million and neither side could accept a compromise. A full scale nationalisation of both BAC and HSA would not only have been more expensive, it would have led to a major political controversy when the government had other problems to face. Throughout the summer and autumn of 1967, deadlines were set and ignored. Tony Benn recorded in his diary that there was 'no solution in sight' and that this kind of merger was likely to produce 'the worst of all possible worlds'. In November, BAC's shareholders demanded to know exactly what the Minister intended. In fact, any interest the government had in forcing the issue was ended by that autumn's economic crisis. On 15 December the companies were told that,

> following devaluation, the Government is conducting a re-examination of their existing policies in a number of fields. It will, therefore, not be possible for the time being to proceed with the negotiations to implement the policy announced last year. I should like to reiterate that, in the Government's view a merger of the aviation interests of these two companies is desirable.[63]

The outcome satisfied BAC and to a lesser extent HSA which would have assumed a dominant position in the new company. However, the failure to create a single, large airframe company to act as a counterweight to Rolls-Royce left the airframe sector vulnerable to an assessment of national aerospace priorities largely shaped by the needs of the engine sector. Although in the short term a forced rationalisation might have generated controversy and caused some disruption, the government's failure to press the issue was a missed opportunity to finish a logical process of industrial rationalisation which would have to wait a decade for completion.

3.9 The Elstub report

The Elstub report provides a useful summary of the condition and problems of aircraft production in Britain during the 1960s.[64] It compared British industry with American, Swedish and, indirectly, French firms. The report began by noting that despite the cancellations of the early 1960s, the industry had changed little since Plowden. Total employment had dropped by just over 4 per cent, to 247,000 – about 3 per cent of the total for the UK manufacturing industry as a whole, with Rolls/BSE accounting for 64 per cent of the aerospace total. The distribution of work between military and civil programmes had also remained at about 3 : 1. Between 1961 and 1967, exports averaged about one fifth of the industry's total output, of which more than half were civil, with engines accounting for 43 per cent of overseas sales (excluding engines in British airframe exports) (see Table 9). Although the early 1960s showed a fall in the proportion of output exported, by the mid 1960s it was over a quarter of the industry's sales and nearly 5 per cent of the UK's total export effort. Overall, in real terms by value, the aerospace industry's output reflected only modest growth since the early 1950s (see Table 10).

The main part of the report concentrated on the efficiency and effectiveness of the industry. The central feature was a 'productivity gap' (measured in terms of value added per man year) between the UK and the US of about 3 : 1. British aircraft and engines could sell at the same price primarily because British labour costs were lower than those of American firms. The disparity between the two industries was not confined to the aircraft industry and was consistent with general comparisons between the US and UK manufacturing industries. But it was sufficient to 'wipe out' any advantage UK companies could derive from their lower labour costs. The committee found that fixed capital per employee in the US was three times higher than in Britain. However, as 'aeroplanes were put together' in much the same fashion in both countries, with little difference, for example, in the use of automation, differences in

Table 9: Aircraft industry exports, 1948–67

	Value (£ million)	% of output
1948	16	13·3
1949	20	14·7
1950	21	14·6
1951	22	13·5
1952	24	9·8
1953	50	16·6
1954	40	11·4
1955	48	14·2
1956	75	20·5
1957	95	23·8
1958	130	32·0
1959	122	30·1
1960	109	26·4
1961	111	22·8
1962	89	19·9
1963	88	19·7
1964	87	17·5
1965	131	23·3
1966	199	34·4
1967	159	27·9

Sources: Plowden (1948–59): Elstub (1960–67).

Table 10: Value of the aircraft industry's output: 1948–68

	£ million
1948	120
1949	136
1950	143
1951	163
1952	225
1953	301
1954	350
1955	338
1956	365
1957	400
1958	405
1959	405
1960	413
1961	486
1962	447
1963	447
1964	498
1965	563
1966	579
1967	570
1968	645

Sources: Plowden (1948–59); Elstub (1960–67).

production method alone were not sufficient to explain the gap. Nor was it simply the case that American workers worked three times harder than their British colleagues. The most important reason for the discrepancy continued to be the scale of production. In short, the British industry was still unable to derive as much 'learning curve' benefit as the US. Fixed costs had to be amortised across a fewer number of aircraft and both prime contractors and their supplier firms had less incentive to invest in manufacturing economies of scale. Suppliers were less inclined to put themselves out to ensure early delivery of relatively small batches of aircraft components. There were also more US specialist manufacturers of sub assemblies, such as doors and tailplanes, who would be able to pass on the benefits of cheaper production to the prime contractors. Finally, the inevitable loss of efficiency at the end of a production run as workers faced uncertainty of employment naturally occurred more frequently in the UK than in the US. Elstub noted that the 'productivity gap' was not confined to the aircraft industry, and was found 'between the manufacturing industries of the two countries generally'. The position of the aircraft industry was certainly no worse than other manufacturing sectors.

Both countries had similar approaches to marketing and sales – an area where the British had improved generally since the 1950s. But there were differences between the two countries – the US paid markedly more attention to delivery times and production control. Again, the difference in scale, especially in the willingness of a company like Boeing to invest heavily in plant and development to support the 747, had a considerable impact on the confidence which customers had in the ability and determination of a firm successfully to carry through a project. Rationalisation had led to some improvements in the economies of scale; the number of factories used by the main groups had fallen by 40 per cent since 1955; work had been redistributed to make better use of resources with increased specialisation of plant and facilities; it was easier for work to be transferred between factories; and there had been a marked improvement in labour productivity. The industry was making more use of computerisation in management services, with savings of up to 10 per cent reported in some instances. Other management techniques such as PERT were having an equivalent impact on operations. Above all, the industry was pioneering the use of Computer Aided Design and Manufacturing (CAD/CAM) – the aircraft industry had installed 25 per cent of the total number of numerically controlled machines used in the UK and, given the complexity of aircraft manufacturing, an even higher proportion of the value of such machines.

Nevertheless, the difference in the scale of production was *the* problem. If American projects had been produced in the same numbers as their equivalent British aircraft and engines, 'they would have cost about twice as much as they actually did'. For this reason, the report concluded that 'the most important step towards raising the productivity of the British aircraft industry is to ensure that projects are produced in quantities large enough to reap the benefits of the labour cost advantage'. In turn, this raised a further vital issue; 'the aircraft produced must, of course, also be sold. Thus the main effort must be directed at capturing for the United Kingdom a larger share of the world aircraft market than it has had in recent years.' This started with the correct choice of project. In civil aerospace, British firms had been unable to derive the benefit of developing families of airliners. Similarly, the timing of the introduction of new projects had sometimes been badly wrong. Above all, Elstub confirmed just how important it was to avoid the 'tailoring' of designs for narrow domestic requirements which had occurred during the 1950s and which was now affecting sales of British airliners. British military designs, if they too were to sell more widely, had to take account of export potential when specifications were drawn up. As we have already noted, although Elstub recognised that collaboration was a way of increasing the scale of production, it did not necessarily increase the efficiency of production if the gains in scale were offset by the increase in costs due to poor organisation, delays in decision-making and politically determined work-sharing agreements.

Elstub could not find any incontrovertible evidence to suggest that the British aircraft industry was less efficient than, for example, the French. The SORIS report, published in 1971, was more critical of Britain's performance compared to the industries of the 'Six'.[65] While it confirmed that European productivity was generally worse than that of the US aerospace industry, it appeared to show that in terms of value added per employee the British aircraft industry was 32 per cent poorer than the EEC average. In absolute terms, the UK was still the largest in Europe, but the value of its output only grew by 1 per cent in the UK during the 1960s, whereas the Community rate was 11 per cent (see Table 11). These results were qualified by the report's authors and challenged by the UK industry. In particular, there were substantial differences in the way the value of sub-contracting and co-operative projects was calculated. The higher rate of growth was also from a much lower base than that of the UK and often the result of deliberate investment in aerospace by European governments. Disputes over the accuracy of cross-European statistical comparisons have never been fully resolved (see Chapter 5), but the overall impression then was that there was considerable room for improvement in the British performance.

Table 11: The output of UK, EEC and US aerospace industries
(\$ million, 1967 values)

	1961	1963	1965	1967
UK	1,634	1,428	1,682	1,610
France	668	782	1,041	1,250
Germany	134	313	225	261
Italy	80	144	164	160
Belgium	11	59	40	27
Holland	67	120	76	60
US	17,576	18,798	18,833	23,258

Source: SORIS.

Finally, Elstub returned to the central relationship between state and industry. In an industry so dependent on public support, Government decisions clearly contributed to the uncertainties which made companies unwilling to invest in production and process technology. The lack of stability undermined long term planning and cost calculations. Elstub recognised that governments had to allow for genuine changes in strategic requirements and for opportunities afforded by new technologies. But it was important for the industry to have a reasonably clear idea of its future loading and to have greater confidence in order to anticipate needs by investing in new plant and facilities. Some form of planning for the industry was therefore highly desirable and recommended to the government. The alternative was for the government to take a more direct role in determining broader investment decisions. If this were the case, and if the government began to play 'an active role in these decisions as well as providing massive launching aid for civil projects and the entire finance for domestic military projects, *it could be argued that the industry might just as well be nationalised'* [my italics].[66]

Compared with Labour's bright new hopes of 1964, the period must be seen as something of a disappointment. It did not see the shift of resources away from aerospace into 'more productive' sectors. If anything, the level of commitment to the aerospace sector grew during this period. By 1973 civil aircraft accounted for 50 per cent of government spending on civil R&D. The Brookings Institute survey of the British economy in 1968 pointed to much the same structural imbalances in the use of skilled manpower as Labour had criticised in the early 1960s. In 1966, aerospace had accounted for 9·7 per cent of qualified engineers in the UK; by 1971 it had slipped to 8·9 per cent but in 1975 it was back to 9·9 per cent. Employment generally in the aircraft industry showed only a modest decline over the period and would not dip below 200,000 until 1977 (see Table 12).[67]

Table 12: *Employment in the aerospace industry, 1965–70*

1965	259,000
1966	249,000
1967	254,000
1968	250,000
1969	246,000
1970	235,000

Source: EEC.

The absorption of the MoA into Mintech was also something of a travesty. Tony Benn had presented it as a 'significant moment for British technology and the British economy, as well as for the aircraft industry'. For the first time, Benn argued, 'it is possible to compare projects across the whole field of engineering and to begin the difficult task of evolving criteria which will allow intelligent choices to be made between developments in different fields'.[68] In the event, the MoA's staff moved as a 'solid phalanx' into the newly enlarged Mintech and in view of the sheer size of the old MoA, some wondered exactly who was absorbing whom. Indeed, according to Elstub nearly 30,000 people were still employed by the Ministry of Technology in aerospace-related administration and research, only 800 fewer than the MoA at its peak in 1965.

As far as the aircraft industry was concerned, the 1960s had begun with rationalisation; they ended with internationalisation. As we have seen, collaborative development and production was not easy and it certainly did not reduce the impact of government on the industry – indeed, collaboration inevitably increased the politicisation of industrial activity by at least the number of participating countries. However, although not so evident at the time, a tapestry of joint projects was emerging which, combined with the growth of an international infrastructure linking the companies of Europe, would bring a greater degree of stability to British aerospace. In the short term, however, another cycle of crisis and doubt would hit the industry. For once this was not caused by government and came from a most unexpected direction – namely Rolls-Royce's determination to stay in the first rank of engine manufacturers.

CHAPTER FOUR

NATIONALISATION
AND
PRIVATISATION
1970–88

Despite the aircraft industry's long and intimate association with the state, until the 1960s nationalisation was never formally considered for the aircraft industry as a whole. Plowden, of course, recommended some form of public holding in the airframe sector and the Labour government made a serious but ultimately unsuccessful attempt to carry it through. It appears as something of a paradox, therefore, that a Conservative government should oversee the first post war nationalisation of a major aerospace company. It occurred not in the airframe sector nor as a deliberate act of industrial strategy, but more dramatically in the aftermath of one of Britain's most catastrophic industrial collapses – the bankruptcy of Rolls-Royce in 1971. By the end of the 1970s, Labour had nationalised BAC and HSA to form British Aerospace (BAe). But by the end of the following decade, both Rolls and BAe were back in private ownership and even Shorts, nationalised since 1943, was on the verge of privatisation. Moreover, following one of the most spectacular political crises in recent British history, a significant part of Westland, Britain's only helicopter company, was in American hands. The main theme of this chapter, then, is the shifting pattern of ownership in the aircraft industry, interwoven with the growing maturity of international co-operation between British companies and firms in Europe, the US and the Far East.

4.1 The collapse and nationalisation of Rolls-Royce

The reasons for Rolls' collapse go back to the early 1960s and its attempts to stay in the big civil engine business. Rolls had done well out of the first generation of jets, but faced potent competition from both P&W, its old American rival, and General Electric (GE), a major military producer but now preparing to enter the civil sector. The focus of the struggle was the very high ratio turbo-fan engine designed for the large wide-bodied airliners being considered in the US and Europe. They would be in essence a new family of engines incurring considerable and expensive launch costs. Development in the US was helped by USAF contracts for the C5A military transport programme and both P&W and GE were able to use this experience to produce civil engines. Without comparable military support, Rolls had to turn to the government for direct assistance in developing the RB178 demonstrator engine. The Rolls board realised that, even with government assistance, the cost of developing a production big fan would be very high and felt that a British or even a European airliner would not offer a market sufficient to justify the risk involved; from the outset, Rolls therefore looked for selection by an American manufacturer. Although Rolls lost the Boeing 747 contract to P&W, 'from this time the company became progressively more and more concerned to secure a major order for its big engine in order to maintain its position as a major world aero-engine manufacturer'. As Adrian Lombard, Rolls' chief civil designer, put it, 'in effect, we have an advanced technical design in search of an aircraft programme'.[1]

In the interim, Rolls turned its attention to the European Airbus. In December 1966, Denning Pearson, Rolls' chief executive, wrote to the Permanent Secretary at the MoA to urge government action in support of a Rolls-engined Airbus. He referred to the government's existing financial interest in the RB178, and cast considerable doubt on the BSE/Snecma combination's expertise in large civil engines. In his view, the obvious step was for the British government to 'nominate Rolls-Royce as the British partner in any European collaboration on the provision of an engine for the airbus'.[2] The government effectively made Britain's involvement in the Airbus conditional on the use of the Rolls 47,500 lbs. thrust RB207 turbo-fan (see Chapter 3). Despite this success, Rolls' main objective was still to win a major American order. As one Rolls executive observed, 'it appeared to us that if we were to stay in the civil business which we had built up since the war, we needed to get into a United States-built airframe as first choice'.[3] The government also hinted that, should Rolls win such an order, it would be willing to help, if necessary beyond the 50 per cent limit on launch aid.

Lockheed were very interested in using the RB207 on its L1011, but by June 1967 the Americans wanted a smaller engine and consequently Rolls offered the 33,000 lbs. thrust RB211. The government responded favourably to Rolls' preliminary request for launch aid provided that nothing should be undertaken which might undermine the European RB207 programme. On that condition, Rolls would be given 70 per cent of the cost of developing the RB211, a fixed sum of £40 million. The RB211, although derived from a common root and sharing several design characteristics with the RB207, would require much the same degree of commitment, and would contain several major innovations including extensive use of carbon fibre material developed by the RAE. The 1971 timescale demanded by Lockheed would certainly test Rolls' ability to deliver a complex engine on time and target. But if it was an ambitious goal, it was seen as necessary for Rolls' survival. Tony Benn and the Ministry of Technology readily accepted Rolls' judgement and in July confirmed its offer of launch aid for both the RB207 and the RB211.

Rolls' successful campaign to win the Lockheed order was viewed at the time as a masterful example to other British companies looking to win export orders. Knighthoods followed for Denning Pearson and for David Hudie, the man who led the sales team from New York. Yet even then there were some warning voices from Derby urging caution as Lockheed forced price and performance concessions from the Rolls sales team. Rolls' American competitors, GE and P&W certainly felt that the eventual price, even allowing for Rolls' labour cost advantages, was far too low for safety. The presumption was that the British government, despite the limit placed on its aid package, would *in extremis* underwrite Rolls' commitments. The deal, described by *Fortune* as a 'bold foreign invasion', was sealed in March 1968. On 1 April, Tony Benn told the House of Commons that the order constituted a 'foothold in the American civil market far bigger than anything which we have achieved before'. It was, he added, 'of special value to the British economy, and above all, an outstanding encouragement for the skills and technology of British industry'. The government and the company congratulated each other on their mutual support and assistance in securing the contract. Crossman observed how 'immensely encouraging' the news was and how he hoped that it would be a 'turn in the tide of fortune for British industry'.[4]

There was some concern that the RB211 contract would draw Rolls' energies and attention away from the RB207, but both government and company moved to scotch any rumours of waning interest in the European programme. After all, Benn noted, the RB211 was 'only' a scaled-down version of the RB207 and although the 'dual programme' would mean a supreme effort by the company, there was 'nothing new about that and we are confident that Rolls can make it'.[5] However, with Rolls' position apparently secured by the Lockheed order, the government had less incentive to support the Airbus programme and by early 1969 the British government had withdrawn from the Airbus (see Chapter 3). Even before this decision, however, it was becoming evident that Rolls itself was looking for a way out of its commitments to the European programme. Developing two large engines, and especially the RB211 to Lockheed's stringent contract terms, was straining its resources. In the summer of 1968, Rolls had to make a £20 million rights issue and raise £10 million more through debenture placing. More seriously, severe technical problems with the RB211's carbon fibre compressor blades forced an expensive shift to a back-up titanium programme. On top of these difficulties, Lockheed wanted to exercise its option on an up-rated RB211 earlier than had been originally planned, which Rolls would have to fund without any extra aid from the government.

The crux of Rolls' problem was not primarily technical but contractual. As subsequent events would show, the RB211 would prove to be a very fine engine, but Rolls had signed a fixed price contract with only a limited provision for inflation. More important, it contained strict and onerous penalties for delay, giving Rolls very little leeway in the event of serious technical or financial problems. Rolls had already received very favourable treatment in obtaining 70 per cent rather than half of the estimated cost of developing a new project, and under the terms of the launch aid agreement Rolls was bound to carry any cost escalation. The launch aid system assumed that a private firm would not, in a rash, ill-considered venture, put at risk its own survival. In this case, the government relied upon Rolls to know its own business. Although the government had not been party to the Lockheed agreement, it had been aware of 'the necessary' concessions Rolls had had to make in order to win the order. Officials had complete confidence in Rolls' commercial judgement and its reputation, built up since the 1930s for superb engineering and better-than-average managerial competence.

The Rolls management was aware of how narrow their margins were, but they were operating in a psychological climate which led them to believe that the government would never, in the words of one official, 'pull the rug out in a major crisis'. They also had a confidence, to the point of arrogance perhaps, in their company's ability successfully to take on massive technical challenges. The assumption of two parallel engine programmes and ambitions for a third (Rolls also hoped to win a contract from MDD for the DC10) was a sign of considerable corporate self confidence. Everything hinged upon trouble free progress with the RB211. Rolls had recovered from difficulties with past engines, such as the Spey, to make a profit. The RB211, however, was a much larger and a more complex programme than Rolls had hitherto taken on; the premature cancellation of the RB178 demonstrator left the design team dependent on parametric studies of the Spey and smaller turbo-fan engines. Worse still, the premature death of Adrian Lombard deprived Rolls of one of the finest 'trouble shooting' engineers in the industry. For their part, ministry officials felt that Rolls' estimates and targets were optimistic 'but not unreasonable'. In the final analysis, however, the Rolls name was its own guarantee. As Benn later admitted, 'I was dealing with not only the most famous British engineering company, but a company that had a blue chip reputation. I am afraid those factors influenced me. I would not have done this with any tin-pot company.'[6] Looking back on this crucial period, Benn was quite adamant that the line had been drawn and had been clearly stated to all concerned. But the government had closely associated itself from the start with the success of the RB211. Rolls had been elevated as a cornerstone in Labour aerospace and industrial strategy and ministers would meet Lockheed officials on their regular visits to the UK. Thus a misperception was formed that provided the basis for an industrial disaster of the first magnitude.

By June 1969, there were indications that Rolls was facing problems. Revised estimates now put the cost of developing the RB211 at nearly £100 million. There was a strong possibility of incurring penalties under the terms of the Lockheed contract. In September, Sir David Hudie reported that the completion of the engine was now 'a formidable task and we are putting the programme on an emergency basis'. Dividends were reduced, a productivity drive instituted, but it was evident that the company needed a large injection of new money. The government chose to use the Industrial Reorganisation Corporation (IRC), which had been set up in 1966 to spearhead the government's interventionist industrial strategy, to channel more money to Rolls without appearing to increase launch aid for the RB211. The IRC undertook a full review of Rolls' position and presented a summary of its findings to the Ministry of Technology in December 1969. It felt that Rolls' problems went beyond a short term liquidity crisis and that substantial changes would have to be made in Rolls' managerial and accounting procedures. However, the IRC did recognise the technological and industrial significance of Rolls and recommended a £10 million loan. Even so, Rolls baulked at some of the IRC conditions and the board hesitated for several weeks. Under pressure of events and from the government, Rolls finally conceded to the IRC terms, with Lord Beeching and Ian Morrow being appointed to the Rolls board.

From here until the General Election of 1970, outwardly Rolls gave every impression that matters were under control. But the RB211 was now six months behind schedule and programme costs were over £169 million and getting worse. The incoming Conservative government soon faced a major dilemma. In opposition, the Conservatives had adopted a policy of 'disengagement' from industry with references to the need to end public support for 'lame ducks'. Admittedly, the aircraft industry had been singled out as a possible exception, but overall the new government wanted to reduce state intervention in industry. It now had a choice between 'bailing out' Rolls or allowing a major industrial and strategically important company to collapse. In September, the government, aware that Rolls was at the brink, needing at least £170 million to complete the programme and unable to escape substantial penalties under the Lockheed contract, put together an emergency financial package. This, however, was dependent on a detailed report about Rolls' position.

The report showed that Rolls' position was almost hopeless without a massive and virtually open-ended commitment by the government. At this point, the government either had to accept that responsibility, or allow the firm to go bankrupt as it was in danger of trading illegally. Some attempts were made to renegotiate the Lockheed contract, but the Americans, with their own problems to contend with and evidently still unable to believe that the government would allow Rolls to go to the wall, refused to do so. On 29 January 1971, the Cabinet decided to allow Rolls to go into receivership. This immediately limited the government's obligations and allowed it to negotiate for a selective purchase of Rolls' assets, especially those with defence implications or involving commitments to foreign *governments*. Although Prime Minister Edward Heath immediately informed the US President of the decision, Lockheed had to wait until 2 February. It was a ruthless step, and Lockheed rightly felt that it had been betrayed by both Rolls and the British government. Other Americans were more blunt; 'this is the sort of thing you would expect from an underdeveloped country'.[7] The government announced that Rolls-Royce (1971) Ltd would be refloated as a limited liability company with the state as sole shareholder. Negotiations would continue in respect of the RB211 engine and Lockheed had little choice but to accept new contract terms. Lockheed's own survival – and that of the RB211 – was decided by one vote as the US Senate authorised a Federal rescue package for Lockheed. In September 1971, Lockheed and Rolls-Royce (1971) signed a new contract and the British government provided the necessary capital to complete development. Thanks to favourable exchange movements, even the first batch of RB211s were delivered at a profit and Rolls had the foundation of a new generation of civil engines.

At the time, however, the Rolls collapse appeared to have few such silver linings. It had a traumatic effect on morale throughout British industry and upon confidence in the economy. Rolls' reputation had attracted thousands of small shareholders; but beyond that, this was *the* British engineering firm and it had gone bust. It was deeply embarrassing for a Conservative government set on industrial disengagement to have to nationalise one of Britain's most prestigious companies and it was hoped that public ownership would be 'only temporary'. However, it was soon evident that Rolls required a long period of convalescence and a sharp taste of internal reform. Pearson, Huddie and the Rolls board took the full brunt of the *post mortem*. There had been fatal flaws in Rolls' management structure and the over dominance of engineers at the top of the company was singled out for particular criticism. As one Rolls man would later put it, 'the first thing we had to learn was that the company was not just a playground for engineers to amuse themselves'. Rolls had to be re-built and Sir Kenneth Keith's appointment as chairman in September 1972 marked the start of the process. According to Sir Stanley Hooker, 'he found a lack of discipline which appalled him' and took on a seven year stint which would lay the conditions for Rolls' revival.[8]

4.2 The Heath government and aerospace

The collapse of Rolls and the evident failure of government to monitor accurately its investment between 1967 and 1970 raised important questions about the relationship between the aerospace industry and the state. As the official investigation into the Rolls collapse observed, the RB211 affair had called into question the 'suitability of companies in the private sector to undertake contracts committing a substantial proportion of their resources to the achievement of major advances in sophisticated technology'.[9] The clearest lesson of the RB211 affair was that government could not necessarily rely upon a 'prudent management' to avoid unacceptably high risks to public money. Rolls' reputation had given reasonable cause for confidence, and for that reason, its failure was all the more shattering. In the short term, the conditions for granting launch aid were tightened, with a much wider review of a firm's ability to sustain its commitments. However, the Rolls bankruptcy and the realisation of the extent of Concorde's commercial failings gave rise to a deeper concern about civil aerospace production in the UK and the proper relationship between the state and a high cost, high risk industry. Indeed, the whole question of aid for civil projects and its poor record of commercial return since 1945 became the subject of a wider and often critical examination.

The case for aiding civil projects was considered by several Parliamentary committee investigations. Officials justified launch aid using a mixture of commercial and broader economic arguments. The prospect of winning a large share of an expanding world market was naturally the major reason for investing in civil projects. But employment, technological spin-off, and the relationship between civil and defence work were other good reasons for giving launch aid. Above all, 'the general theme or philosophy underlying launch aid has been more than anything else the earning of foreign currency or the saving of imports of aircraft from abroad'. One Labour MP felt that was a rather dubious rationale: 'if we ever got to the happy situation of not having balance of payments difficulties, then what you are virtually saying is that there are only minor reasons why any government should maintain an aircraft industry'.[10] The Expenditure Committee, with a wider brief, concluded that with the general expansion of public money committed to complex, high risk projects, 'it is not surprising that Government and industry have stumbled from time to time'. The need was to draw the right lessons for control and management. One trenchant critic of current policy, Lord Beeching, who had served as the IRC representative on the Rolls board immediately prior to the crash, told the committee that governments had wasted 'an enormous amount of money on things justified by the pursuit of high technology – an almost childlike desire to play with toys'. The Public Accounts Committee was equally direct: launch aid seemed to have been little more than an implied subsidy for unprofitable and uncommercial projects – a view shared by at least one DTI economist.[11] However, neither committee considered in depth the relationship between civil and military technology, and it was plain that strategic interests still carried considerable weight in justifying the maintenance of a UK aircraft industry.

The Heath government had been 'shaken stiff' by the Rolls affair. Although it refused aid for the BAC 3–11 and turned down an invitation to rejoin the Airbus programme it would have to face requests for more money for civil and military projects, including aid to maintain Rolls' position in the civil engine market. Some 30 per cent of the firm's business was tied up in the RB211 and officials admitted that for the medium term at least, Rolls and its products could not be judged by strict economic criteria.[12] The government also had to find money for Concorde and it was soon apparent that any hope of offsetting the costs of development or even production against overseas sales was illusory. The government was sufficiently concerned about the level of expenditure on aerospace and the control of projects to undertake two official reviews of aerospace and procurement policy.

The first of these, conducted by Sir Derek Rayner, led to the establishment of a Procurement Executive within the MoD to act on behalf of the Services in the purchase and monitoring of defence and launch-aided civil programmes.[13] The Procurement Executive combined the functions of the Ministry of Aviation Supply (a holding department for aerospace matters created following the dissolution of the Ministry of Technology) and the MoD's responsibility for defence aerospace procurement. Given the 'indivisibility of aerospace technology between civil and military applications', Rayner had debated the possibility of making the MoD responsible for all aerospace matters. However, this solution could have led to a conflict between the MoD's duty to provide the best and cheapest equipment for the Services and an obligation to protect and to promote the interests of the aerospace industry. It was desirable, therefore, to make a clear distinction between the cost and technical requirements of military procurement and commercially related activities. Rayner hoped to limit the traditional preoccupation on the part of both user and industry sponsoring departments with technological advance at the expense of financial and economic considerations, but without threatening a 'progressive erosion of the Government's civil aerospace interests'. Rayner felt, therefore, that that policy towards aerospace should be integrated into government policy towards manufacturing and technology generally. Responsibility for general aerospace policy and civil aerospace R&D was, therefore, retained by the newly created Department of Trade and Industry (DTI).

In order to co-ordinate aerospace and defence procurement and to provide a forum for resolving policy differences between the DTI, MoD and other interested parties, he also recommended the creation of a Joint Ministerial Aerospace Board (JMB) to 'oversee the collaboration between the two departments and to be the authority for instructions and policy guidance to the Procurement Executive on civil aerospace matters'. In the event, this suggestion was not implemented, on the grounds that most officials felt that existing channels provided by the Cabinet and its sub-committees would be sufficient to ensure co-ordination and to resolve policy disputes. The Rayner procedures helped to tidy up some of the loose ends of procurement policy and to reinforce the MoD's contract supervision system. It did not entirely solve the problem of how to manage large scale and complex defence and aerospace programmes. Equally, the shift of aerospace responsibilities to the

DTI made no real impact on the substance of policy. Significantly, some eighteen years after Rayner, the issue of reconciling defence procurement and national industrial and technological interests would be central to the Westland affair and would lead one Commons Committee to resurrect the idea of a 'JMB' for aerospace (see below).

The second and confidential report by Sir Robert Marshall, Permanent Secretary at the DTI was a more wide-ranging exercise. Several officials appear to have expressed some doubts about the desirability of maintaining a comprehensive UK design and production capability. On balance, it was accepted that there was insufficient cause to run the industry down either in the civil or military sectors. The future, however, clearly lay with more extensive use of collaboration. Here there was a division between 'Atlanticists' and 'Europeans' within the Ministry, with a strong case being put to build on links with the US, especially now that US firms were beginning to look for overseas partners. In the event, the government's own strong European sentiments indicated that European collaboration would have priority. In many respects, the Heath administration came to much the same conclusions as its predecessors; aerospace had to be supported for a mixture of commercial and general economic reasons and that collaboration offered the best chance of limiting its cost.

On the face of it, the government appeared to be moving towards a more comprehensive European strategy. In 1971, a junior minister told the House of Commons that 'the collaborative projects in which we are currently engaged have taken us some of the way down the road towards the goal of an integrated European industry. Very valuable lessons have been learned, but I think we need to move well beyond *ad hoc* collaboration on particular projects to some more permanent form of industrial association.'[14] The theme of industrial integration was enthusiastically promoted by his superior, Michael Heseltine, who resurrected the spectre of the 'American challenge' to urge the formation of a single European aero-engine company and two airframe groups in Europe. He certainly believed that *ad hoc* collaboration had led to a confused and potentially disruptive pattern: 'it's virtually impossible to start a new project without cutting across existing arrangements and policies of governments and the firms they support'.[15] Heseltine was also a prime mover in the creation of a European Space Agency

(ESA) to co-ordinate and to promote European efforts in launchers, satellite applications and space research generally.

Collaboration was now well established as the basis for major airframe projects and, by association, most military engine developments. But Heseltine's call for a more integrated approach was greeted with some scepticism. Allan Greenwood of BAC supported the general principle, but not necessarily in the short term: 'my view of the philosophy of company integration across national boundaries is that it is probably right in the long run'. For the present, 'the multi-project consortium or joint companies seem to me to show the way ahead'. He did accept that the pattern of co-operation was 'chaotic' and 'somehow order must come from this confusion and it is my belief that the more permanent mergers or consortia which can grow from these existing partnerships will only be brought about when the governments of Europe show with greater clarity the political will to rely upon the European aerospace industry'. Sir George Edwards spoke for many in the industry when he said that collaboration had to follow the market; that is to say, to be based on commercial needs rather than political initiatives. European mergers, even allowing for the practical difficulties which stood in their way (the absence of a common European company law or taxation policy for example), were not 'lightly entered into'. They had to have a genuine and continuing purpose. Integration might eventually arrive, but there was no reason to force the pace unnaturally. Finally, the SBAC underlined the importance of treating the industry, airframes, engines and equipment, as an integrated whole. In negotiating collaborative programmes, the government had to give equal consideration to all three sectors and avoid work sharing agreements which compromised British technological leadership.[16]

Rolls-Royce was again more sceptical about collaboration – especially with Europe and certainly in large civil engines. After the bankruptcy, it was suggested that Rolls would find its rightful place within Europe, but although Rolls and Snecma discussed prospects for the joint development of a 'ten tonne' civil engine, both companies preferred links with US firms. Sir Kenneth Keith made Rolls' position quite clear in evidence to a House of Lords Committee. Rolls had its own family of engines on which to base future development and while the airframe industry might have to look to Europe for large scale civil projects, Rolls could still compete with the US 'on all fours'. In other areas, it would collaborate, especially in the military sector, but again collaboration did not just mean with Europe; Rolls and P&W were working together to produce and improve the Pegasus vectored thrust engine and generally there was much to be said for working with the US. In this respect, Rolls stood amongst equals, where there were possibilities for exchanging technology. The problem with European co-operation, he suggested, was that it was usually in a 'one-way direction, with Rolls-Royce on the giving end'.[17]

In fact, Rolls' main objective during this period was to develop the RB211 as the core of a 'family' of designs in order to satisfy a range of airliner requirements. The market for engines was becoming even more competitive now that GE had joined P&W as a major supplier of large civil turbo-fans and was making considerable progress helped by its links with the French engine industry and the European Airbus. With the advent of three competing 'families' of turbo-fans, the airlines now had a choice of engines and were not necessarily committed to the 'launch engine' adopted by the aircraft manufacturer. Although it was still commercially advantageous to provide the 'launch engine', every airliner order could trigger an intense competition to secure the engine contract. Under these circumstances, technical merit was clearly important, but a deal could also depend upon sophisticated financial and export credit packages often supported by governments. Rolls' plans included a joint programme with P&W to develop a 'ten tonne' thrust engine. Discussions began in 1973, and two years later the two companies announced that they would collaborate on the development of an engine based on the P&W JT10D to compete with the GE/Snecma CFM56. The agreement appeared to mark a significant extension of Rolls' American strategy. Sir Kenneth Keith, for example, said that henceforth 'all major commercial engines will be undertaken as trans-Atlantic collaborations'.[18] In the event, Rolls' continued development of the RB211, in this case a 'cropped fan' RB211–535, to cover a gap between the larger RB211s and the new joint engine, helped to undermine the agreement with P&W which was terminated in the spring of 1977. Nevertheless, the parting was 'amicable' and in time the partnership would be renewed (see below). Significantly, Rolls did not have an engine suited to the Airbus and showed little interest in developing one.[19] In retrospect, this proved to be a major commercial misjudgement by Rolls; but even if the later success of the Airbus family could not have been forseen, Rolls' preference for American airframes nevertheless underlined the presence of divergent interests in the British civil aircraft industry.

For the airframe sector, exhortations to form trans-national companies, however desirable they might have been, meant little to industry unless backed by work. After a decade of problems, the military sector was in a reasonably healthy state. The Tornado programme, and in the shorter term, Jaguar production, at last promised some stability for BAC's military division. The company was also reaping the benefit of the 1966 Saudi Arabian deal. The £100 million air defence package had centred on Lightnings, Thunderbird SAMs and Strikemaster jet trainers, associated equipment, and an agreement to provide pilot and ground staff training. BAC demonstrated an impressive ability to deliver and manage a complex package, which was the beginning of a long, and for BAC and its successor BAe, a very profitable relationship with Saudi Arabia. In time, this would almost entail the provision of a complete modern airforce and its ground support facilities. The creation of a 'service' sector was one of the major indirect benefits for the UK industry which British Aerospace has since broadened and expanded (see below). HSA's military programme was boosted by a 1971 agreement with MDD to develop the Harrier, and its military prospects were further improved in 1971 with the launch of the HS1186 Hawk strike trainer. Although the Hawk used the Adour engine so that a hint of European co-operation remained, it was the first independent military aircraft started in Britain since the early 1960s and was a direct competitor with the Franco-German Alpha jet – an indication, perhaps, that the government's commitment to expanded European co-operation had a pragmatic side.

Civil production was a different matter. As Sir Arnold Hall of HSA put it, the reality was 'that Concorde and the RB211 together will fully absorb what is available (from the state) and therefore unquestionably other projects are going to be and are being starved'. Geoffrey Knight, head of BAC's Commercial Division, underlined the industry's worries. Without further help, he said, HSA and BAC would 'progressively lose their capability, and if that happens we have little or no chance of taking a lead position in European projects in the future'. BAC was the least well placed; production of the BAC 1–11 was running down and there was little prospect for a successor. The company was under pressure from

GEC, which held 40 per cent of the company's shares, to limit civil development and 'impose a very strict economy regime' on the company.[20] GEC's stance caused considerable bitterness within BAC as it was evident that GEC wanted to be free of its involvement with aircraft, but at the same time to keep hold of BAC's systems and missile business. BAC's results for the early 1970s were modest – in 1971 £2·4 million profit on a capital employed of nearly £64 million. Although BAC was able to avoid plant closures, nearly 2,000 employees were made redundant in the company's commercial division. By 1973, reorganisation and the growing return from BAC's military programmes helped to improve matters, but the long term prognosis for civil aircraft was decidedly bleak unless BAC could find European partners. Both HSA and BAC joined several European civil design consortia, but the turmoil generated by the 1973 oil crisis, and Britain's reluctance to expand on HSA's private (and highly profitable) links with the Airbus programme, rendered much of this activity academic. HSA also launched its own small airliner, the American engined 146, which competed directly with the VFW-Fokker 614. Again, the government's pragmatic view of aircraft projects was shown by its favourable reaction to HSA's request for launch aid. As one minister put it, international collaboration was still the 'natural route for the larger, more expensive aircraft', but it was better to see 'a viable national project than an unsuccessful joint venture'.[21]

In fact, the government's main concern was not the encouragement of European mergers but domestic restructuring. The Marshall report had considered the desirability of a merger between BAC and HSA but it had also noted the advantages of keeping the two separate, especially if the aim was to facilitate the emergence of European trans-national firms such as VFW-Fokker. However, to the government, the logic of a domestic merger was more appealing; it would end the pretence of competition between the two companies, prevent unnecessary duplication of research and, hopefully, further improve the capital and technological base of the British airframe sector. In practice, the obstacles to a negotiated merger remained as strong as they had been in 1967; neither company was that keen to amalgamate and the government was not sure exactly what shape it preferred the industry to assume. The problem was partly a question of personalities. Neither Sir George Edwards of BAC nor Sir Arnold Hall at HSA would have found it easy to work under the other. BAC's industrial shareholders had different interests: the Receiver simply wanted the highest price for Rolls' residual shareholding; Sir Arnold Weinstock, chairman of GEC, made plain his lack of interest in the aircraft business, but wanted BAC's missile work; and while Vickers might have sold its airframe interests if the price was right, it was not interested in investing in a GEC-led electronics subsidiary. HSA was a profitable part of a larger industrial conglomerate, the Hawker Siddeley Group, but the Hawker Siddeley board was not so committed to aerospace that it would not have settled if the terms were right. All concerned felt that some form of backing from the government was a vital precondition for any deal.

Despite the complexity of the negotiations, Charles Gardner believes that, had the General Election of 1974 not intervened, 'there might have been a voluntary and freely negotiated merger'.[22] This would also have retained the link between aerospace and wider manufacturing and the financial and commercial advantages which that brought. In the event, the new Labour government not only wanted to see a merger between BAC and HSA but also wished to nationalise the joint enterprise. To many in the Labour Party, the problems exposed by Concorde and the RB211 represented a clear case for public ownership. The scale of public investment in private firms and the government's dependence on private decisions was so grotesquely out of balance that nationalisation could be presented simply as a way of regularising industry's dependence on the state. The Labour Party was determined that if public money was to be given to advance commercial aerospace, the state *ought* to have a direct stake in the business – it was a matter of public accountability and democratic control.

4.3 The formation of British Aerospace

During the early 1970s, the political controversy surrounding publicly funded civil aerospace programmes, combined with the leftward shift inside the party, led Labour spokesmen to argue the case for nationalisation with increasing vehemence. The nationalisation of Rolls-Royce, albeit as a 'temporary measure', also helped to strengthen the case for public ownership. Accordingly, the nationalisation of aerospace and shipbuilding was included in Labour's

Programme for 1973, with strong support from the TUC and the engineering unions and was formally adopted by the National Executive of the Labour Party in July 1974. Following Labour's second General Election victory that year, the Queen's Speech contained a proposal to nationalise both industries in a single legislative measure. Draft legislation and a consultative paper was published in January 1975 and a Bill was introduced towards the end of the year.

Labour's case for nationalisation was much the same as Plowden's in 1965, namely that little of substance in the relationship between the state and industry would in fact change. As the industry's largest customer and source of launch capital for civil projects, the government would always play a major role in determining the industry's overall strategy and workload. Nationalisation would merely regularise the relationship and facilitate a more relaxed approach to monitoring and project control. The government was aware that it would now be directly involved in commercial decision-making and that nationalisation had not always been synonymous with sound commercial judgements. To counter this weakness, the new nationalised company, British Aerospace (BAe) would be given substantial managerial autonomy and would not be hindered in its ability to make independent commercial judgements. Public ownership would resolve problems of public accountability associated with publicly funded civil projects by removing the ambiguity of 'launch aid' which had contributed to the Rolls crash. BAe's relationship with the government would be arranged to give the greatest degree of flexibility and autonomy consistent with the needs of public accountability. The powers assumed by the Secretary of State for Industry would be the minimum to secure the government an effective influence over corporate strategy and to protect public investment in individual projects. The new company would also have greater freedom to diversify into related areas of technological and industrial activity. But above all, the process would force the airframe industry into completing a rationalisation which everybody felt to be financially and technologically desirable.

Vesting day was set for 1 January 1976, and a junior minister in the Department of Industry, Lord Beswick, was appointed chairman designate. Beswick's appointment was attacked by the Conservative Opposition as a sign that government intervention in the industry would be closer than it had admitted. Beswick, in fact, had

had a long association as politician and journalist with the aircraft industry. He insisted on the 'clearest devolution of autonomy and responsibility' and later would prove that he could resist government pressure to move in a direction opposed by BAe's management. Beswick took the chair of the Organising Committee for BAe comprising representatives of BAC and HSA. Initial concern that the government would either hive off the guided weapons work or seek to integrate the airframe with the engine sector proved groundless. Shorts was excluded, primarily to protect Northern Ireland's special interests. Other decisions to include or exclude the smaller airframe companies were largely pragmatic. The upper limit of £10 million in aerospace related turnover for a company to fall within the scope of the Act was reduced to £7·5 million following representations from Scottish unions and Labour MPs to include Scottish Aviation (the makers of the ex-Beagle Bulldog trainer and the Handley Page Jetstream). However, this would have roped in Fairey and Westland and neither were keen to become part of BAe. In particular, Westland feared that helicopters would have less priority in the new company and would bear the brunt of subsequent rationalisation. Combined management and union pressure led to a 'redefinition' of aerospace business which got both Fairey and Westland off the hook. With the benefit of hindsight, this left Westland dangerously dependent on a single market; as one influential Tory backbencher later remarked, 'Westland was about the only part of the British aerospace industry which actually should have been nationalised' (see below).[23]

The debate on the Bill was dominated by the twin themes of control and accountability.[24] The industry could no longer be regarded as a 'genuine example of private enterprise'. In the past, huge sums of public money had been spent in private industry which had necessitated a regime of detailed and intrusive monitoring. Now that the government would have a direct role in investment decisions, official involvement in detailed management activity could be reduced. Government control would be largely exercised through ministerial approval of BAe's annual corporate plan, its capital investment, R&D programme and operational budget. The Secretary of State would have to approve all new civil aircraft, while the Secretary of State for Defence would have similar authority for military projects. The Industry Secretary also retained the power to direct BAe 'in the national interest' and to appoint members of the board. However, BAe would be answerable directly to the Secretary of State and not through the National Enterprise Board (NEB), Labour's new holding and industrial investment company which now 'owned' Rolls-Royce (see below). Finance in the form of loan capital could be authorised by the Secretary of State under specific provisions in the Act, or through the existing Industry Act, or from the National Loan Fund. As a public corporation, BAe was no longer eligible for launch aid under the Civil Aviation Act of 1949, but Section 45 of the Aircraft and Shipbuilding Act gave the Secretary of State the specific right to provide money for the promotion of the 'design, development and production of civil aircraft'. Sums over £50 million, however, would require formal Treasury authorisation.

Industrial and Conservative critics were unimpressed by the government's diagnosis of the past weaknesses in the relationship between state and industry. Labour was accused of slandering the industry's commercial record: the industry was not a 'feather bedded, weak sister' in need of caring and careful attention. The history of dependence in civil projects could not be hidden, and undoubtedly the government was its key customer, but the industry's exports for 1975 of £800 million and the past contribution to the balance of payments were seen as proof of the industry's contribution to the economy. Several military projects had been sold on fixed price contracts and the BAC 1–11 had been a strong commercially led programme. Since the early 1970s, reforms had been effected in launch aid procedures and other contractual issues relating to defence programmes which had increased control and accountability. Indeed, there was a greater likelihood of efficiency in public procurement if the customer was not financially involved with the constructor. Moreover, decision-making under nationalisation would be slow and cumbersome, affected at all stages by political and official interference. The promise to abstain from detailed intervention was a 'pious thought' which would 'last as long as the first crisis' which, in turn, would 'bring a demand from the Secretary of State for Industry for cash, and the Treasury will respond with the ruthlessness with which it controls the rest of the public sector'. Speaking for the Opposition, Michael Heseltine promised that they would 'return these industries as far and as fast as possible to the private sector'.[25]

Both BAC and HSA resisted nationalisation. Although

aerospace represented only 25 per cent of Hawker Siddeley Group turnover, HSA was especially vigorous in its opposition with Sir Arnold Hall saying that he would fight all the way. But it was apparent that opposition would be futile. Allan Greenwood, who succeded Sir George Edwards as BAC chairman at the end of 1975, said it would be a 'waste of adrenalin' to fight the government and he certainly felt that a union of HSA and BAC would lead to a stronger unit.[26] On balance, the clear logic of rationalisation helped to undermine the case against nationalisation. In a sense, the industry had only itself to blame for the government's actions, since a voluntary merger had not been forthcoming and it had lost its chance of forming a solid industrial unit which might have negotiated a more flexible arrangement with the state. The question of compensation was more problematic and became the subject of a long drawn out wrangle. Payment was to be based on an average Stock Exchange quotation during a six month period ending 29 February 1974. But neither BAC nor HSA were publicly quoted companies and their shareholders argued that the Stock Exchange was too volatile to form a basis for calculating the value of such a long term business as aerospace. The government was effectively offering about half of the notional estimate of the two firms' net worth of between £150 and £200 million. In the event, the debate over compensation dragged on beyond the lifetime of the Labour government and was finally settled by the European Court of Justice.

The government's only real problem stemmed from misdrafting in parts of the Bill related to ship repairing. After a record fifty-eight meetings in Committee, the government was holding all of its provisions when, in May 1976, a Tory backbencher claimed, rightly as it proved, that the Bill was 'hybrid'. The whole timetable of nationalisation was thrown out and it required another series of heated Parliamentary debates which included the 'Red Flag singing' and the Heseltine 'Mace waving' incidents, to complete the legislative process. As a result, BAe's vesting day slipped from 1 January 1976 to 29 April 1977.

The impact of nationalisation on the aircraft industry and its relationship with government is difficult to gauge, primarily because it lasted for such a short period. Within four years, the Thatcher government began the process of privatisation and the only decisions of consequence during the nationalised period both related to civil projects – the re-launch of the HS/BAe 146 and Britain's re-entry to the Airbus consortium as a full partner (see below). Funding for the latter was provided under Section 45 of the nationalisation Act, whereas money for the 146 formed part of the £250 million allowed for in BAe's first capital plan. More important, and of course, more long lasting, the formation of BAe completed the process of rationalisation which had started in the 1950s. It created one of the strongest and most capable aerospace companies in Europe with some 70,000 employees with net assets of over £300 million and an annual turnover of £700 million. Senior BAe management now concede that nationalisation was perhaps the best way of finally forcing HSA and BAC into a single entity. However, in the short term, the creation of BAe severed the links between aerospace and other commercial activities which would leave it exposed when the company first returned to the public sector. A narrow definition of 'aerospace' business also limited the firm's ability to expand associated activities such as simulation technology while in public ownership.

4.4 Aerospace decisions under Labour

The protracted campaign to nationalise the airframe industry meant that many important decisions, particularly in respect of civil projects were delayed. Neither BAC nor HSA were prepared to invest further in their operations while valuation and compensation was still uncertain. For its part, the BAe Organising Committee had no authority to take major decisions until after vesting day. The main issue was the future of Britain's commitment to the Airbus programme. This boiled down to a straight but by no means simple choice between Europe and several US options and involved again Rolls' determination to secure a position on American aircraft and especially those of the market leader, Boeing.

Throughout the early 1970s, HSA remained a major subcontractor to Airbus Industrie, with responsibility for the wing and acting as a design consultant to the consortium. Although the contract proved very profitable for HSA, the company had no guarantee of future work on any subsequent project developed from the A300 design. Without the support of a national government, it also lacked the 'political clout' of full membership. There was no shortage of new ideas and proposals in both Europe and the US for new airliners. However, the inflation and economic stagnation during the early 1970s caused considerable confusion and uncertainty. Design studies proliferated while companies on both sides of the Atlantic manoeuvred for partners who would help cover the financial risks involved in launching new aircraft. In Europe, BAC and HSA joined the so-called 'Group of Six' (later Seven) consortium to investigate various design concepts. The intention was to anticipate airline requirements and to develop a common front against the Americans. It was clear, however, that all roads led to Toulouse. The French and German governments were so deeply committed to Airbus Industrie as the focal point for European civil aerospace that in practice, prospects for Britain in any new European civil project soon hinged upon a relationship with Airbus Industrie. Although British industry could live with this, the British government and its officials were more sceptical of the Airbus organisation and its products.

In any event, the government was not going to commit itself to anything until the nationalisation process had been completed. HSA and BAC, and later the BAe Organising Committee could discuss matters with their European colleagues, but firm decisions would have to wait until after vesting day. BAC and HSA were less sanguine and warned that the French in particular wanted to move quickly and might seek partnerships with American firms if discussions with their European partners were delayed. In February 1976, it appeared as if French patience had run out when an agreement was announced between Boeing and Aerospatiale, linking new Boeing projects to developments of the Airbus. This was followed a few months later by an accord between Dassault and MDD. In fact, neither agreement was binding, and in many respects they were contradictory – but the French had signalled that they wanted action faster than the British government was prepared, or able, to move. BAe also had American options to consider. Both Boeing and MDD had discussed the possibility of forging links with the UK, and during 1976 Boeing made a serious proposal which would involve BAe collaborating on one of its new projects (the 7N7/757) with the Rolls Royce RB211–535 providing the 'launch engine'. The importance of this order to Rolls was clear: 'if we do not get these orders there will be no Rolls-Royce at all in three years time'.[27] The proposal also had the support of British Airways (BA was the result of a merger in the early 1970s between BOAC and BEA), who wanted to buy the aircraft. A campaign was soon under way to convince BAe and, more important, the British government that this would a better prospect for all concerned than any development of the Airbus.

For the British government, the attractions of BAe joining Boeing were evident. It would satisfy in one package all three elements of British civil aerospace. The airframe industry would be involved in a large American programme which, in the view of many officials and ministers, was more likely to be commercially successful than a European aircraft. Rolls would expand its American beachhead and British Airways would get an optimal aircraft and engine package. The key issue was the extent to which BAe could and should reorientate its civil activities towards the US. However, the supposed advantages to BAe contained a number of serious qualifications. Boeing would lead the programme and although BAe would have an important role in the design process, overall responsibility for systems integration would remain with Boeing. The Americans would also dominate most of the commercial aspects of the programme. In effect, BAe would be a subcontractor to Boeing with no guarantee of future work to follow the 757. In the Airbus or a comparable European programme, BAe would be an equal partner with greater access on a long term basis to the complete process of design, development and commercial exploitation. Faced by these conflicting interests, the government took a neutral position on the issue, arguing that while it was aware of the dangers associated with dependence on the US, it was not going into civil aerospace 'for prestige, but to make money and secure employment'.[28]

In June 1977, BAe joined another European design consortium – the Joint European Transport (JET). JET was remitted to review all the main ideas for a 150–170 seat airliner. The consortium made considerable progress, and by December the companies were ready to discuss more substantive project proposals. Although JET was not linked to Airbus, and the JET designs did not compete with either derivatives of Airbus or the Boeing 7N7/757, the French and the Germans argued that it made sense for any new European development to be run by Airbus Industrie. In the event, the European alternative was narrowed down to a smaller version of the Airbus, the A310. In February 1978, Boeing made BAe a formal offer: it would lead the programme and have responsibility for final assembly, while BAe would design and produce the aircraft's wing. This would be a fixed price contract determined by estimates based on Boeing's in-house costings. BAe had grave reservations about the Boeing offer and asked for more time to consider the alternatives. BAe was accused of being frightened of the efficiency demands of working with Boeing. However, BAe felt that it was being asked to do the most difficult part of the 757 based on data derived from Boeing's total programme costs. In short, if BAe were to take on such a contract under these conditions, there was a grave danger that it could face a substantial loss. Although Boeing made an improved offer, it still fell somewhat short of being an acceptable risk for BAe. After weighing up the options, BAe became convinced that its future lay with Europe. Despite its own reservations about Airbus Industrie, full membership would reinforce BAe's position in all aspects of large civil airliner production and would guarantee the company a place in other projects.

The British government was far from convinced that Airbus Industrie was capable of sustaining a commercially viable operation and edged towards Boeing. The Treasury was especially keen to see the British aircraft industry tied up with the Americans. The Prime Minister, James Callaghan tended to favour Boeing or an alternative, but vaguer proposal which had been made by MDD. Lord Beswick and his board, however, were now determined on the European option. They brooked no interference in their commercial judgement and were prepared to resign over the issue. In September, facing the prospect of open revolt from its 'own' creation, and under considerable pressure from other European governments to show a commitment to European technology, the Cabinet decided that BAe could join Airbus as a full partner, at a cost of £100 million for BAe's share of A310 development. Rolls also received £250 million in launch aid for the RB211–535 and BA were allowed to order the 757 – an investment of over £600 million. The decision, although it suited all three industrial parties, underlined the divergence between the British civil airframe and engine industries. As *The Times* put it, 'after many years of argument over whether Britain should look to the US or Europe for partners in a new generation of aerospace products, this country has emerged ... facing both ways'.[29]

With hindsight, BAe undoubtedly chose the right course of action. BAe has since assumed a major role in three more Airbus derivatives, including the high technology A320, to date Europe's most successful civil aircraft. Although there are still problems with Airbus Industrie's overall commercial and industrial effectiveness, if the Airbus programme does achieve an overall commercial success to match its undoubted technical excellence, it will provide the basis for European civil aerospace development well into the next century. It has already transformed the scale of civil production in the UK and Europe and has seriously challenged US dominance of civil markets. Rolls has done well out of its American strategy, although it has come to regret its failure to appreciate the potential of the Airbus programme and has subsequently developed engines for later Airbus types (see below). Although sales of the 757 were initially disappointing, and the aircraft only began to sell in quantity in 1988, the RB211–535 has become Rolls' baseline engine, setting high standards for fuel efficiency and reliability. In short, the importance of this decision cannot be overstated; had BAe taken the US route, it would have had a profound effect, not only on the direction of British aerospace, but on the cohesion and long term credibility of the European civil aircraft industry.

The second major decision taken by the government affecting BAe during this period was the 're-launch' of the HS146. The HS146 feeder liner had originally received launch aid under the Conservative government, but the post-1973 slump in demand for civil aircraft hit the HS146 very hard. Matters were made worse by the onset of very high rates of inflation which made cost control very difficult. HSA had a reputation for hard nosed financial evaluation – its contract with Airbus Industrie had been a very carefully thought out exercise – and the company feared that the project could threaten the viability of HSA's entire aircraft operation. In July 1974, it informed the DTI that the 1973 launch aid agreement could no longer justify continuation of the project. Tony Benn, then Labour Industry Minister, took a different view. He was concerned to protect employment and the future BAe's civil design capability. Benn argued that HSA should be held to its 1973 agreement. This led to a row with HSA and its strong-minded chairman, Sir Arnold Hall. Benn felt that a 'conjectural' rate of inflation was an inadequate basis for cancellation. Hall, on the other hand said that his company still had the right to make decisions on its own behalf, that HSA had fulfilled its obligations, and hinted that he was prepared to settle the issue in court if necessary. HSA denied accusations that nationalisation had anything to do with the decision, but clearly Hawker Siddeley wanted to avoid tying up any more of its resources in project development in advance of public ownership.

The government conceded that the 1973 agreement had to be amended, with the state assuming more of the risk. In the event, HSA and the government reached a compromise whereby full scale development was 'suspended' pending nationalisation and a future review of the 146's prospects. In the interim, the DoI would finance design work and market studies and HSA would pay between £6 and £10 million in compensation to subcontractors affected by the decision. This was an important point of principle, for Benn had clearly rejected the commercial judgement of HSA (and some of his officials) concerning the HS146. The project was 'suspended' for the next two years, during which £2·5 million was authorised to cover the cost of further design work. In March 1978, BAe decided that the 146 should be 're-launched' and in July received permission to allocate £250 million of company funds to full development. Additional money would be available if needed from the National Loan Fund. BAe's decision was in advance of firm orders and constituted a major risk but the government pointed to it as proof that the nationalised BAe could take independent commercial decisions. In the event, the BAe 146 has done reasonably well, and as a 'quiet jet' it has found customers in environmentally sensitive areas of the US. It has also benefited from the deregulation of US airlines and the emerging need for smaller 'feeder liners'. However, break even is still some way off and it has yet to be shown that the BAe 146 programme will be commercially viable. It does, however, have a significant place in BAe's overall civil aircraft strategy (see below).

4.5 Rolls-Royce, 1971–88

The formal relationship between the government and the nationalised Rolls-Royce was laid down in a Memorandum of Understanding signed in 1971. This specified that Rolls should continue to operate as a private company and that the state, as sole shareholder, would not interfere in day-to-day management. On the other hand, the government would be consulted on the firm's forward planning and about any financial commitment implied by new projects. Rolls also undertook to keep the sponsoring department fully informed about its operations. In 1974 the Labour government inherited the nationalised Rolls-Royce. Despite earlier assurances to the contrary, Rolls was placed in the hands of the National Enterprise Board (NEB). Rolls' chairman, Sir Kenneth Keith, was unhappy with this decision, believing that the NEB would add an unnecessary layer of bureaucracy between it and the government: 'two people cannot run a business. Rolls-Royce is a complex business. We understand it – and we cannot be backseat driven by people who do not.'[30] Under a new MoU between Rolls, the Industry Department and the NEB, the company retained direct access to the DoI and MoD, its main customers and sources of development capital. It was hoped that this would allow Rolls sufficient freedom of action in a highly competitive environment without preventing the NEB from exercising its statutory duties.

Initially, Rolls and the NEB worked reasonably well together and co-operated to persuade the government to support a major campaign to win orders for RB211 derivatives from Boeing (see above). Relations between Keith and the NEB's second chairman, Sir Leslie Murphy, were not so cordial. Keith described the NEB as a 'bureaucratic contraceptive', while Murphy was increasingly sceptical of Rolls' managerial competence. The primary cause for concern was the large loss taken by Rolls on dollar contracts which in 1979 pushed Rolls into a deficit of £58·4 million. In 1982 and 1984, it lost £93 million and £115 million respectively, almost all attributable to the foreign exchange risk associated with its American contracts. The Rolls management had decided not to 'cover forward' its exchange risk and was badly caught by the appreciating pound during the first years of the Thatcher government. It was a decision which a later Rolls chairman described as being 'very unwise'. The government and the NEB had not been directly consulted about Rolls' fiscal strategy but had trusted the Rolls board to know its business. However, according to officials, the NEB's intermediary position had made oversight more difficult than usual.[31]

The issue was brought to a head by the election of a Conservative government opposed to bodies like the NEB and to any form of state intervention in manufacturing. In the event, the new Conservative government, intending eventual abolition of the NEB, agreed to return responsibility for Rolls to the Industry Department. Sir Leslie Murphy and most of his board resigned with predictions that the DoI would be a 'soft touch' for Rolls. Shortly after, Sir Kenneth retired to be replaced by Sir Frank McFadzean. The affair showed yet again the problematic nature of government involvement in complicated and high risk choices involving aerospace. Publicly owned or otherwise, in the final analysis, governments had to trust the company. As McFadzean put it, 'as chairman of this company I have no intention of going and clearing everything with civil servants; otherwise I would never run the company. You would never run a business on that basis'. In his view, if the government was dissatisfied with the way Rolls was being managed, the only legitimate course of action was to change the management.[32]

In due course, the Thatcher government's solution was to return Rolls to the private sector. The Conservative campaign to reduce public borrowing, to reduce government intervention in industry and to spread 'popular capitalism' through wider share ownership turned the privatisation policy into the centrepiece of three administrations. Furthermore, it was dogma that private companies were more efficient than those in the public sector and that the heat of competition would benefit industry and the consumer alike. In the case of aerospace, even though there was ruthless competition from overseas and various forms of state intervention pervaded the whole fabric of industrial activity, the government saw no reason why BAe or Rolls-Royce should stay in public hands. As one minister put it, 'the business of aerospace must pay its way. Defence considerations apart, there is no reason why aerospace should not be subject to the financial discipline and opportunities of the marketplace.' As a private company, it was asserted that BAe would also have more 'freedom to determine its own future'. The government's view of the new relationship was that it would become more like a 'public banker' than an 'industrial planner'. More bluntly, in the view of Norman Tebbit, then Industry Minister, 'the aerospace industry is for making profits, it is not a form of occupational therapy'.[33]

Rolls-Royce remained nationalised for most of the first two Thatcher administrations. After the successful sale of BAe (see below), it was evident that the aero-engine company would eventually be sold. The Rolls flotation of May 1987 raised £1·36 billion. The government retained a 'Golden Share' to prevent a foreign take-over and foreign holdings were limited to a total of 15 per cent of Rolls shares. It was accompanied by a capital injection of £283 million, substantially more than the £140 million the government's financial advisers had suggested because the Rolls chairman, Sir Francis Tombs, had insisted that the company had to be largely free of debt before it could be taken back into the private sector.[34] Despite privatisation, Rolls still relied heavily on government aid for civil programmes, though in recent years less so than BAe. Between 1971 and 1982, successive governments provided equity injections of some £550 million which helped Rolls to compete with the Americans. Between 1979 and 1988, Rolls-Royce also obtained £437 million in launch aid for its various civil engines, of which £111·7 million was repaid from sales levies.

During the 1980s, Rolls' sales have continued to rise, with about 70 per cent of the total exported, over a quarter to the US (see Table 13). After the losses of the late 1970s, Rolls' profits have steadily grown to £156 million in 1987. This represents a pay-off from money sunk in the RB211, and returns from RB199 and other established military programmes, as well as the build-up of spares revenue – indeed, about a third of Rolls' civil turnover was from this source. In 1988, the distribution of work between civil and military engines was about equal but its civil output is expected to grow faster than Rolls' defence business. Prior to privatisation, Rolls embarked upon a major productivity drive. Union leaders were taken to the US on visits to Rolls' US competitors where they were able to appreciate the multiple machine-tending practices employed by American firms and the extent of their productivity advantage. In six years Rolls shed 26,000 jobs, about one-third of its work force, and its long term target is to reach a total UK employment of 34,000 by 1994, about half the 1967 level. Rolls has also consolidated its forteen sites, introduced more automated production techniques and other cost saving measures which have dramatically reduced inventory costs and improved production times.

Table 13: Rolls-Royce performance 1982–88 (turnover, £ million)

	Civil	Military	Other	Total
1982	520 (35%)	742 (50%)	231 (15%)	1,493
1983	388 (29%)	706 (53%)	137 (18%)	1,331
1984	446 (32%)	735 (52%)	228 (16%)	1,409
1985	577 (36%)	735 (46%)	289 (18%)	1,601
1986	757 (42%)	740 (41%)	305 (17%)	1,802
1987	943 (46%)	820 (40%)	286 (14%)	2,059

Source: Rolls-Royce.

Rolls has continued to develop its own 'family' of engines, with the aim of keeping the company in every market 'from the smallest in helicopters to the very largest in jumbo jets'. The centre of its civil range was, of course, the RB211. By 1978, the RB211 series could offer a range of engines from 40,000 lbs. to 70,000 lbs. of thrust. In 1988, the company launched the largest RB211, the -524L to meet the demand from the very largest 747s, the A340, the MD11 and the long range twins. This will cost £300 million, and if the government does not grant the £100 million in launch aid Rolls has asked for, the company will almost certainly go ahead anyway to meet this vital market requirement. Rolls will certainly seek collaborative partners to cover up to 20 per cent of the cost. Collaboration has also filled another important gap in Rolls' civil range. Rolls has a major share of the International Aero Engines V2500 programme with P&W, a Japanese group, MTU of Germany and Fiat, all of which came together in the late 1970s. This started as a bilateral project with the Japanese, but under pressure both from its Japanese partners and the British government to cut the costs, Rolls renewed its links with P&W to form IAE. The V2500 was an all-new engine in the 20,000 lbs. class aimed primarily at the Airbus A320. Unfortunately, Rolls encountered development problems in its part of the programme and, embarrassingly for the British company, P&W had to assume overall responsibility for the engine. Although the problems have been solved, this setback has cost IAE a number of important A320 sales.

In 1984, Rolls also concluded a risk- and revenue-sharing agreement with GE covering the RB211–535E4 and the GECF6–80C. Both firms had 'gaps' in their range which were filled by the other. However the partnership fell apart in November 1986 when Rolls decided to launch a more powerful version of the RB211 – an event which caused some bitterness at GE and which may yet haunt Rolls' reputation as a reliable partner. Rolls has completed its civil range with the £100 million development of the 12–15,000 lbs. Tay, a combination of Spey and RB211 technology. Between 1976 and 1985, the company only had 13 per cent of the total market for civil engines, a weakness almost entirely a result of Rolls' failure to have an engine for the burgeoning market of Airbus A300s and A310s. Unlike GE and P&W, Rolls does not offer a jet engine for the complete range of civil aircraft currently on the market (five types to GE's nine, and P&W's ten). It does, however, have an engine for three out of the four Boeing airliners, including 29 per cent of the high value 747 market. Rolls expects to benefit from the rapidly expanding market for airliners, with hopes of obtaining a substantial share of a total market put at $110 billion over the next twenty years.

Although Rolls has been wary of European collaboration in civil engines, and quite selective in its dealings with the Americans, the majority of its military engines are collaborative projects. As Sir Ralph Robins, Rolls' managing director observes, 'in the military business, it is absolutely vital', a view reinforced by Gordon Page, Rolls' military engine chief: 'European based collaboration is absolutely essential if we are to ward off US domination'. As in the case of European military airframe co-operation, the continuity of partnership has improved efficiency and development effectiveness.[35] The success of the Tornado has, of course, provided the core of Rolls' military production in co-operation with MTU and Fiat. Following on from the RB199, Rolls and its Turbo Union partners are now developing the EJ200 for the Eurofighter. Rolls also has links with the Americans in the defence field through work on the Pegasus and other advanced VTOL concepts as well as the Adour for the MDD/BAe Goshawk. (see below)

Rolls-Royce remains a unique force in the world aero-engine business. It is one of only three companies with a design and development capability in virtually every engine market. But unlike its main American competitors, GE and P&W (UTC), which are divisions of large conglomerates, Rolls is largely dedicated to aero-engine manufacturing leavened only by some marine and nuclear engineering interests. In 1987, aero-engines were only 17 per cent of GE's total sales and 33 per cent of UTC's turnover, compared to Rolls' 85 per cent. The two American firms also benefit from a near duopoly of the US military market, worth about $5 billion a year. Rolls, on the other hand, can only count on about £1 billion in total military sales.

This clearly puts pressure on Rolls' R&D resources. In the late 1980s, Rolls' 1986 spending on R&D of over £250 million, or about 9 per cent of turnover, was similar to GE's engine division, but GE's total spending on R&D was $1 billion a year (see Table 14). Nor does Rolls have access to the large government funded general purpose R&D programmes such as NASA's propfan research project. Following the experience of the original RB211 programme,

Rolls has adopted conservative R&D practices, making extensive use of demonstrator rigs to explore design configurations and to assess the range of technological unknowns. Advances in computer simulation have also served to reduce the risk of hardware-based development. About 25 per cent of the R&D phase is now spent in this preparatory work. Rolls' position has been helped by the fact that no-one expects a technological leap of the kind which occurred in the 1960s; the majority of engine requirements until well into the next century will be based on incremental improvements in existing engine technology.

Table 14: The 'Big Three' engine companies, 1986

	Turnover	R&D spending
United Technologies (includes P&W)	$15·67 billion	$853 million
General Electric (includes engine division)	$28·28 billion	$1,069 million
Rolls-Royce	£1·80 billion	£255 million

Source: Financial Times, 22 April 1987.

The main exception may prove to be the propfan or unducted fan (UDF), a combination of advanced technology propeller and high efficiency turbo-fan engine. The UDF promises considerable savings in fuel and could revolutionise engine design in the next century. Both P&W and GE (in co-operation with Snecma) have flight tested basic UDF designs. However, several technical and, more important, commercial questions remain to be resolved,not the least of which is the cost of fuel, for while it remains low, few airlines will want to incur the extra cost of a UDF engine. In the meantime, Rolls has not committed itself to a propfan programme and a proposed 'SuperFan' engine to be built by IAE was abandoned. If the engine does enter service more rapidly than Rolls expects, the company will have a critical decision to make; whether to launch its own design at considerable cost (over £1 billion) or to try to seek a partnership with one of the Americans. But the signs are that the introduction of propfan engines may be delayed until the late 1990s, in which case Rolls can afford to wait. The uncertainty surrounding the UDF is a reminder, however, of the level of risk in the civil engine industry and the importance of spreading that risk through a range of engines and industrial partners.

The risks of Rolls' exposure as a dedicated aero-engine manufacturer in a volatile commercial environment are obvious. The company may have to consider some degree of diversification (it has recently begun to look at expanding its electricity generation turbine business), but for the present its strategy is still very much to concentrate on the core engine business with its risks covered by collaboration and a broad spread of products. It is unlikely that Rolls and the other main European engine firm, the French Snecma, will join forces. The strained relations during the 1960s have taken the two on divergent paths. Snecma has a long term partnership with GE and the opportunity for co-operation on a major military programme passed when the French dropped out of the EFA project. Within the UK, Rolls remains a 'national champion' and it is inconceivable that any government would allow a major engine contract to go to one of Rolls' competitors. 31 per cent of Rolls' sales still go to the MoD, but, like BAe, under a more competitive procurement regime, Rolls has had to fight harder for British military contracts, the more so now that GEC of Britain has linked with GE to develop turbo-shaft engines for helicopters. Rolls can certainly expect no quarter from its foreign competitors, even though in some projects they may be working in tandem. However, the design and development of large aero-engines is a very rare skill, and while Rolls-Royce has always had the technical competence, the experience of the last two decades has also honed its managerial skills.

4.6 Westland and the helicopter industry; 1945–88

The history of the British helicopter industry is in some senses a microcosm of the post war dilemmas faced by the aircraft industry at large. It suffered from the problems of industrial fragmentation, developing too many designs for a small domestic market, coming belatedly to rationalisation and having a mixed experience with European collaboration, although the helicopter sector has been more successful in forging close and mutually beneficial links with the United States. The main British helicopter company, Westland, escaped nationalisation but its independence in the end became a liability and in 1986 was not only the centre of a major commercial crisis but also the focus of a dramatic political upheaval in the Conservative government. The origins and resolution of this crisis provide an interesting insight into the state-industry relationship which has pervaded the history of British aircraft manufacturing.

The modern helicopter dates from the Second World War, although the idea of vertical lift is much older. In the 1920s and 1930s the 'hybrid' Cierva Autogiro, driven by a conventional propeller with lift sustained by an unpowered rotor, had some popularity.[36] In the mid 1930s, the RAE undertook some research on VTOL and in 1938 the Weir W5 made the first British direct lift flight. During the Second World War, helicopter research in the UK all but ceased, although an autogiro Squadron was used to calibrate radars. The first true helicopters were developed in Germany and the United States, pioneered in the latter by Igor Sikorsky. A number of post war British helicopter projects were started including the ill-fated Weir 'Air Horse', at the time the largest of its kind in the world. Weir had acquired the Cierva company which was itself taken over by Saunders Roe in 1950. In turn, Saunders Roe developed a series of light helicopters primarily for naval and army use. In 1944, Bristol formed a helicopter division, developing the Bristol 171 Sycamore which adopted the basic design concepts worked out by Sikorsky. The B171 flew in 1947 and in 1949 became the first British helicopter to be granted a Certificate of Airworthiness. It was operated in substantial numbers by the RAF, the German government and BEA. Bristol also developed a twin-rotor aircraft, the B192 Belvedere as a transport and ASW helicopter. However, the Belvedere became an early victim of the inter-Service disputes which have bedevilled British helicopter development and only twenty-six were built with the Navy preferring the Sikorsky-Westland S58 Wessex.

Fairey Aviation entered the helicopter business in 1945 with the Gyrodyne 'compound' helicopter – a lifting rotor with forward motion through a propeller which in 1948 established a world helicopter speed record of 124 mph. The Gyrodyne led directly to the larger Rotodyne designed as a heavy transport flying for the first time in 1957. The Rotodyne was conceived as a 'city-to-city' airliner with 40–50 passengers for BEA or as a military transport for the Army. However, noise and other technical problems and a dispute between BEA and the MoS over its funding dogged its development. It was eventually cancelled in 1962 at a cost of over £4 million. Westland itself entered the field in 1946 with a licence from Sikorsky to build the S51. This was the start of a long and fruitful relationship between the two companies. In the 1950s, Westland 'anglicised' the S55 and, as the Whirlwind, it became the mainstay of Royal Navy search and rescue operations. The Whirlwind was extensively modified, including a new engine which produced a substantially improved aircraft. Westland would later perform the same trick on the Wessex (Sikorsky S58) and Sea King (Sikorsky S61). In the mid 1950s, Westland designed a large transport helicopter for the Army and BEA called the Westminster, but this was cancelled in favour of the Rotodyne. Between 1945 and 1965, a total of 1,510 British helicopters were built with over 20 different designs. The Whirlwind with 417 and its Wessex successor with 348, were by far the most successful – about five in every six British helicopters during that period was built by Westland.

In 1960 these disparate helicopter interests were merged into a single company, Westland. Westland's performance was described by Plowden as the 'most successful and consistent profit record of all the major groups in the aircraft industry', and was based on diversification into equipment ventures both in and outside the aircraft industry and on a low risk R&D strategy which had not strained company resources.[37] Even then, American domination of the world market was evident, compounded by fierce competition from French, Italian and German companies. The government had also made it clear that, although it would try 'as far as practicable to concentrate' its orders on the group, it reserved the right, 'in the public interest', to purchase helicopters from overseas. The development of independent British helicopters, especially in the larger categories, was always marginal – the more so with all three services often varying markedly in their helicopter requirements. Even within the army, changing doctrines about air lift would continually affect helicopter specifications. Then, as now, the main customers for helicopters were the military, and civil use, although it has since expanded with the growth of off-shore oil exploration and servicing, has always been a relatively small part of the business. Helicopter manufacturers have also had to contend with the problem that helicopter forces have usually had to fight for priority in defence budgets, often losing out to more central service requirements.

As we have seen, following Plowden, the government looked to collaboration to solve the problem of small numbers and high costs. Westland was involved in several collaborative programmes during the 1960s, culminating in the Anglo-French 'package' of 1967 (see Chapter 3). However, the Lynx, Gazelle and Puma package did result in substantial savings in reduced unit costs and increased export sales, with production of the three types reaching over three times the original forecast of 835 aircraft. Despite Westland's bad experience with the French, in 1975 it joined the other European companies in a MoU on future collaboration. It was certainly imperative to start a new round of projects if the European helicopter industry was to survive. In 1978, the Labour government joined with fellow European governments in signing a 'Declaration of Principles' in which Britain, France, Germany and Italy would together build a 'family' of helicopters to hold off the powerful American helicopter industry, although the possibility of working with the Americans was not excluded.[38] The result was a patchwork of joint projects. Westland, with Agusta of Italy were to develop a large naval helicopter, the EH 101, to replace the Sea King in a £1·5 billion programme. The second, an agile 'battle field' design, formed the basis of a Franco-German project, the PAH2/HAC. Westland later joined the Italians in working on a competitor – the A129. A third European project was the NH90 medium sized transport which the British eventually rejected. However, it was evident that co-operation had not led to any rationalisation in the European helicopter industry, and by the mid 1980s it was suffering from considerable over-capacity. Westland chose this moment to develop its own aircraft, the W30, aimed primarily at a civil market, with £40 million in launch aid from the Conservative government. As a largely military and UK MoD orientated company, this was something of a gamble for Westland, although it had some hopes that the design would be taken up by the British Services. The government also helped to arrange an aid-based sale to India.

Westland was excluded from the Aircraft and Shipbuilding Act and throughout the late 1970s and 1980s became something of an anomaly in the world aircraft industry – an independent helicopter manufacturer. Its main competitors, and certainly its European colleagues, were parts of wider industrial or aerospace groupings. Aerospatiale's helicopter division represented only 20 per cent of the company's overall activity; only 5,000 of MBB's 36,000 employees worked on helicopters, and Agusta was a subsidiary of the state holding company EFIM. In the US, specialisation and rationalisation had allowed Sikorsky-UTC, Bell-Textron,

Hughes-MDD and Boeing (again divisions of large firms) to achieve significant economies of scale and to derive cost advantages. Westland also had other interests in aircraft equipment, but in 1985, helicopters still accounted for some two-thirds of company turnover. Along with other manufacturers, Westland had to contend with increasing inter-generational costs, in some cases as high as 200 per cent. The world market was dominated by the US with 72 per cent of the world's military inventory. Of the Europeans, Aerospatiale was the largest, with a market share equal to that of Agusta, MBB and Westland combined. In short, 'Westland lacked the resilience of the other producers. Westland's worsening problems in 1984 and 1985 therefore had a direct effect on its viability.'[39]

Between 1981 and 1984 the market for both military and civil helicopters collapsed, putting even the Americans in some difficulty. But for Westland, it was a disaster, with heavy debts incurred as a result of the W30 and facing the prospect of a substantial short term production 'gap' – it had no orders at all for 1986–90. Westland's hopes of selling the W30 to the British military were badly dented by chronic inter-Service rivalry and vacillation over specific requirements for helicopters. There was also some interest in buying the Sikorsky Black Hawk and in 1982 the Americans went so far as to propose a partnership, first with Westland and then with Shorts, in order to improve their prospects of penetrating the UK and European markets. However, Michael Heseltine, the Minister of Defence, said that there was neither a requirement nor funds for a helicopter of that type. In the spring of 1985 one of Westland's most trenchant critics, the helicopter operator Alan Bristow, made a bid for the company and opened discussions with Sikorsky about the possibility of building the Black Hawk under licence. Bristow backed out when he discovered just how weak Westland's finances were and found that the government would not give any further financial support. However, the government decided that an effort should be made to save the company from bankruptcy and helped to engineer a change of management with Sir John Cuckney replacing Sir Basil Blackwell, Westland's chairman. Well connected to the Whitehall establishment, Cuckney had a clear brief to take the necessary commercial judgements to save the firm. This rapidly took the form of a closer relationship with Sikorsky. Neither the DTI nor, at that time, the MoD expressed any fundamental opposition to the prospect of Westland passing into some form of overseas control. Cuckney, therefore, increasingly looked to the pragmatic solution of linking more formally with a long standing partner and one of the strongest helicopter firms in the world.

As the deal shaped up, it was evident that Sikorsky was looking for a major opening to the European defence market. In return for a substantial holding in Westland, Sikorsky would inject new capital into the company, give a licence for Black Hawk production and rights to sell the helicopter in Europe and elsewhere (though not in the US, Japan or several other important markets). Sikorsky also guaranteed two million man-hours of production to tide Westland over until the EH101 was in production. In the autumn of 1985, a 'European' flavour was added when Fiat joined the Sikorsky bid. It was equally clear that Cuckney had put together a powerful lobby in favour of the deal with Sikorsky, which included Mrs Thatcher. The other European manufacturers belatedly woke to the danger and MBB and Aerospatiale, with help from BAe and GEC, put forward an alternative proposal. However, perhaps rightly, Westland believed that no European company, especially the French, had shown any interest in saving Westland until Sikorsky had came into sight. It would have suited them to have seen a reduction in a large European over-capacity in helicopter production. Nevertheless Michael Heseltine, with a deep commitment to European weapons collaboration, believed that a European solution to Westland's problems should be considered.

The European 'rescue package' left much to be desired. It was vague and dependent on a series of interrelated project decisions, some of which were mutually incompatible. Heseltine had the backing of the European National Armaments Directors for a European helicopter programme. This was not good enough for Cuckney, nor did it encourage Mrs Thatcher to change her support for an American solution for Westland. Leon Brittan, the Industry Minister, supported the Thatcher/Cuckney line. From this point, the political aspects of the Westland 'affair' exploded into one of the most bitter Cabinet disputes of the Thatcher years, culminating in the resignation first of Michael Heseltine and then of Leon Brittan, accusations of dictatorial government, questionable actions by Mrs Thatcher's and Leon Brittan's aides, late night 'pressure' applied to the BAe chief executive, Sir Raymond Lygo, and the possibility that Mrs Thatcher herself might have gone. In the event, the Sikorsky deal went through, accompanied by a last minute struggle with

Bristow and some murky share transactions. UTC and Fiat finished up with 21 per cent of Westland voting shares, but it was evident that the Americans would have an important role in Westland's future and a 'close involvement in the day-to-day policy and practices' of the company.[40]

Since 1986, Westland's fortunes have been mixed; profits and turnover have fluctuated, but the trend has been unfavourable – in 1988 it reported a 5 per cent fall in turnover to £185·8 million with a trading profit of £13·1 million. Its non-helicopter work, including subcontract work for MDD, Boeing and Airbus, has been relatively buoyant. The continuing shortage of production work led to a cut of one-third in the company's 6,000 workforce. The BAe-led deal with Saudi Arabia in August 1988 was of critical importance in transforming its order book (see below). Worth £500 million, it has effectively given Westland a breathing space while the EH101 comes on stream in 1992. For the future, the basis of helicopter technology is changing. The 'tiltrotor' concept may challenge the helicopter's unique characteristics as well as offering fixed wing performance. Westland remains sceptical of the largely civil orientated 'Eurofar' research programme and has down-graded its participation to a mere 6 per cent. However, Westland could be under pressure from technological innovation in the late 1990s. BAe, for example, is collaborating with the Americans on 'tilt wing' research. Even 'conventional' helicopters, such as the US LHX, will use very advanced equipment and design concepts which will push up R&D costs still higher. There will be pressure on all of the European manufacturers and especially Westland either to respond or to join a collaborative programme with the US.

Why the control of Westland should have led to such a dramatic crisis is somewhat baffling. The Defence Committee drew attention to the notion of a *defence industrial base* (DIB) which the UK needed in order to maintain some security of development and production of key 'weapons platforms'. Aerospace, or at least certain elements of aerospace, falls into this category. The Committee noted a range of opinions on whether helicopters were so important to the UK that it had to have an indigenous capability. Michael Heseltine had no doubt that the main point at issue was the collaborative dimension; that the Westland case was an 'acid test' of European co-operation and of Europe's ability and determination to prevent US domination of key sectors of weapons production.

Set against this, the Committee heard the views of Leon Brittan and Westland who held that the commercial judgement of a private company which was quite clearly in favour of the Sikorsky option should have been paramount. By failing to order the W30, Heseltine had not helped the company in the 'national interest', and as a result it had had the right to choose its own salvation. There were cases where important principles such as European collaboration should lead a government to override commercial factors, but this had not been one of them. Indeed, Westland believed that the European option was potentially the more damaging for British helicopter interests. The Committee itself reached no specific conclusion as to whether this had been a case where the government should have gone against the views of a private company; here the *government as a whole* identified no compelling national interest in Westland choosing a European solution'.[41] The Committee finally observed how a 'Ministerial Aerospace Board' as recommended by the Rayner Report would help to resolve conflicts of interest between the MoD as customer and the DTI as sponsor of the aerospace industry (see above).

With hindsight, this was undoubtedly the wrong case about which to make a stand on the principle of European defence solidarity. There was, and is, a clear case for some degree of rationalisation in the European helicopter industry and Westland, sad though it might be for the UK, would have to prove that its operation should not be much reduced in scale. Equally, given Westland's strong tradition of working with the Americans, if this was the best way to secure that future, the imposition of a European solution was absurd. On the other hand, for ministers to say that the future of Westland was simply a matter for 'market forces' was a facile observation that either failed to note the deep and pervasive state-industry relationship in any defence contractor or aerospace company activity or was utterly and cynically disingenuous. Finally, the root cause of the whole fiasco lies in the failure to place helicopter manufacturing within a more powerful industrial grouping. For a variety of reasons, union and regional interests, corporate pressure to stay independent and some residual political preference, Westland was left to fight it out in a ruthlessly competitive environment against better financed and better supported companies. As part of British Aerospace, a 'helicopter division' would have been under pressure much earlier to show a positive return and unquestionably a substantial degree of rationalisation would have taken place. Although Westland has weathered one major crisis, its position as an indepedent, dedicated helicopter manufacturer will remain vulnerable. Its future may yet lie in becoming a part of a stronger engineering grouping. In this respect, GKN's purchase of 22 per cent of the company and the possibility of buying out UTC's shareholding could point the way to a more secure base for helicopter development in the UK.

4.7 British Aerospace, 1978–88

BAe remained in public hands for only four years. In November 1979, the Conservative government announced that BAe would be 'privatised'. BAe was sold off in two instalments between February 1981 and May 1985. As in the case of Rolls-Royce, the government retained a 'Golden Share' to prevent the company from falling into foreign ownership and overseas holdings were limited in total to 15 per cent. A Government Director was also appointed to the board, primarily to protect the government's liabilities in respect of the Airbus programme. BAe welcomed privatisation, however, believing that it would lead to a sharpened concern for commercial realities. Sir Austin Pearce, who succeeded Lord Beswick as BAe chairman in 1980, said that it 'causes you to set up the commercial and financial disciplines which apply to all capital and operating expenditures, wherever they come from'. This, he suggested, solved the problem of accountability in publicly financed programmes, and generally sharpened BAe's concern for efficiency. Nevertheless, there was a clear role for government; he was against reliance on 'pots of government gold', but the company needed help on programmes such as Airbus.[42] BAe could raise money through the normal means of loans and rights issues, and was again eligible for launch aid under the 1948 and 1949 Civil Aviation Acts. Indeed, over the last ten years, BAe has received a total of £700 million in launch aid, primarily to support two new Airbus projects. In both cases, BAe received rather less than it wanted and has complained that this has put it at a disadvantage in relation to its partners in the Airbus programme.

The MoD, of course, remained BAe's single most important customer and the source of most of its R&D funding. However, changes in defence and procurement policy under the Conservative government have had an impact on BAe's operational environment. The government's adoption of 'value for money' procurement, with its emphasis on competitive tendering and fixed price contracting, has affected BAe, although as a 'prime contractor' and 'national champion' in aerospace alongside Rolls-Royce it has suffered less than the equipment and electronics companies.[43] BAe seems to have responded well to the new regime, reasonably happy to negotiate fixed priced contracts for all but the most complex aspects of a new programme. As one senior BAe manager put it, fixed price contracting entailed 'greater risks but with good management there are bigger upside prospects'. The main problem was that the MoD had not adapted to the 'hands off' approach to monitoring associated with fixed price contracting and still behaved as though BAe was working to cost-plus agreements.[44] BAe has also found the government rather less keen to support long term projects such as the Hotol space vehicle and, like many firms in the high technology sector, has expressed concern about the government's funding of national R&D (see Chapter 5).

Over the last five years, BAe has mounted an ambitious and aggressive campaign to deepen its core business in defence and aerospace and to diversify its operations in high technology and manufacturing. Nationalisation had cut the links with the electronics and engineering industry which had helped to provide a measure of long term protection against the cyclical nature of aircraft production. The privatised BAe was suddenly vulnerable to new pressures, such as fluctuations in share prices, which the airframe sector had not faced directly since rationalisation. Two take-over bids for BAe in 1984 rammed home the importance of broadening the company's range of activities.[45] At one level, BAe has sought to expand its systems and electronics activities. This has partly reflected a search for new business opportunities in 'smart weapons' and electronic based equipment (including an advanced drug 'sniffing' device) as well a determination to protect its core aerospace capability. As military aircraft have grown more reliant on electronics and systems, BAe's status as a prime contractor and weapons system integrator has depended upon its own skills in these areas. BAe has improved an already sophisticated in-house software and systems design capability as well as taking a 25 per cent share in one of Britain's most important independent software houses, Systems Designers. The growing proportion of value added work in a military aircraft attributable to electronics (rising towards 42 per cent) has further encouraged BAe to enter the equipment market in its own right. BAe is a major producer of aircraft and missile gyroscopes (helped by its acquisition of Sperry), navigation equipment and, for its own use, custom designed micro-circuitry. BAe is now the sixth-ranked defence electronics company in Europe and the third largest in the UK. But the main objective is to keep BAe in the forefront of European and world aerospace: 'the ability to deal with the whole aircraft is vital. In Europe the common feature of international collaborative programmes has been the agreed workshare. When the EC becomes more common in 1992, we feel that we will be better able to compete if we retain a full capability.'[46] In this respect, BAe is following a line of development which is already well under way in the US and which is steadily blurring the distinction between aerospace and electronics manufacturers.

Since BAC's involvement in Saudi Arabia in the 1960s, BAe has expanded its defence 'service' sector including training and infrastructure development. In 1987, BAe bought the Dutch airfield construction company Ballast Needham which has reinforced BAe's ability to offer a complete, 'turn-key' air defence/air force package. BAe's other ancillary activities have embraced aircraft and missile simulators and pilot training which has been enhanced by the purchase of Reflectone, a US military simulator company which will help BAe gain access to the US defence market. Similarly, BAe's use of advanced CAD/CAM techniques has led to spinoff sales of software and expertise in this area. However, BAe's most radical acts of diversification were the purchases of Royal Ordnance (RO) and Rover, the last British-owned volume car manufacturer.

BAe bought the RO from the government in April 1987 for £190 million. Although the deal was hedged with constraints to prevent BAe from deriving an unfair competitive position in areas such as rocket motors, it was still largely structured to BAe's advantage. BAe acquired a profitable company free of debt, with assets of £235 million and with a strongly growing order book. RO had a turnover of £515 million in 1986, with 80 per cent of sales going to the MoD and in 1987, it made a profit of £45 million. Through buying RO, BAe became the West's largest defence contractor outside the US.

BAe took over a firm with 16,300 employees on fifteen sites, historically dispersed against enemy attack. BAe put in five of its own men to head the board, including the chairman, Dr Maurice Dixson, who had previously been commercial director of BAe's military division. This team rationalised plant, cut the work force and even cancelled contracts for its own rocket motors which were not up to scratch. BAe invested in new plant where improvements could be made to RO's productivity and efficiency, essential if the RO was to meet the government's demands for fixed price contracts on small arms and ammunition. BAe also built up the company's marketing and sales team. BAe provided the RO with a more effective link to overseas markets and better access to high technology to up-grade its products and manufacturing processes. In turn, the RO extended BAe's product range to include such items as ammunition with quicker returns on capital which will have beneficial effects on BAe's cash flow. The merger has also provided an opportunity for vertical integration: RO was already a leading subcontractor for Alarm, Rapier and Sea Wolf amongst other BAe missiles, and the company could realise savings on development and production as well as having a 'turn-key' missile capability to compete more effectively for MoD and foreign orders. In short, RO was a flabby company with considerable potential that needed a sharper commercial outlook. As Lygo put it, 'RO was an organisation looking for a home. It was a very similar business to BAe, but was heavily bureaucratised and run by former civil servants.'

The RO take-over, although in some respects taking BAe into the 'low technology' end of military products, was at least in a sector within BAe's established area of interest and where there were obvious links between the two companies' activities. However, BAe's March 1988 bid for Rover stunned both the City and industrial analysts. Although there have been successful car/aircraft combinations, notably Saab of Sweden, the advantages to BAe of taking on the 'albatross' of Rover were not immediately apparent. The government accepted BAe's offer with alacrity; it would push Rover into the private sector several years earlier than expected, ending the company's dependence on public money and, equally important, Rover would be sold intact to another British firm. Again, BAe obtained extremely generous terms; BAe would pay £150 million for Rover, but the government would write-off £1·6 billion in accumulated debt as well as providing a cash injection of

£800 million. Rover also had assets of some £333 million, potentially very valuable land from rationalised plant, and an operation which was at last beginning to show a profit (£27 million in 1987) after decades of losses. In the event, the EC Commission, looking to outlaw government subsidies to ailing industries, intervened to force a modification to the terms. As a result, the government reduced its cash injection to £469 million, but BAe still had Rover at a give-away price.

BAe's chairman, Professor Roland Smith (very much the architect of the deal which was known in advance to only five people in BAe, Rover and the DTI) argued that the new company would generate 'synergy' – a positive interaction of each side's different strengths, exploiting a pool of over 23,000 engineers. The car company would bring knowledge of highly automated manufacturing processes; aerospace would provide access to very advanced technology and a growing electronics sector. Both had a considerable competence in systems engineering and Land Rover's military vehicles would complement the RO's activities. However, as similar mergers between Hughes and General Motors, and Daimler, MTU and Dornier in Germany have shown, such synergistic effects are not immediately apparent and have to be worked on for some years. It was noted that in these cases, large car companies had taken over aerospace/electronics firms and not the other way round. Similarly, although most of Rover's capital requirements for the next decade have been made and the link with Honda will also reduce development costs, BAe will still have to find substantial sums (about £1·5 billion according to Rover's 1988 corporate plan) to support Rover's future needs at a time when it will be incurring heavy liabilities associated with the Airbus and other civil aircraft programmes. On balance, in the short term the deal offered BAe rather more financial than industrial advantage. Like the RO acquisition, Rover's quicker turn round on capital would help BAe's earnings per share and broaden its capital base. The new company had a combined turnover of over £7 billion and employed 120,000 people. The merger has made BAe the UK's seventh largest company and third placed manufacturer – the twenty-forth largest company in Europe and one of the world's top one hundred firms.[47]

4.8 Aerospace: the core business

In 1986, before the purchases of Royal Ordnance and Rover, BAe employed 75,480 people of which 51,785 were in its aircraft divisions. In 1965, the constituent companies had over 87,627 workers. Development and production work was on twenty sites compared with over thirty at the time of Plowden (see Table 15). The bulk of capital investment in new plant has largely been focused on Stevenage, Warton and Filton, but extensive rationalisation would be too expensive. Surplus capacity at Woodford (Manchester), for example, meant that it was cheaper to open a second BAe 146 production line there than at Hatfield. Most of BAe's activity was still based in the south and south-east, but 37.5 per cent of BAe's workforce was located in the north-west. During the nationalisation period, BAe shed over a 1000 employees and since 1985, production work was ended at Hurn and the old Vickers factory at Weybridge with a loss of 2,500 jobs. Most of the lost jobs were from BAe's civil division. However, further job losses were announced in 1988 and 1989 in a reorganisation and rationalisation of BAe's military and guided weapons divisions which will lead to a reduction of 3,900 by 1990. This was again part of BAe's continuing drive to improve productivity to reach US standards.

Out of a total turnover of £3,137 million, 24 per cent was in civil aircraft, 38 per cent in military aircraft, 32 per cent in guided weapons and systems, and 6 per cent in space and communications, making BAe the ninth largest aerospace company in the world and the largest in Europe (see Tables 16 and 17). With nearly two thirds of turnover sold overseas, even before the Rover purchase, BAe was already Britain's most important exporter of engineering goods and fifth-placed exporting company overall. The company was also a major user of British goods, with 72 per cent of its purchases coming from UK companies, supporting some 29,500 jobs in the equipment industry alone. Between 1978 and 1986, BAe profits have shown a steady improvement with guided weapons and systems providing the best rate of growth. Its most profitable activities were the defence related military aircraft, missiles and systems divisions. On the other hand, BAe's civil programmes have consistently showed a loss since 1985 and have been the source of considerable concern for BAe management (see below).

Either independently, or in collaboration with European or US companies, BAe has one of the most comprehensive product lines in the world, certainly in Europe. The only major gaps are in strategic bombers, long range missiles, and helicopters. BAe's military programme has included two important collaborative agreements with the US. In 1981, a MoU with MDD to build the AV8B/Harrier 2 gave BAe 40 per cent by value of the airframe and 25 per cent of final assembly work. However, what originally had been a clear UK lead in VTOL development was lost as a result of government vacillation and corporate uncertainty during the protracted process of nationalisation. Fortunately, the link with MDD has enabled BAe to stay in the business of advanced VTOL research. The Harrier 2 was at the time the largest joint military programme between the US and the UK and the largest co-operative agreement for the development and production of combat aircraft between any West European and American company. Although BAe lost the leadership of the VTOL programme, the relationship has allowed BAe to stay in an area where otherwise cash-flow problems might have forced it to leave. It has certainly improved the scale economics of what had been a rather specialised product.[48] BAe's partnership with MDD also proved a decisive element in the sale of Hawk trainers (the T-45A Goshawk) to the US Navy in 1981 in a contract worth £2·7 billion. About 60 per cent of the work will be done in the UK, including Rolls Royce's share of the Adour engine. On balance, therefore, BAe has gained considerably from this trans-Atlantic partnership, providing a significant counterpoint to the firm's European programmes, allowing it a direct *entrée* into the tightly controlled US military market. The Hawk itself has evolved into a potent strike/trainer and is currently one of the best selling aircraft in its class. BAe has launched a privately financed upgraded version – the Hawk 200 – in order to maintain its market share.

The Tornado remains BAe's most important military production programme. In addition to developing an air defence version (ADV) for the RAF, export sales to Saudi Arabia have extended the lifetime of Tornado production well into the 1990s. In two deals, this has led to orders for a total of over 112 aircraft worth over £7 billion (including orders for other BAe military equipment and services). These sales, with twelve more from Malaysia in 1988, will take the Tornado production run almost up to US levels, with a strong possibility that the total could exceed 1,000 units. This

Table 15: BAe factories and responsibilities, 1986

Military aircraft division

Weybridge	HQ military aircraft, BAe HQ staff.
Kingston	Harrier, Hawk 200 assembly.
Brough	Harrier, Hawk, Tornado, 146 sections.
Hamble	Components for Harrier, Hawk, 146. Specialist materials.
Warton	Tornado final assembly and sections, A320
Preston	wing components, EAP/EFA design and development,
Samlesbury	Tornado support, components.

Civil aircraft division

Hatfield	146 and 125 design and development, 146 final assembly.
Chester	125 final assembly, A300/310 wing production.
Filton	A320 wing production, 146 centre section, aircraft overhaul.
Chadderton	748/ATP design, development and production,
Woodford	second 146 assembly line.
Prestwick	Jetstream production.

Guided weapons and electronic systems division
  Naval

Filton	Sea Dart design and development, circuitry.
Weymouth	Tracked Rapier.
Bracknell	Aircraft instruments, fire control systems, navigation systems, gyroscopes.

  Air weapons

Hatfield	Sea Eagle, Skua, Alarm Skyflash.
Lostock	

  Army weapons

Stevenage	Rapier design, development & production, Swingfire and Milan, Trigat development, missile components and integrated circuits.

Space and communications division

Stevenage	Satellite design, development and production, Hotel development shared with Filton and Warton.

Source: British Aerospace.

success will provide work for the company and its European partners until they can bring the next generation of European combat aircraft on stream, the EFA, or Eurofighter. Built by the same combination of companies with the addition of Spain, the EFA represents the 'cutting edge' of aerospace technology utilising 'fly-by-wire' and computer controlled 'unstable' aerodynamics. The project will also act as a powerful software and systems driver, stimulating research into new structures and materials, expert systems and artificial intelligence. At an estimated cost of over £20 billion, it will be one of Europe's most expensive defence projects.

The origins of EFA and the diplomacy of its inception recalled the traumas of the 1960s. In the late 1970s, along with other European

Table 16: British Aerospace performance, 1983–86
(£ million)

	1986	1985	1984	1983
Turnover				
Civil aircraft	761·7	650·2	572·0	434·6
Military aircraft				
and services	11,68·0	945·2	995·1	1,030·5
Guided weapons/				
systems	1,011·1	922·9	791·3	692·1
Space	196·1	129·4	109·5	143·1
TOTAL	3,137·0	2,647·7	2,467·8	2,300·3
Trading Profit				
Civil aircraft	(7·7)	(2·5)	7·5	13·6
Military aircraft				
and services	146·0	148·3	114·3	104·7
Guided weapons				
and systems	139·7	127·8	104·9	80·3
Space	1·9	(2·0)	(15·2)	(14·2)
R&D	(62·7)	(54·9)	(45·3)	(38·7)
TOTAL	217·2	211·1	166·2	112·0
Employees				
Aircraft	51,785	51,800	52,928	55,927
Guided weapons				
and space	22,508	22,588	22,310	21,351
Others	1,187	1,157	760	720
TOTAL	75,480	75,645	75,998	75,980

Note: Figures in brackets denote a loss.
Source: British Aerospace.

Table 17: British Aerospace results, 1987 (incorporating Royal Ordnance)

	£ million
Turnover	4,075
Civil aircraft	753
Military aircraft/services	1,854
Weapons/systems	1,315
Space/communications	153
Exports	2,801
Trading profit	217
Employees: 86,800	

Source: British Aerospace.

and American firms, BAe was working on advanced fighter designs. Following the publication of a European airforces' joint requirement, in April 1980, MBB, BAe and Dassault reached an 'industrial agreement' and began serious discussions on a common programme. In order to support research into the advanced avionics and structures needed for a modern high performance fighter, BAe put together a privately financed group of British equipment firms to explore the necessary concepts. In 1983, the BAe-led consortium and the MoD agreed jointly to fund the £165 million EAP demonstrator with some contribution from BAe's 'Panavia' colleagues. The French decided independently to develop a similar demonstrator aircraft, the Dassault ACX (Rafale). In December 1983 the French, British, German and Italian airforces reached a 'European Staff Target' and in July 1984 the four national defence ministers agreed to a joint feasibility study for what was now designated the European Fighter Aircraft, EFA. At this point, rivalry between Dassault and BAe became open, with the French laying claim to 'design leadership' of the programme. The French government and air force also argued strongly for a lighter, less 'capable' aircraft (albeit one designed with exports in mind) than the others required, a tactic designed to support a case for basing development on the ACX.

Negotiations dragged on through the spring and summer of 1985. BAe and its British industrial partners began to accuse the government of failing to defend British industrial interests as effectively as the French appeared to be doing for their industry. Certainly, the British Minister of Defence, Michael Heseltine, was known to be strongly in favour of a five-nation programme. But it was evident that while the 'Panavia' group had learnt the lessons of collaboration, the vigorously independent Dassault had not and its leadership claims were alienating its European colleagues. There were also suspicions that the French were trying to delay the start of a new programme in order to protect sales of the Mirage 2000. On the other hand, the French believed that the established consortium would dominate the programme and felt excluded from the close relationship which had grown up between MBB, BAe and Aeritalia. In August, the British, Germans and Italians decided to go ahead without the French. A new organisation, Eurofighter was set up to run the programme, but this would draw upon the Panavia experience and share Panavia's Munich Headquarters. Programme costs were estimated at over £10 billion based on an initial order of over 650 aircraft. For their part, the French committed themselves to full development of the Rafale and sought to attract other

Europeans to a joint project. In the event, Spain went with the EFA, and to date the French have failed to internationalise the Rafale, and will face an estimated $5·6 billion bill for development with up to $42 billion for production alone. The final decision to go ahead with EFA was not taken until the spring of 1988, following considerable uncertainty over funding in Germany. The British government's insistence on tight contractual terms, with as many fixed price agreements as possible also caused friction between the governments as their industrial contributors were less confident of meeting cost targets than BAe.

EFA has assured the future of Britain's and Europe's combat aircraft design capability. However, the cost of building EFA is likely to put considerable pressure on the UK defence budget. The competition with Rafale will inevitably divide the European market and the US will be pressing equally hard to sell developments of the F16 and F18. With inter-generational costs set to carry on rising, there must be a possibility that EFA will be the last wholly European advanced fighter programme. Pressure to share the cost of future defence programmes with the Americans is likely to grow and in this context EFA may well be the foundation for Europe's stake in a later generation of trans-Atlantic programmes. For the moment, EFA will be the heart of BAe's military work when Tornado production ends, and maintains a line of development stretching back to the English Electric P1 and reflects BAe's standing as a world class aerospace company.

BAe has its own 'family' of civil products. At the bottom end of the market, it builds the ex-HSA 125 and ex-Scottish Aviation, ex-Handley Page Jetstream executive aircraft/feederliners. Over 700 125s have been sold, with exports worth over £1·5 billion and in 1988, BAe joined with Rockwell of the US to bid for a $1·5 billion USAF training system based on the 125. The BAe 146 is the most important of BAe's own designs. Although it has made considerable headway (total orders in 1987 stood at 107) towards a break even point of about 200 aircraft, the programme is still a drain on BAe's resources. The Advanced Turbo-Prop (ATP) was launched in 1984 at a cost of over £100 million as a 748 replacement. This has begun to sell moderately well in a highly competitive market sector, but it too has contributed to BAe's heavy losses on civil aircraft.

The core of BAe's civil effort is still the Airbus. Since 1978, the Airbus 'family' has been extended to include the 150-seat, 'fly-by-wire' A320 and the A330/340 'dual programme' – two aircraft being developed in tandem with shared structures and systems. In each case, BAe sought and received launch aid from the government. However, BAe had to fight hard to convince a reluctant government and an even more reluctant Treasury that the investment would be justified. In the event, the strength of BAe's commercial arguments, combined with the powerful momentum of a politically high profile collaborative venture were sufficiently convincing. Even so, the launch aid formula was less generous than BAe had expected. In the case of the A320, some of the government's money will have to be repaid from corporate profit and not just from a sales levy. BAe also received only 57 per cent of the £437 million it asked for, leaving BAe to find a total of £637 million for its share of development. However, with over 600 sales to date, the A320 is proving to be Europe's most successful civil airliner and should eventually provide a handsome return.

The decision to finance BAe's share of the A330/340 programme was, perhaps, even more marginal. The government had considerable reservations about the A340, a four engined long range aircraft designed to cream off some of the market monopolised by the Boeing 747. It was also in direct competition with MD11 and as such was likely to face a hard fought struggle in the market. Deteriorating relations with the Americans over 'unfair subsidised' competition in civil aerospace added an extra complication. In the event, US pressure to curb European practices misfired and helped to convince the British government that it should support the A330/340. This time, BAe received a conventional launch aid package, but at £450 million, it was again substantially less than the company had asked for. BAe's commitment to the Airbus programme now exceeds £630 million in development funding alone, and has taken BAe and Europe into the 'big league' of civil production, passing MDD to become the world's second most important airliner manufacturer, albeit still a long way behind Boeing. It represents the kind of volume and continuity of investment that the UK industry could only dream of in the 1950s and 1960s. BAe is part of a complex European design, development and production system and it would now seem inconceivable that BAe could ever leave Airbus Industrie. However, the programme as a whole is still some way from commercial viability. The A320 will provide positive returns, but the investment (mainly French and

German) in the earlier types has been effectively written off. The future costs of the A330/340 will bear heavily on BAe, increasingly sensitive to City judgements about its profitability and liabilities. BAe has become increasingly concerned that Airbus Industrie and its other European partners should be more conscious of economic realities and has pressed hard for reforms in the Airbus system to make it more commercially sensitive.

The burden of developing BAe's family of civil aircraft, including the company's share of Airbus launch costs, has put pressure on the firm's profitability. In 1983, BAe made an 'exceptional provision' of £100 million in its accounts to cover the development of the 146 and other civil projects. More seriously, in 1988, a weak US dollar accentuated BAe's difficulties. As a result, BAe charged all of its expected foreign exchange costs up to 1990 to its 1987 account, leading to a £159 million net loss. The company has also put pressure on its suppliers to bear some of the burden and has begun to subcontract work overseas in lower-cost or dollar-based economies. Despite these problems (and a hint that it might leave Airbus if matters did not improve), civil aerospace remains a key element in BAe's corporate strategy. The potential market for sales of large airliners into the next century has been estimated to be worth over $222 billion. According to Sir Raymond Lygo, BAe's chief executive,

> we decided to go into civil aircraft because it was and is an area of substantial growth. We were in it for the long term and we were looking to 1995 before making a real profit. Nothing has changed. If we lose our nerve half way through we would lose our shirt and trousers. Even twelve years after start-up we would lose our trousers.[49]

In September 1987, on taking over the BAe chair from Sir Austin Pearce, Professor Smith said that BAe's strategy would not be revolutionary. 'BAe is doing well and has done well. It's not a case of requiring enormous changes, but obviously in the next five to ten years there will be different pressures exerted upon this business than was the case in the previous ten years'.[50] The Rover deal will be a risk, though clearly a reasonably containable one especially given the value of any land released following rationalisation. Should it mature into a sound and effective partnership, generating the financial and industrial 'synergy' expected of it, the balance of BAe's activities will be irrevocably changed (see Table 18). Moreover, the acquisition of Rover is unlikely to be the end of BAe's expansion plans. The target companies are all likely to be in the high technology/engineering sectors, and could cover Europe and the US. Indeed, at the time of writing, BAe is discussing the possibility of forging links with the French electronics company, Thomson-CSF, and other European defence firms. The implication is that BAe may be looking to become a multinational enterprise, anticipating the opportunities offered by '1992' and the opening up of European defence and other public markets.

Table 18: The changing nature of British Aerospace

	Percentage of turnover					
	Civil aircraft	Military aircraft	Weapons/ electronics	Space	Construction	Cars
1987	18	46	32	4	–	–
1988[a]	13	23	17	2	6	39

Note:[a] estimated
Source: Sunday Times, 4 September 1988.

The thrust of BAe's corporate strategy, then, is to develop a technological, industrial and, above all, the financial base to survive what will be a very uncertain period for a dedicated aerospace manufacturer or even a diversified defence contractor. Market forecasts predict substantial returns from civil aircraft, but launch costs remain high and sales cannot be guaranteed. Defence agreements, such as the Saudi deals, suggest an equally profitable future. However, these can go sour; political uncertainty, changes in defence policy and budgetary restrictions can rapidly change the business outlook. The British government's search for 'value for money' in defence procurement has squeezed margins and forced defence companies like BAe to put more of their own money into R&D for defence programmes. Moreover, British defence spending could fall in real terms over the next decade with a depressing effect on domestic demand for defence equipment. BAe, along with the other established aerospace companies, can also expect to face growing competition from new entrants in South America and the Far East.

BAe's diversification strategy, although it brings its own problems, spreads commercial risk by introducing several overlapping cycles of investment and returns. The equalisation of highs and lows in demand has been the standard case for having both a military and a civil aircraft capability; BAe's strategy has been simply an extension of that logic. As Roland Smith put it, 'we have business like space and communications which are on the frontiers of technology, but it is no good being on those frontiers if you do not have mature operations on which you are making profits'.[51] At over £9 billion, BAe's turnover is approaching that of Boeing, is on a par with MDD and is £1 billion more than Lockheed. In European terms, BAe has become one of the largest manufacturing companies, and certainly far bigger than Aerospatiale or MBB (now part of the Daimler-AEG conglomerate). BAe-Rover now exports more than GEC, Ford(UK) and Rolls-Royce combined, or 5 per cent of the UK total. Turnover alone, of course, does not constitute industrial strength or power and BAe still has much to do to achieve an efficiency to match that of its American competitors (see Chapter 5). Equally, a diverse set of business activities can create conflicts of interest as investment plans and divisional crises compete for managerial attention and corporate resources. The privately-owned status of BAe also brings constraints; the concern for share price and return on capital are not always consistent with long term investment in R&D and long lead-time projects.

In some senses, the Rover deal and BAe's other acquisitions mark a return to the origins of aircraft manufacturing as an offshoot of the motor industry and general engineering. At BAe, the transformation from a fragmented and rather limited set of enterprises which began in the late 1950s, is nearly complete. Structural changes made in 1988 were designed to make all parts of the operation more cost and profit conscious and finally to break down old plant and company loyalties which for some employees extended back to the time before rationalisation, let alone the formation of BAe. The nature of aircraft manufacturing has undergone several radical changes in its history, but with the new technologies of electronics and systems integration, the industry is becoming a more diversified and complex business. The present BAe, and Rolls-Royce for that matter, are a very long way from the 'hero designer-firms' of the 1920s and 1930s with their 'penny packet' factories. The modern Rolls-Royce and BAe are not entirely reliant on public markets and state aid, but both are still 'government orientated' companies, and without their relationship with the state they are, perhaps, as vulnerable as the 'family' of the 1920s and 1930s. In this respect we should never forget that aerospace is not a 'normal' industry and never has been.

CHAPTER FIVE

EVALUATION

5.1 Retrospect

We have traced the evolution of an industry from its earliest days as a novelty for enthusiasts to one of the most important manufacturing sectors in the British economy. We have seen how the effect of war was twice to transform the scale of its operations and finally to elevate it to a place of permanent, though not unquestioned prominence in British industrial life. Military needs led to the creation of a recognisable aircraft *industry*, and in the immediate post-war years the industry was sustained by the state as a strategic asset, by 'drip-feeding' a select group of firms with military contracts. This protected the industry from the worst of the depression, but it also tended to discourage inventiveness and innovation. By the early 1930s, a few highly publicised achievements could not hide a general weakness in British aircraft design and, more important, production skills. The success of British aircraft during the Second World War was a tribute to a *cadre* of brilliant designers who were able to incorporate innovations made overseas and a world class engine industry. However, the pressures of rearmament and war revealed serious deficiencies in industrial structure and organisation. More understandably under the circumstances, only a limited commitment to advanced R&D was permitted which meant that the UK industry, with the exception of jet propulsion, would have to make up considerable ground after the war, albeit with considerable help from the state.

The post-war period was characterised by a losing battle against

the competitive might of the US aircraft industry. Although technically British aircraft were often as good, if not better, than their
American counterparts, the UK lacked the base market and the
scale of production to match US manufacturers. Both industry and
government were reluctant to address the issue of industrial fragmentation. The problems which stemmed from fragmentation –
undercapitalisation, duplication and dispersion of R&D effort –
were exacerbated by the volatility of government policy towards
both military and civil development. Although output rose during
the 1950s, the constraints of dependence on a limited national
market and the particular requirements of national customers, had
a deleterious effect on the industry's product range. In short, firms
were not big enough to take on the US without the support of
national customers, but the effect of parochial requirements all too
often constrained their ability to make more progress in international markets. The limitations of British development and
production were further underlined by the rising costs of development attendant on the increasing technological complexity of
aircraft. One result was that Britain successively opted out of manned bombers, long range missiles and long-haul civil airliners. The
Sandys' defence review finally precipitated a government-induced
process of industrial rationalisation. However, the regrouping of
1959–61 was still only a partial solution to the problems facing the
UK industry. The establishment of four main groups was not
accompanied by any long term or consistent strategy for the
industry. The shift to international collaboration during the 1960s,
however flawed in practice, was the only realistic long term option
for British aerospace.

The early 1970s were a crucial watershed. The Rolls collapse
shook the whole industry to the core and the Concorde, for all its
technical brilliance, served to emphasise the fundamental commercial inadequacy of post-war British civil aerospace. Although the
Tornado, Hawk and Harrier promised a brighter future, two generations of core military projects had also been lost. If aerospace had
been 'just another' manufacturing sector, this may well have been
the point at which it would have shrunk to more modest proportions, along with other manufacturing sectors such as the British-
owned car industry and shipbuilding. But aerospace was still perceived as an irreplaceable national asset making a vital, if often
unquantifiable, contribution to national security and the economy

at large. Equally important, international links were in place which would hopefully reduce the cost of aerospace and which were difficult politically to abandon. Internationalisation has been the salvation of the aircraft industry. Since the 1960s, UK aerospace development has been increasingly centred on a network of collaborative programmes, and even many of those defined as 'national' products have a substantial overseas input. Above all, joint ventures have provided a stable core of business for both Rolls and BAe and have led to a scale of operation which has taken the British industry closer to American levels.

From the perspective of the late 1980s, the prospects for the British aerospace industry were very healthy. Total orders for 1988 stood at over £20 billion. Aerospace companies employed some 200,000 people (including 35,000 in the equipment sector), producing £9 billion in total turnover. In 1987, the industry exported over 60 per cent of turnover, with a record trade balance of £2·4 billion. UK companies were well established on a wide range of civil and military projects. Globally, the market for aircraft, engines and guided weapons is expanding. Although traditional defence markets, especially in the UK itself, will be tighter as defence budgets decline and tougher contracting policies bite, the UK is now the third placed arms exporter, with aerospace products well to the fore. The world market for civil aircraft and engines is estimated to be worth $400 billion over the next twentyyears. British firms, either independently or in collaboration, are well placed to take a substantial share of these expanding markets.

5.2 Evaluation

(i) Technical status

In technical terms, the international position of the British aircraft industry has never been higher. This is clearly seen in the aero-engine sector, where Rolls-Royce stands with GE and P&W as one of only three wholly capable engine companies in the western world. Development of the RB211 was, of course, nearly fatal, but the main source of failure was managerial rather than technical deficiency. Since then, the RB211 family has achieved an outstanding record for efficiency and reliability and will provide the core of the company's civil activities well into the next century. Rolls, of course, has been in the forefront of jet engine technology since the Second World War and its only major technical problem was in developing large turbo-prop engines – one shared by most of its contemporaries. The firm was relatively late into supersonic military engines, but this was largely due to delays in developing suitable airframes. However, it did avoid a 'lost generation' thanks to the use of Spey engines in the UK's Phantom purchase. In subsequent European military programmes, Rolls has consistently led development – in practice if not formally. Rolls still has a lead in VSTOL engines and is co-operating as an equal partner with P&W on the development of more advanced designs. The French firm of Snecma has made tremendous progress, especially in civil engines thanks to collaboration with GE, but has not yet shown a capability independently to design and develop its own large engines. MTU, the German engine company, is still only a junior partner in collaborative programmes. Japan, potentially a major competitor, also has several important technical deficiencies.

The status of the airframe sector is more complicated and far more tied into international programmes. Since the war, the British airframe industry has had several opportunities to exploit technical leads. The Comet and Viscount were particularly important examples. Indeed, at a technical level, few of the industry's postwar programmes have been outright failures. The Canberra, Hunter, Lightning and the V bombers were technically on a par with their contemporaries. Moreover, it should be noted that several of the American 'century series' of supersonic fighters were woefully inadequate; the B58 supersonic bomber was dangerous to fly and the F111 proved far less capable than promised. The British problem has been either projects developed too late to match the competition, or with specifications which were too narrowly drawn to achieve export success. There have also been significant discontinuities in the pattern of development due to changes in government policy. Of the contemporary range of British/international projects, Tornado is at least as good as, if not better than its American equivalents, and EFA promises as much. In both cases, although the UK has shared development responsibilities with German and Italian firms, again the technical lead in critical areas, such as systems integration, has tended to come from the UK. On the other hand, in the area of VTOL, BAe has had to take second place to the US, a position primarily dictated by financial exigencies. Concorde remains a technically unique aeroplane and through working in the Airbus programme, the UK shares a technological lead in medium-haul airliners. BAe also retains a fully independent civil design and development capability.

Finally, since the Second World War, the British equipment industry has emerged as a powerful international competitor with the most comprehensive range of capabilities outside the US, and with a turnover equal to that of France and Germany combined. With some justice, the equipment industry has often felt that its interests have been sacrificed to those of the airframe and engine sectors, especially in collaborative programmes. Nevertheless, in many areas such as ejection seats, landing gear and head-up displays, British companies have world class products and are included in several important foreign-built aircraft. However, there is some concern, in Europe as well as the UK, that a comparative technological weakness in materials and electronic components may constitute a danger for the future.

In Europe, the UK industry has rarely fallen behind French or German standards, and in many respects led both. Until very recently, the French aircraft industry lacked the comprehensive capability of the British and there are still gaps in the French engine and equipment sectors. The Germans too have acquired considerable design and technical strength, but their presence in the postwar industry has been based on collaboration with their neighbours which, for the most advanced military projects, has come to mean with the UK. They also have a record of over-ambitious and ill-considered projects, most notably the VFW614 feeder liner. There will be increasing competition from newer aerospace centres, but few will able to approach the overall technical competence of the UK without huge financial commitments. The most formidable challenger is likely to be Japan, with a clearly expressed ambition and with the established technical base to become a major power in world aerospace. Although BAe and Rolls may not be directly threatened, at least for the remainder of the century, they may have to concede to the Japanese increasingly large shares of collaborative programmes. The British equipment industry, however, has a more immediate cause for concern, with Japanese electronics firms already targeting aerospace markets.

The only underdeveloped sector in British aerospace is space technology. In many respects, the British space programme has been a sad case of neglect and missed opportunities. Unlike the French, the UK withdrew from long range missiles and the British government has rarely been enthusiastic about taking on the US in satellite launchers. The ELDO project fell apart in the late 1960s when the British pulled out for economic reasons. Although the British government later helped to establish the European Space Agency (ESA), British industry has concentrated, with considerable success, on satellite technology, leaving France and Germany to develop the highly successful Ariane launcher (although British firms do have a number of important subcontracts). However, space development world-wide is largely dominated by state funded activity and British governments have been consistently reluctant to invest as heavily in space research as their European neighbours. The net result is that Britain's budget for space has fallen well behind that of Italy and considerably below that of Germany and France, the leading European space nations (see Table 19).

Table 19: Expenditure on civil space, 1986

	$ million	% of GDP
US	7,200	0.17
France	934	0.20
Japan	804	0.04
Germany	545	0.06
Italy	460	0.15
India	183	0.10
UK	174	0.03
Sweden	53	0.04

Source: HoL Paper 41-1 (1987-7).

In 1985, a British National Space Centre was set up to co-ordinate British space policy and to formulate a national space plan. However, the Conservative government not only proved unwilling to extend Britain's publicly financed space programme, but it also alienated its European partners by dismissing the current ESA programme as a grandiose waste of money. Domestic initiatives, such as the BAe/Rolls-Royce Hotol project – a revolutionary satellite launch system – have also failed to attract more than a modest degree of government support. The government's view is that space activities must be 'market-led', with private industry carrying the burden of development costs. It has not accepted the argument, as the French, Germans and Japanese have, that space represents a potentially new dimension of technological and industrial activity which should not be left to the US and Soviet Union. The ESA programme did have several questionable aspects, but the debate over space technology in the UK brought into sharp focus questions about the contribution aerospace makes to the wider economy and the role of the state in supporting aerospace development.

(ii) Commercial and economic performance

If the technical dimension of the British aerospace industry has, on balance, rarely given cause for concern since 1945, the commercial and economic aspects of the industry clearly have. An objective commercial and economic evaluation is made difficult from the outset by aerospace's status as a 'strategic' industry – an area generally perceived as vital for the attainment of security goals or broader national purposes. The notion of a 'strategic industry' is itself vague and subjective. On the one hand, it can refer to an element of the 'defence industrial base' – another ill-defined term – which is seen as being essential in the provision of equipment for the Services where reliance on foreign suppliers could entail a dangerous degree of dependence. Even if cost precludes a comprehensive capacity, it may still be felt desirable that a substantial part of national procurement comes from indigenous sources – or at least from a source that has a strong national presence.[1]

Aerospace, it is often asserted, is 'strategic' in a broader sense – as an industry particularly able to stimulate technological activity which has a positive and widespread impact on the economy at large. Even if aerospace tends to exploit innovations in other areas rather than to create new technology and processes, because its standards are so rigorous and demanding it 'drives' innovation in several sectors such as electronics and materials. Equally, the complexity of aerospace programmes has generated managerial and systems-integrating skills of a very high order. The aerospace industry is also a high value-added, export-orientated sector of manufacturing where high entry costs bestow a competitive advantage on those few nations which have the capability. Such arguments have been advanced for maintaining aerospace, not only as a British national asset, but as part of a wider European capability. For example, in 1975 the EC Commission asserted that '[aerospace] is one of the chief representatives of a type of employment – highly skilled, commanding sophisticated technologies and a high level of investment – toward which the Community must necessarily move in the future as the industrialisation of the Third World proceeds and a wider division of labour unfolds'.[2]

In this context, commercial return, especially in 'civil' aerospace, is an important, but not necessarily the decisive criterion for investing in aerospace. 'Externalities', such as the balance of payments effect, tend therefore to predominate in the rationale for government support for the aerospace sector. The industry, especially the current management of BAe and Rolls-Royce, does stress the importance of 'bottom line' performance in determining the success or failure of their business. As Sir Arnold Hall, one of the most hard-nosed of the industry's leaders in the 1960s and 1970s put it, 'there's only one eventual way of judging the viability of an aeroplane, just as on any other commercial product, and that is, "Does the profit and loss account look right?" I found it very difficult myself, to take a view that aeroplanes were any different from most other things in this respect.'[3]

The industry has certainly sought to improve its comparative efficiency. Although the increase in scale brought by collaboration has helped to redress the advantages of long production runs in the US, studies by BAe analysts in the early 1980s revealed that the British aircraft industry was still less productive than the Americans. The key finding was that 'learning' in the US went on much longer than in the UK. This was attributed to several factors, including a more systematic approach to cost control and production management, and the small but cumulative gains associated with the greater use of powered hand tools. The greater flexibility of labour ('hire and fire') was also seen as important over the long term. Although European practice emphasising greater stability of labour (due to more stringent conditions attached to redundancy) increased skill levels and therefore manufacturing quality, it did affect overheads. It should be emphasised that many of these problems were characteristic of European practice and not confined to the UK. However, it was accepted that the French industry could be up to one and a half times more productive than the British, although the French advantage was balanced by higher wage costs.[4] The aerospace industry has not been unique in this respect – until very recently, factories in the British car industry using the same machinery performed significantly worse than their counterparts in Europe.

However, the extent of the problem as revealed by a simple

turnover per head calculation can be misleading. The degree of subcontracting in US and continental European industry, the complication of collaborative transactions and the absence of uniform accounting procedures tends to underestimate British productivity (see Table 20). If the productivity of BAe and Rolls was so poor, they could hardly have competed on price in international markets and, at the same time, achieved a reasonable profit. Compared to Aerospatiale, MBB and recently even Dassault, the two British firms have in recent years consistently shown a profit and have expanded their share of export markets. Similarly, in collaborative programmes, BAe has been able to match or, in most cases, better, the man-hour calculations made by its partners which are used as the basis for estimating the value of various tasks. Nevertheless, both BAe and Rolls have committed themselves to increase productivity – an improvement which is evident in Table 20.

Table 20: Productivity in the world aerospace industry
(turnover/1,000s of ECUs per employee)

	1986	1980	% change
Boeing	140	64	115
MDD	130	57	128
Lockheed	110	43	156
Rockwell	140	50	140
General Dynamics	100[a]	41	143
P&W	140[a]	NA	NA
GE	200[a]	61	227
Aerospatiale	110	65	84
Dassault	141	110	37
Snecma	110	52	111
MBB	70	50	60
MTU	80	42	90
BAe	60	30	100
Rolls-Royce	60	31	94

Note: [a] 1985 figures.
Source: EC Commission.

In this respect, the current reorganisation of BAe into profit centres is instructive. Admittedly, the nature of BAe has recently changed from (or more accurately, perhaps, reverted to) being just an aircraft manufacturing company into a very large industrial conglomerate. However, the aim is finally to break down the distractions of old company and even factory loyalties and instil a commitment to sectoral efficiency and profitability. The pre-nationalised firms were moving in this direction and were well able, for example, to undertake fixed price contracts. It is evident that BAe will be quite ruthless in seeking even higher standards of productivity. Part of their strategy is to put pressure on their own suppliers to cut prices and to involve them in a shared commitment to 'drive cost' out of programmes. Aircraft are increasingly 'designed for production' and new programmes, such as the EFA, will have the benefit of new technology and flexible manufacturing techniques which, compared with the Tornado, should lead to a substantial reduction in manpower requirements. By early 1989, BAe were able to claim that they were matching US efficiency standards.

However, the extent to which the benefits of new manufacturing techniques can be fully realised is constrained by the complexity and individuality of aircraft construction, and by the legacy of older programmes. The 146, for instance, can be retrospectively 'redesigned for production', but only in part and where the cost of the change can be justified by long term savings. BAe has also begun to look to cheaper overseas manufacturers to subcontract assembly work. However, improving productivity is as much an attitudinal change as a set of substantive organisational reforms. As Sir Austin Pearce noted back in 1985, as a non-'aerospace man' he found the history of the business a fascinating tribute to the 'dictators' who had founded it. Technical excellence was their primary goal: 'very low on their priority list was the question of finance'. The development of people also took a low priority and their commitment to plant and a project as a physical entity was 'of greater importance than its cost, marketability and profitability'.[5]

The evaluation of aerospace's effect on the economy involves much broader questions than the viability of individual projects and the the efficiency of British firms. At frequent intervals over the last twenty years, expenditure on aerospace and its effects on the industrial economy have attracted numerous critics.[6] Admittedly, the attack is more often directed at the consequences of over-commitment to defence-related R&D of which aerospace has taken a major share, rather than at the resources devoted to aerospace *per se*. However, the drift of their arguments is clear: Britain has spent too much on aerospace for the return it has obtained. The the spin-off effect cannot be calculated and has been grossly over-estimated.

Other industries could have achieved equally good export performance with similar levels of assistance. It has deprived other high
technology and manufacturing sectors of scarce engineers and
technicians. In short, public funds could have been better spent on
other areas generating more employment and greater long term
technological benefits.

Keith Hartley has been particularly sceptical of the value and
utility of a state-supported UK aircraft industry – even in a
European context. He has consistently advocated a free market
solution to the provision of civil and military aircraft for the British
military and airlines. In a 1974 paper, he noted that as past policy
has failed to achieve satisfactory results, it would be better to cut the
ties between the state and the industry, and to allow the latter to find
its own salvation. This would mean an end to launch aid and a fully
open market for military procurement. Industry would inevitably
face a much reduced status and would be forced to seek commercially based partnerships with European or American companies.
More recently he has concluded that, as the American competitive
advantage in military aircraft production remains so great,
European governments should, perhaps, buy the majority of their
aircraft from the US with commensurate budgetary gains.[7]

This line of argument plainly has some strength, and the trend
towards more competitive procurement policies throughout
Europe is to be welcomed. However, Hartley and other critics tend
to underestimate the potential political effects of dependence in key
areas of high technology such as aerospace. Moreover, the political
dimension notwithstanding, the life cycle costs of overseas purchases and lost revenue from export sales would represent a considerable hidden cost should the UK (or the European) industry
substantially decline. The absence of effective competition for US
industry could also lead in time to higher unit prices. In the civil
sector, Boeing already profits considerably from its monopoly of
long haul wide-bodied aircraft; but where the Airbus has competed
with Boeing and MDD, prices have been highly competitive. To
suggest that new entrants would be attracted by the higher margins
and that thus price competition would return, underestimates the
qualitative problems of acquiring a capacity to develop the more
complex aircraft and engines and the growth of implicit specialisation in the US aircraft industry.

However, the weight of evidence suggests that British commitments to defence R&D, of which aerospace has been a major element, has had some deleterious effects on economic performance. But exact cause and effect has proved more difficult to pin down. It is probably the case that the *way* in which British defence R&D has been conducted is at least as important as the concentration of resources. The pervasive effects of secrecy and 'in-house' research activity have undoubtedly reduced the value of money spent in the defence sector to the economy at large. Undoubtedly, France and the US have seemed to make better use of their defence/aerospace R&D to stimulate wider industrial use of new technology. Over the last few years, the British government has become sufficiently concerned to encourage a more open dissemination of defence technology and to use the procurement process to sharpen the competitive and commercial instincts of defence orientated companies such as those which predominate in the aerospace sector.

The shortage of scientists and engineers in Britain was (and still is) a fundamental issue of educational provision. Although aerospace has attracted a large proportion of the total, the real problem has been the absolute number of engineers and scientists available to industry. Since the war, the aircraft industry has had a solid record on apprentice training – in the 1960s, they comprised 11·2 per cent of the industry's skilled workforce, and in 1985, BAe alone had 3,100 trainees of all grades, just over 4 per cent of its total number of employees. One might also add that a number of people may have been motivated to become engineers by the existence of an aircraft industry. Finally, and perhaps more worrying, the manufacturing sector generally has been losing a battle for qualified engineers, scientists and computer specialists to the higher paid service sectors. Indeed, BAe has had to buy into Systems Designers Ltd, one of Britain's major software and systems houses, to ensure its access to this expertise. In the longer term, BAe hopes that its link with Rover will create 'synergistic' effects in both product and process technology through the cross-fertilisation of aerospace and auto engineers.

However, the aerospace industry has undoubtedly emerged as a powerful force in Britain's overseas trade. Aerospace's export performance over the last decade has been very strong indeed. Overall, the aerospace industry is responsible for nearly 3 per cent of all UK manufactured goods and just under 8 per cent of manufactured exports. In the 1960s, the UK share of world aerospace markets was 10 per cent, by the mid 1970s, 14 per cent, and in the 1980s, nearly 17 per cent. The industry has had a positive balance of trade – despite the fact that the major domestic airline has tended to buy American airframes. It has also maintained a higher share of world aerospace markets than the average market shares for British manufacturing generally (see Figure 2). Moreover, even allowing for collaborative

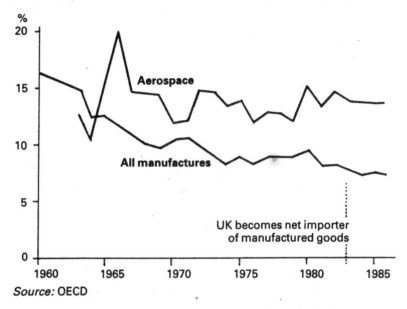

Figure 2 UK industry and aerospace share of world trade

transactions, with most of its components and subsystems 'bought in' from UK sources, the industry has less difficulty in maintaining a 'British' identity than a motor industry dominated by multinational operation and 'intra-company' imports.[8] Turnover has increased from £2·5 billion to £9 billion, a 50 per cent increase in real terms. Exports have risen from £1 billion to £5·6 billion – two and a half times in real terms. According to the SBAC, only oil and chemicals (especially pharmaceuticals, where the industry surplus in 1986 was £2·5 billion, £850 million from drugs) have produced a consistently positive balance of trade and aerospace has never had a negative balance in the ten years since 1977 (see Figure 3).[9] Mechanical engineering has seen a steady erosion of its international position,

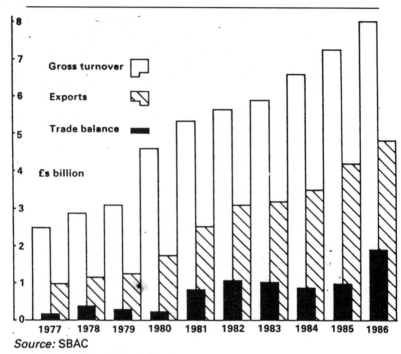

Source: SBAC

Figure 3 Britain's aerospace industry performance, 1977–86

and in the 1950s the textile industry was second only to US, but the overall trade balance is now in deficit. In the electronics sector, with the exception of defence and avionics, the UK 1986 balance of trade was £2 billion in the red.

The question of ownership is also significant. Rolls- Royce, BAe and most of the major equipment firms are British owned. Although it is short sighted to ignore the benefits of inward investment and adhere to nationalist positions heedless of cost, UK control does ensure retention of design, innovation and commercial expertise. Increase in output is also based on solid productive return and not just on currency transactions within multinationals taking advantage of fluctuations in exchange rates.[10] In the final analysis, the British aerospace industry is now a major manufacturing sector and one of the few in the UK that is of world class with a chance of maintaining a competitive place in international markets; to pursue policies which might threaten that position would be folly. The nature of the international industry is such that British interests can only be served by operating on the basis of a strong national capability which can compete, but which can also collaborate from a position of technological and commercial strength. The United States has been increasingly concerned to protect its national aerospace capability, for as in the UK, it is one of the United States' few trade surplus industries. France has traditionally promoted its aerospace industry and both Germany and Japan have consistently sought to build a strong national industry. The logic of argument by emulation can be highly dubious, but in this respect, the example of every major industrialised state looking to aerospace as one of its industrial and technological investments for the next century is hard to gainsay. In all of these cases, directly or indirectly, the state plays a significant role in encouraging these developments. The British aerospace industry obviously bears a clear responsibility for shaping its own destiny; rationalisation and increased productivity are a necessary feature of future planning but aircraft development and production is now, as it always has been, a partnership of state and industry.

(iii) State and industry

The industry's relationship with the state has been close and vital to its long term survival. This, above all other factors, explains its continuing position in the economy. It is equally evident that neither side has always been happy with the relationship. The industry, despite the support which it has had from the state, has often faced considerable uncertainty as a result of oscillations in government policy. As Sir Arnold Hall of Hawker Siddeley observed, 'one of the difficulties which we have got to face is that moods change because ministers change, but projects do not change'. This, he continued, was perhaps the inevitable price for democracy, but it was 'inevitably disruptive' and hardly conducive to 'good engineering'.[11] Sir Stanley Hooker's observations about collaboration in the 1960s echoed those of Sir Arnold: 'Over a period of years we were in, we were out, we were in, we were out. It was more like a boat race than a policy to follow.'[12] British industrialists have frequently cast envious eyes at the apparent consistency of French aerospace policy, the explicit commitment of West German governments to building an aircraft industry as a national asset and, more recently, Miti's 'vision' which will shape Japanese aerospace policy into the next century. The feeling that greener grass exists on the other side of the Channel may be responding to a chimera; certainly the success of French 'planning' for aerospace can be much over-rated. Nevertheless, there has been a greater degree of continuity in other European national programmes and the SBAC, for example, has called for a more 'strategic' approach to the aerospace sector.[13] In practice, and perhaps more important than any 'plan for aerospace', the aerospace sector has achieved greater stability through the existence of mature collaborative programmes which have proved less vulnerable to Treasury-induced cuts. Nevertheless, British industrialists have bemoaned the absence of a consistent, long term view about aerospace.

On the other hand, politicians can feel helpless in the face of complex technology and the legacy of long term commitments. The Concorde inevitably provides the classic example. Its origins illustrate the influence of a well established 'technological lobby' in Whitehall pushing for advances in the aircraft industry even when, as in this instance, the industry was itself initially lukewarm about the prospect of an SST. Then, of course, successive governments were 'locked-in' by the Treaty and by the momentum of events. As Crossman put it, the Labour government had 'to go on with that confounded 'plane'. He also noted how the Cabinet had solemnly debated the Black Knight rocket with no real knowledge of its technical aspects. 'How can Cabinet', he recalled, 'come to a sensible decision when none of us have the vaguest idea what these things really are?' Finally, Crossman quotes Roy Jenkins, Chancellor of the Exchequer when the decision was made to go ahead with the MRCA/Tornado. Jenkins is reputed to have said: 'I suppose we have to have it, but I suspect that when it comes to action it won't be for ten years and by then our successors will be as sceptical and as mystified as to how we made our decision this morning as we were about the TSR2.'[14]

In some respects, the current government has provided a source of stability. Although yet to achieve the longevity of the Conservative administrations of 1951–64, the Thatcher government has generally retained a higher degree of internal consistency of policy than any post-war British government. This has not always been to the taste of manufacturing industry, especially when fiscal policy has led to an over-valued pound and increased pressure on export margins. Nevertheless, the commitment to a strong defence has been of benefit to the aerospace sector and certainly more attractive than the uncertainties of Opposition policies. The government has also sought to place more responsibility for cost control on industry itself. The privatisation process, which is set to be completed when Shorts is sold sometime during 1989, has sharpened the industry's commercial and financial senses. Although there must be some danger that privatisation has opened up an essentially long term industry to the problems of 'short termism' in respect of financial assessment and an increased sensitivity to the fluctuation in share values, on balance it has proved to be a change for the better. Sir Raymond Lygo, for example, believes that the 'act of privatisation has released enormous energies – without it [the expansion of BAe] would not have been possible'.[15] Privatisation notwithstanding, the government has continued to support a wide range of civil and military programmes, including three new Airbus types and EFA. In this respect, the aerospace industry remains something of a special case even for a 'free market' government.

However, the key issue remains the degree to which the state remains committed to long term support for aerospace technology and the research base on which it stands. In 1988–89, in launch aid and support for R&D, aerospace received £219 million out of the DTI's £500 million programme of support for science and technology. However, the government appears to be responding to criticisms of over-spending on defence R&D and will be seeking to apply tighter 'value for money' criteria in its evaluation of research and development proposals generally.[16] The government has been equally concerned to limit, in absolute terms, the money it is prepared to provide for advanced R&D and basic science. It is determined, perhaps obsessively so, to force private industry to back 'commercially' orientated research where other governments have recognised the importance of backing long term investment in high risk technology. The advent of the Single European Market and possible changes in the structure of the European arms industry and national procurement practices could also imply significant adjustments in the relationship between the British aerospace industry and the British government. These developments could diminish the direct links between state and the industry and further dilute the national character of aerospace. However, such are the costs of aerospace technolgy, some form of public support will still be required for the foreseeable future.

In this respect, the aerospace industry has suffered a major setback in its hopes to match international levels of funding in space activities. The House of Lords' report on British space policy accepted that Britain's standing as a technological power would not 'disappear' if it only had a small space programme, but the important thing was to have a meaningful presence in the area. Space was not just

> another technological endeavour calling for funds, in competition with information technology, medicine, nuclear power and the like. Space is a new domain. Man has fought for control of the land, the sea and the air, and he is now tackling the challenge of space. The United Kingdom has to accept this challenge, as the other major industrial countries are doing. The reasons are political, cultural, military, economic, commercial and scientific; these arguments stand together the major technological powers are making up their teams for the race. The United Kingdom has the chance to join in. Unless we do so now, we shall never be in the running.[17]

As the British aerospace industry looks forward to the technological challenge of the next century, it may have to accept that the state will be less willing to provide support for large scale, speculative development. Given that its competitors do have the backing of their governments, there is a clear danger that a significant part of the industry may be under some threat of a long term erosion of its technical standing.

In 1965, the Plowden report stated that there was 'no predestined place for an aircraft industry in Britain'; but if the industry recognised 'some overwhelming economic realities' and embraced a European solution, it could look forward to a future where an industry, 'smaller but stronger', could make a 'valuable contribution not only to the British but to the European economy'. These predictions, perhaps rather more by accident than by design, have been realised. Over the two decades since Plowden, the British aerospace industry has emerged a stronger and more powerful entity. No industry is 'irreplaceable', but the loss of the British aircraft industry, or a significant reduction in its present scale, would surely leave a substantial hole in the UK economy.

NOTES

Note to Introduction
1 *Report of the Committee of Inquiry into the Aircraft Industry*, London, 1971, cmnd. 2538, para. 469

Notes to Chapter One
1 C. H. Gibbs-Smith, *Aviation, a History*, London, 1970, p. 139.
2 *ibid.*, p. 163.
3 I. Lloyd, *Rolls-Royce: the Years of Endeavour*, London, 1978, p. 120.
4 J. D. Scott, *Vickers*, London, 1962, p. 120.
5 Lloyd, *Rolls-Royce: the Years*, p. 132.
6 P. Fearon, 'The formative years of the British aircraft industry', *Business History Review*, No. 4, 1969, pp. 490–3.
7 Lloyd, *Rolls-Royce: the Years*, p. 131 and C. M. Sharp, *De Havilland*, Shrewsbury, 1982, p. 34.
8 Sharp, *De Havilland*, pp. 90–156.
9 P. Fearon, 'Aircraft manufacturing', in N. K. Buxton and D. H. Aldcroft, *British Industry between the Wars*, London, 1979, p. 222.
10 *ibid.*, pp. 222–8.
11 M. Postan, D. Hay and J. D. Scott, *Design and Development of Weapons*, London, 1964, pp. 97–100.
12 B. Gunston, *By Jupiter: the life of Sir Roy Fedden*, London, 1978.
13 Scott, *Vickers*, p. 200.
14 See the exchange of opinions between Fearon and Robertson in the *Economic History Review*, November 1975.
15 It should be noted that by the 1930s, the Ministry system was also more flexible.
16 C. Barnett, *The Audit of War*, London, 1986, p. 128
17 D. Hickey, 'The government and civil aircraft production', University of London Ph.D. dissertation, 1988, pp. 45–52.
18 Sharp, *De Havilland*, pp. 157–63. For Airspeed, see Neville Shute, *Slide Rule*, London, 1968.
19 Hickey, 'Government and aircraft production', pp. 220–1.
20 Barnett, *Audit of War*, p. 128.
21 Fearon, 'Aircraft manufacturing', pp. 217–18.
22 J. Wood, *Wheels of Misfortune*, London, 1988, p. 73; Gunston, *By Jupiter*, p. 82
23 R. J. Overy, *The Air War*, London, 1980, p. 163.
24 Lloyd, *Rolls-Royce: the Years*, pp. 179–85.
25 M. Smith, British Air Strategy between the Wars, Oxford, 1984, p. 320.
26 Barnett, *Audit of War*, p. 140; Scott, *Vickers*, p. 211; Gunston, *By Jupiter*, p. 90.
28 Postan *et al.*, *Design and Development*, p. 67.
29 *ibid.*, pp. 105–7; I. Lloyd, Rolls-Royce: the Merlin at War, London, 1978, pp. 66 and 76.
30 Postan *et al.*, *Design and Development*, pp. 27–30; Gunston, *By Jupiter*, chapters 9–10.
31 Barnett, *Audit of War*, p. 131.
32 Postan *et al.*, *Design and Development*, pp. 16–24

33 Barnett, *Audit of War*, p. 148. See also *Aeronautical Journal*, January 1966, p. 216.
34 Lloyd, *Rolls-Royce: the Years*, pp. 165–9; Sir Stanley Hooker, *Not Much of an Engineer*, Shrewsbury, 1984, p. 27; Scott, *Vickers*, p. 211.
35 M. Postan, *War Production*, London, 1952, p. 391, cited in Barnett, *Audit of War*, p. 154.
36 Lloyd, *Rolls-Royce: the Merlin*, pp. 198–9; Hooker, *An Engineer*, p. 59; Gunston, *By Jupiter*, p. 121.
37 Lloyd, *Rolls-Royce: the Merlin*, pp. 28–31.
38 Hickey, 'Government and aircraft production', p. 227.
39 For the impact of the jet and other technical developments, see R. Millar and D. Sawyers, *The Technical Development of Modern Aviation*, London, 1968.
40 Postan *et al.*, *Design and Development*, pp. 182–7; P. Pagnamenta and R. J. Overy, *All Our Working Lives*, London, 1984, p. 60.
41 J. Golley, *Whittle*, Shrewsbury, 1987, chapter 5.
42 *ibid.*, pp. 92–100; Postan *et al.*, *Design and Development*, pp. 181–6.
43 Golley, *Whittle, chapter 12; Postan et al.* Design and Development, pp. 190–1.
44 Postan *et al.*, Design and Development, p. 194.
45 Golley, *Whittle*, pp. 137–8.
46 Postan *et al.*, *Design and Development*, pp. 204–6.
47 Sharp, *De Havilland*, pp. 200–5; Postan *et al.*, *Design and Development*, p. 203.
48 Golley, *Whittle*, pp. 178–84; Lloyd, Rolls-Royce: the Merlin, pp. 136–8.
49 Postan *et al.*, *Design and Development, p. 212.*
50 *Golley, Whittle, pp. 189–91, 201–5.*
51 Hooker, *An Engineer*, pp. 73–4.
52 Postan *et al.*, *Design and Development*, pp. 224–5.
53 *ibid.*, pp. 228–233,
54 Golley, *Whittle*, pp. 209–10, 229–30.
55 Details of the MAP's deliberations can be found in PRO AVIA, 15/1915. 9a, 11a, 16a, 25a, 4a, 64a, 92a; PRO AVIA 15/1916 RC(44)16 of September 1943 to March 1944.
56 Barnett, *Audit of War*, p. 127.
57 War Cabinet Minutes, PRO, WM35(43);38(43); PRO AVIA, 15/1912 2b, 15/1912, 28 dc and 37a.
58 Hickey, 'Government and aircraft production', p. 288.
59 Barnett, *Audit of War*, p. 146.
60 *ibid.*
61 Overy, *Air War*, pp. 160, 165 and 176.

Notes to Chapter Two

1 C. H. Barnes, *Handley Page Aircraft since 1907*, London, 1976, pp. 44–6.
2 A. Robertson, Lion Rampant and Winged, private publication, 1986.
3 S. Ransom and R. Fairclough, *English Electric*, London, 1987, p. 58.
4 Hooker, *An Engineer*, pp. 100–22.
5 Rolls Royce Companies Report, p. 15.
6 Sharp, *De Havilland*, chapter 36.
7 Hooker, *An Engineer*, pp. 125, 135–43.
8 Edwards, Sir George, 'U.K. Aerospace – a personal view', *Aeronautical Journal*, November 1972, pp. 633–40.
9 House of Commons Debates, 27 July 1948.
10 A. Reed, *Britain's Aircraft Industry*, London, 1973, p. 29.
11 Hickey, 'Government and aircraft production', pp. 419–22.
12 *ibid.*, pp. 350–1.
13 Pagnamenta and Overy, *Working Lives*, p. 62.

14 Hickey, 'Government and aircraft production', pp. 380–91.
15 K. Hayward, *Government and British Civil Aerospace*, Manchester, 1983, pp. 16–18.
16 Pagnamenta and Overy, *Working Lives*, p. 63.
17 Cited in Hayward, *Government and Aerospace*, p. 23
18 *ibid.*, pp. 18–27.
19 *The Supply of Military Aircraft*, cmnd. 9388, 1955; House of Commons' Select Committee on Estimates, *The Supply of Military Aircraft*, 1956–7, HC34, paras. 20 and 23.
20 *ibid.*
21 A. Brooke, *The V Bombers*, London, 1982.
22 D. Wood, *Project Cancelled*, London, 1975, p. 32.
23 cmnd. 9388.
24 Pagnamenta and Overy, *Working Lives*, p. 66.
25 K. Hartley, 'Development timescales for British and American aircraft', *Scottish Journal of Political Economy*, June 1972; HC34, para. 8.
26 *Report of the Committee of Inquiry into the Aircraft Industry*, London, 1971, cmnd. 2538 (hereafter referred to as Plowden), paras. 47–58; C. Gardner, *The British Aircraft Corporation*, London, 1981, p. 16; M. C. S. Dixson, 'Parliament and the aircraft industry', University of Oxford Ph.D. dissertation, 1972, p. 30.
27 Plowden, paras. 66–72 and 100–3; HC34, paras. 62–4.
28 HC34, para. 109.
29 *Flight*, 9 November 1956.
30 HC34, para. 115; Dixson, 'Parliament and the aircraft industry', pp. 208–9.
31 Gardner, *British Aircraft Corporation*, p. 19.
32 House of Commons Debates, written answers, 25 March 1957.
33 I am very grateful to Stephen Twigge for the use of his material on the post-1945 British guided weapons programme.
34 *Times*, 3 December 1957; *Economist*, 31 August 1957.
35 See Hayward, *Government and Aerospace*, pp. 30–1
36 Dixson, 'Parliament and the aircraft industry', pp. 209–11.
37 Gardner, *British Aircraft Corporation, p. 25.
38 ibid.*
39 Hayward, *Government and Aerospace*, pp. 38–9.
40 Gardner, *British Aircraft Corporation*, pp. 33–8.
41 *Flight*, 15 January 1960.
42 Gardner, *British Aircraft Corporation*, pp. 35–83.
43 Committee of Public Accounts, 1966–67, HC647, paras. 66–76.
44 *Flight*, 17 February 1961; 6 January 1961; 25 July 1963.
45 House of Commons Debates, 22 March 1962.
46 Hooker, *An Engineer*, p. 179.
47 Sir Reginald Verdon-Smith, 'BAC – the first ten years', *Aeronautical Journal*, January 1974, p. 46. *Flight*, 17 February 1961; 6 January 1961; 25 July 1963.
48 K. Hartley, 'The mergers in the UK aircraft industry', *Aeronautical Journal*, December 1965, p. 848.

Notes to Chapter Three

1 *Flight*, 30 March 1961.
2 Plowden, para. 435.
3 *Flight*, 15 November 1962.
4 House of Commons Debates, 20 November 1963.
5 *Report of the Steering Committee on Development Cost Estimates*, (the Downey Report), London, HMSO, 1968.
6 For the most detailed and objective analysis of the TSR2, see G. Williams *et al.*,

Crisis in Procurement: a Case Study of the TSR-2, London, RUSI, 1969.

7 *The Management and Control of R&D*, (the Gibb–Zuckerman Report), London, HMSO, 1961

8 Gardner, *British Aircraft Corporation*, pp. 101–3.

9 *First and Second Reports of the Committee of Public Inquiry into the Pricing of Ministry of Aviation Contracts*, July 1944 and February 1965, cmnd. 2428 and 2581.

10 Hayward, *Government and Aerospace*, pp. 47–53.

11 House of Commons Debates, 23 March 1962; Dixson, 'Parliament and the aircraft industry', pp. 107–8.

12 A. Reed, *Britain's Aircraft Industry*, p. 55.

13 House of Commons Debates, 9 February 1965.

14 House of Commons Debates, 1 July 1967.

15 *Flight*, 6 July 1967.

16 House of Commons Debates, 9 December 1964; H. Wilson, *The Labour Government, 1964–70*, London, 1971, p. 113.

17 Reed, *Aircraft Industry*, p. 52.

18 *Times*, 20 June 1964.

19 House of Commons Debates, 9 February 1965; A. Reed, *Aircraft Industry*, p. 59.

20 Reed, *Aircraft Industry*, p. 62.

21 B. Gunston, *Attack Aircraft of the West*, London, 1974, p. 38; House of Commons Debates, 13 December 1965; *Flight*, 15 April 1965; *Times*, 19 June 1965; Hooker, *An Engineer*, p. 148.

22 Plowden.

23 House of Lords Debate, cited in *Flight*, 10 March 1966.

24 House of Commons Debates, 1 February 1966.

25 Cited in Hayward, *Government and Aerospace*, p. 75. See also, *Times*, 8 December 1965 and *Flight*, 16 September 1965 and 3 February 1966.

26 House of Commons Debates, 13 March 1965; *Economist*, 2 September 1966.

27 Cited in Hayward, *Government and Aerospace*, p. 59.

28 *Times*, 18 April 1957 and 23 April 1957.

29 *Flight*, 30 March 1961, 16 November 1961 and 25 July 1963.

30 B. Myles, *Jump Jet*, London, 1986, p. 103.

31 *Sunday Times*, 8 June 1976.

32 A. May, 'Concorde', *International Organisation*, Autumn 1979; Hayward, *Government and Aerospace*, pp. 56–8.

33 Owen, *New Shape in the Sky*, London, 1982, p. 47; Hayward, *Government and Aerospace*, p. 63.

34 Owen, *New Shape in the Sky*, p. 47.

35 Owen, *New Shape in the Sky*, p. 124.

36 Hayward, *Government and Aerospace*, chapter 5.

37 Owen, *New Shape in the Sky*, p. 24; Hayward, *Government and Aerospace*, pp. 124–5.

38 Hayward, *Government and Aerospace*, pp. 140–4.

39 P. D. Henderson, 'Two British errors: their probable size and some possible lessons', in C. Pollet *et al.*, *Public Policy in Theory and Practice*, London, 1979.

40 Cited in Hayward, *Government and Aerospace*, p. 67.

41 *Flight*, 27 May 1965; *Times*, 1 March 1965.

42 Gardner, *British Aircraft Corporation*, p. 142.

43 House of Commons Debates, 13 July 1967.

44 *Times*, 25 May 1967 and 14 December 1967.

45 B. O. Heath, 'MRCA', *Aeronautical Journal*, September 1979.

46 House of Commons Paper, HC141, 1971–2, Q1808.

47 Gardner, *British Aircraft Corporation*, p. 129.

48 For a detailed history of the Airbus, see Hayward, *Government and Aerospace*, chapter 3.

49 *Flight*, 3 June 1965.

50 *Flight*, 13 November 1969.

51 M. Rich *et al.*, *Multinational Coproduction of Military Aerospace Systems*, RAND, Santa Monica, 1981, R-2861.

52 The Downey Report; Roy Jenkins, *Flight*, 3 June 1965.

53 *Productivity of the National Aircraft Effort*, London, 1969 (hereafter referred to as Elstub).

54 Second Report of the Select Committee on Science and Technology, *Defence Research*, HC213, 1968–9, Qs 1155–85.

55 *Flight*, 3 July 1969; Hayward, *Government and Aerospace*, p. 93; R. H. S. Crossman, *Diaries of a Cabinet Minister*, Vol. 1, London, 1975, pp. 413 and 530; Vol. 2, London, 1976, pp. 103, 642 and 762; Vol. 3, London, 1977, pp. 20 and 776.

56 *Flight*, 22 October 1970.

57 *Rolls-Royce Limited: Investigation under Section 1965(a) (i) of the Companies' Act*, London, HMSO, 1973 (hereafter referred to as the Rolls Company's Report), p. 14.

58 House of Commons Debates, 17 November 1965; *The Public Accounts Committee*, 1968–69, HC362, Q428.

59 Rolls Company's Report, pp. 22–3; Hooker, *An Engineer*, p. 182.

60 Rolls Company's Report, pp. 22–30.

61 Gardner, *British Aircraft Corporation*, p. 123.

62 House of Commons Debates, 21 November 1966; Gardner, *British Aircraft Corporation*, pp. 150–56.

63 Gardner, *British Aircraft Corporation*, p. 160; Tony Benn, *Out of the Wilderness*, London, 1987, p. 510.

64 Elstub, sections 2 and 5.

65 SORIS, *The Aeronautical and Space Industries of the Community*, Brussels, 1971.

66 Elstub, para. 294, my emphasis.

67 K. Pavitt, 'The choices and targets and instruments for government support of scientific research', in A. Whiting (ed.), *Economics of Industrial Subsidies*, London, 1976; R. Caves, *Britain's Economic Prospects*, London, 1968, pp. 471–6.

68 Hayward, *Government and Aerospace*, p. 72.

Notes to Chapter Four

1 Rolls Company's Report, p. 116; *Aviation Week*, 29 May 1967, p. 273.

2 Rolls Company's Report, p. 20.

3 Hayward, *Government and Aerospace*, p. 87.

4 *ibid.*, pp. 88–91; Crossman, *Diaries*, Vol. 2, p. 754.

5 *ibid.*, p. 90.

6 *ibid.*, pp. 101–4.

7 *ibid.*, p. 116.

8 John Wragg, head of Rolls-Royce Military Engines Interavia, August 1988; Hooker, *An Engineer*, pp. 197–8.

9 Rolls Company's Report, para. 553.

10 Cited in Hayward, *Government and Aerospace*, p. 154.

11 House of Commons Paper, HC347, para. 280; House of Commons Paper, HC537, para. 67; See N. K. A. Gardner, 'The economics of launch aid' in Whiting (ed.), *Economics of Subsidies*.

12 Hayward, *Government and Aerospace*, p. 153.

13 *Government Organisation for Defence Procurement and Civil Aerospace*, cmnd. 4641, London, 1971.

14 House of Commons Debates, 15 December 1971.

15 *Flight*, 18 May 1972.
16 Gardner, *British Aircraft Corporation*, pp. 237–9.
17 Cited in Hayward, *Government and Aerospace*, p. 175.
18 *ibid.*, p. 169.
19 It should be added that the French were none too keen on welcoming Rolls into the European fold.
20 HC347, Q1041 and 872; Gardner, *British Aircraft Corporation*, p. 231.
21 Hayward, *Government and Aerospace*, p. 158.
22 Gardner, *British Aircraft Corporation*, p. 239.
23 Sir Cranley Onslow, cited in M. Linklater and D. Leigh, *Not With Honour*, London, 1978, p. 28.
24 For these debates, see House of Commons Debates for 2 December 1975, 17 March 1975 and 2 December 1975.
25 Hayward, *Government and Aerospace*, pp. 193–5.
26 *Flight*, 5 December 1974.
27 Hayward, *Government and Aerospace*, p. 175.
28 *ibid.*, p. 170.
29 *ibid.*, p. 182.
30 *ibid.*, p. 200.
31 *ibid.*, pp. 200–8.
32 *ibid.*, p. 207.
33 *Flight, 13 October 1979 and 6 September 1980; Interavia*, August 1984.
34 See National Audit Commission report, cited in *Financial Times*, 27 January 1988.
35 *Interavia*, August, 1988.
36 For early history of UK helicopters, see R. Hafner, 'British rotorcraft', *Aeronautical Journal*, January 1966, pp. 235–42; Wood, *Project Cancelled*, chapter 7.
37 Plowden, para. 372.
38 For details of the Westland 'affair' see Linklater and Leigh, *Not with Honour*; Report from the Defence Committee, HC518, 1985–86; P. Creasey, 'European defence firms in co-operative agreements', in P. Creasey and S. May, *European Armaments and Procurement Co-operation*, London, 1988.
39 HC518, para. 90.
40 HC518, para. 129.
41 HC518, para. 173, author's emphasis.
42 *Flight*, 25 July 1981.
43 For example, the cancellation of the Nimrod AEW aircraft in favour of the Boeing AWACS cost GEC far more than BAe.
44 D. Parry, head of BAe Military Division, *Interavia*, August 1988.
45 The bids were from GEC and Thorn-EMI.
46 D. Parry, head of BAe Military Division, *Interavia*, August 1988.
47 According to one analysis, BAe can hardly fail to profit from the purchase of Rover. See *Financial Times*, 2 August 1988.
48 Creasey, 'European defence firms', pp. 122–5.
49 *Financial Times*, 21 January 1988.
50 *ibid.*, 14 September 1987.
51 *ibid.*, 5 March 1988.

Notes to Chapter Five

1 For an analysis of UK defence industrial issues, see T. Taylor and K. Hayward, *The UK Defence Industrial Base*, London, 1989.
2 *Action Programme for the European Aeronautical Sector*, Brussels, 1975, R/2461/75, p. 3.
3 Pagnamenta and Overy, *Working Lives*, p. 48.

4 See R. A. Harvey, 'Learning to improve productivity and cut costs', *Aeronautical Journal*, May 1981, pp. 169–73; P. Jefferson, 'Productivity comparisons with the US', *Aeronautical Journal*, May 1981, pp. 179–84; M. Rich *et al.*, *Multinational Coproduction*.

5 *Aerospace*, October 1985.

6 K. Pavitt (ed), *Technological Innovation and British Economic Policy*, London, 1980; P. Stoneman, *The Economic Analysis of Technology Policy*, Oxford, 1987, chapter 13; see also Taylor and Hayward, *UK Defence Industrial Base* for recent debate on the economic affects of defence R&D.

7 K. Hartley, *A Market for Aircraft*, Hobart Paper 57, London, Institute for Economic Affairs, 1974; *NATO: Arms Co-operation*, London, 1983.

8 Some 72 per cent of BAe's annual spend is with British companies.

9 SBAC, *Britain in Aerospace*, London, 1988.

10 *Financial Times*, 23 November 1987.

11 Cited in Hayward, *Government and Aerospace*, p. 9.

12 Pagnamenta and Overy, *Working Lives*, p. 75.

13 K. Hayward, *International Collaboration in Civil Aerospace*, London, 1986, chapter 1; SBAC evidence to House of Lords Committee on Overseas Trade, HL 238-1 July 1985.

14 Crossman, *Diaries*, Vol. 1, p. 580; Vol. 2, p. 126; Vol. 3, p. 479; see also Hayward, *Government and Aerospace*, pp. 22–5.

15 *Sunday Times*, 2 October 1988.

16 *Financial Times*, 3 December 1988.

17 House of Lords Select Committee on Science and Technology, *UK Space Policy*, 1987–88, HoL 41-1.

FURTHER READING

There are very few books which cover the full development of the industry. The series published by Putnam detailing the histories of individual aircraft companies tends to focus on the aircraft they produced. However, most provide useful summaries of company histories. Biography and autobiography also provide some useful, but by definition limited coverage of the evolution of the British aircraft industry.

For the years up to 1945
Barnett, C. *The Audit of War* (London, 1986).
Golley, J. *Whittle* (Shrewsbury, 1987).
Lloyd, I. *Rolls-Royce: Growth of a Firm* (London, 1978).
Lloyd, I. *Rolls-Royce: the Years of Endeavour* (London, 1978).
Lloyd, I. *Rolls-Royce: the Merlin at War* (London, 1978).
Postan, M., Hay, D. and Scott, J. D. *Design and Development of Weapons* (London, 1964).

For the period since 1945 and general
Evans, H. *Vickers Against the Odds* (Sevenoaks, 1978).
Gardner, C. *The British Aircraft Corporation* (London, 1981).
Harker, R. W. *The Engines were Rolls-Royce* (London, 1979).
Hayward, K. *Government and British Civil Aerospace* (Manchester, 1983).
Hooker, Sir Stanley. *Not Much of an Engineer* (Shrewsbury, 1984).
Owen, K. *Concorde, a New Shape in the Sky* (London, 1982).
Reed, A. *Britain's Aircraft Industry* (London, 1973).
Scott, J. D. *Vickers* (London 1962).
Sharp, C. M. *De Havilland* (Shrewsbury, 1982).
Wood, D. *Project Cancelled* (London, 1975).